AN ANNOTATED
BIBLIOGRAPHY OF

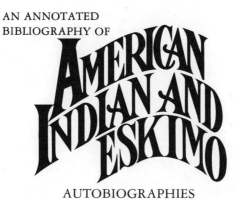

AUTOBIOGRAPHIES

AN ANNOTATED
BIBLIOGRAPHY OF

AUTOBIOGRAPHIES

H. David Brumble III

UNIVERSITY OF NEBRASKA PRESS / Lincoln and London

**Library of Congress Cataloging in Publication Data**

Brumble, H          David.
  An annotated bibliography of American Indian and Eskimo autobiographies.

  Includes indexes.
  1. Indians    of    North    America—Biography—Bibliography.    2.
Eskimos—Biography—Bibliography.  I.  Title.
Z1209.B78  [E89]     016.970.004'97  [B]     80-23449
ISBN 0-8032-1175-9

*For Harriet*

# Contents

# Acknowledgments

For this book I am largely indebted to librarians. My most particular thanks must go to Linda Delowry, Hazel Johnson, and Sue Crosby at the University of Pittsburgh's Hillman Library, but I am grateful as well to librarians at the New York Public Library, the University of Michigan, the University of Texas, the University of Minnesota, and the Library of Congress. For their kind willingness to read what must have seemed overlong portions of this work, I wish to thank Professors Roger Acord, Robert L. Gale, Paul A. Olson, John M. Roberts, and William S. Simmons. My department chair, Professor Mary Louise Briscoe, has provided me encouragement, assistance, criticism, and even time. Pat Buddemeyer, who set this book up on a word processor, has been more a collaborator than a typist.

Finally—well, how I can find words to praise the virtues of a daughter who claims to *enjoy* proof reading?

AN ANNOTATED
BIBLIOGRAPHY OF

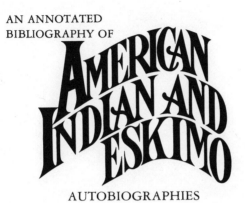

AUTOBIOGRAPHIES

# Introduction

## About American Indian Autobiography

Many of those who look through this book will be surprised at the number of entries--over five hundred autobiographical narratives, well over one hundred of which are book length. The earliest date back to the eighteenth century; the latest reference is to a book still in press. Here are mothers, fathers, warriors, G.I.'s, preachers, pilots, pitchers, authors, artists, shamans, doctors, hunters, Peyotists, Methodists, visionaries, spiritualists, politicians, and at least one cannibal (no. 116).

Some of the earliest of the American Indian autobiographies, tales of conversion and missionary life (see nos. 14, 251, 252), were read as evidence of the marvelous ways in which nineteenth-century America's God worked, his wonders to perform. But even the pious must have relished those narratives the more because of the glimpses they offered of an utterly alien way of life. By the twentieth century this interest had been professionalized; anthropologists began to trade their colored beads for Indian autobiographies literally by the hundreds. And the anthropologists were not alone. Indian enthusiasts of many persuasions began to record these narratives, and to urge Indians themselves to write them. Spiritualists, nostalgia mongers, newsmen, sensationalists, liberal activists, poets, amateur historians, all found their appropriate Indians.

Of course they all, anthropologists and enthusiasts alike, shaped the material they received, sometimes to a large extent, sometimes very little, some by questioning, nearly all by editing, many by merely suggesting that an individual could tell his life at all. Even where the Indian wrote of his own volition, without the aid of an editor--and there are many such autobiographies--one could argue that white society plays the role of collaborator. It is the white society which provided the pen and the letters, the questions and the occasion for written autobiography.

Laments as to editorial distortions of Indian autobiographies are commonplace. For example, in his appraisal of Sun Chief (no. 483) Clyde Kluckhohn regretted that Leo Simmons had edited out so much of what Don Talayesva, the Sun Chief, had written. The 381 pages of narrative which Simmons prints is, after all, only one fifth of what Talayesva had supplied him.

> From the point of view of popular interest, the editor has done a fine job, but the serious student wants to know at first hand on what subjects [Talayesva] did tiresomely repeat himself. Every omission by the editor, every stylistic clarification takes us one more step away from what Don actually said. (Kluckhohn, 1945, p. 97)[1]

Some such lament is common to almost every account of Indian autobiography I have read. Of course those interested in the recovery of aboriginal Indian life ways must join in these lamentations. But many, quite apart from those who share "the point of view of popular interest," ought to disagree. Those who study the effects of cultures in collision, the effects of literacy, the history of autobiography, literature and literary theory, those interested in a culture's developing awareness of history, or in the rise of a sense of the individual, all these can be happy to have Sun Chief and many of the rest of these bi-cultural documents as they are. Indeed, as I read through these more than four hundred autobiographical narratives--shot through as they are with the often conflicting interests of two or more quite different cultures--I became ever more convinced that much of the fascination was a result of, rather than in spite of, their being so often collaborative.

I would not wish to be mistaken. I am not arguing in favor of bad field work or irresponsible editing. I am arguing that we have much to learn from what might, from a purely ethnological perspective, be considered mistakes. I am arguing that, for example, the relationship of Simmons and Talayesva is one of the continuing fascinations of Sun Chief. However we might feel about the consequences for the Indian of white contact, we must be intrigued by the impact Simmons's questions, assumptions, prestige, and money had upon Talayesva and his community. Had Simmons asked fewer questions, or none at all, what he gleaned from Talayesva might have been closer to a glimpse of pre-contact Hopi life, but we would know less about the impact of literacy, money, and other effects of external contact upon pre-literate people.

Thanks to the work of Michael Castro (1979) and Sally McCluskey (1972), as another example, we now understand how John Neihardt shaped and added to Black Elk's narrative. Are we to prize Black Elk Speaks (no. 66) the less because we now know that Neihardt himself composed the oft-quoted passage about the death of a people's dream? Are we to prize Black Elk Speaks the less

---

1. Complete references are to be found below in the section titled "References."

because we now know that the tragic sense which pervades the book is largely Neihardt's own working out of the implications--as he saw them--of Black Elk's life?  If our interest is ethnological description of the Oglala Sioux, yes.  If our interests are at all comparative, if we are at all interested in the impact of one set of aesthetic or narrative assumptions upon another, we might prize Black Elk Speaks all the more for Castro's and McClusky's revelations.

May I sketch, at rather greater length, another example of what might be done?    Karl J. Weintraub (1975, 1978) has written stimulating accounts of the relationship between the development of a people's sense of history and the development of a sense of the self as an individual, and the rise of autobiography.  According to Weintraub it took Western man some two thousand years to move from pre-literacy to a real awareness that a self might, perhaps ought to, be unique.  Whatever else the American Indian autobiographies may be, they are the record--and to some degree the means--of much the same transformation being wrought among the Indians in less than 150 years.

Weintraub begins his history with the Greeks and Romans.  Some of the ancients, Weintraub says, "wrote of great deeds done (res gestae);" and the Indians had their coup tales, a fair sampling of which is preserved in the written record (e.g., nos. 160, 417, 467). Some of the ancients, Weintraub says, "wrote on memorable events they had witnessed (memoir);" several of the Indian narratives cited below could well be accounted memoirs in Weintraub's sense (e.g., nos. 55, 132).  Others of the ancients "reported why and how they sought to become wise men (philosophers' Lives);" many Indians have similarly reported on why and how they became shamans (e.g., nos. 66, 73, 107, 116).  "But," Weintraub concludes, "none  of  the ancients  opened up their souls in the inwardness of true autobiography" (1978, p.1); the reluctance of early Indian "informants" to open up "their souls in the inwardness of true autobiography" is widely remarked upon.    Simmons's attempts  to break through Talayesva's reserve, for example, are well known and typical of the ways  in  which  many  professional  and  amateur  anthropologists handled what they regarded as a research problem.

Now it is certainly true that these Indian narratives differ in many ways from their Greek and Roman counterparts.  But some, at least, of these differences can only add interest to comparisons. Many of the Indian res gestae, memoirs, and "shaman's Lives," for example, are products of pre-literate cultures, and so seem to take us back in history beyond the literate Greeks and Romans.  Another large difference,  especially in the case of the memoirs, is that a white collaborator usually decided for his Indian informant what was memorable, what was to be recalled, what was to be cut, what kept; indeed, one of the broadest traditions of Indian memoirs, the Custer memoirs, is largely a result of interest sparked by persistent Anglo questioning.  But even in the case of memoirs, by studying the nature  of  Indian  resistance  to  memoirs,  by  discovering  the differences between what the Anglo wished to have recalled and what the Indian was inclined (or able) to recall, we might learn something significant about the individual Indian, his particular culture, and perhaps even something about the differences between literate and pre-literate societies in general.

Weintraub devotes only a little space to Greek and Roman autobiographical writing (those who want more detail--much more--should turn to Georg Misch, 1949-50), for it is in Augustine's Confessions that Weintraub sees possible beginnings of true auto-biography. He begins his chapter on Augustine as follows:

> The historian often finds a rich harvest in the great periods of crisis when the lives of Western men take decisive turns . . . . The Ages of Crisis, in which the firm assumptions about man and his world are being called into question, force upon the individual the task of doubting and reinvestigating the very foundations upon which his self-conception traditionally rested. (1978, p. 18)

Weintraub goes on to argue, then, that The Confessions is at once a mirror and a result of "an age of the most profound cultural changes Western man experienced" (1978, p. 18). True autobiography is almost impossible to imagine as a product of a monolithic age, but the more large questions hang in the air, the more assumptions are open to question, the more an individual is likely to try to define his self as a distinct entity, distinct from the other selves he might have become. Weintraub is not surprised that the Christian Middle Ages produced nearly as little in the way of autobiographical inwardness as did the Greco-Roman age; neither is he surprised at the number and complexity of autobiographies written after 1800, for where there is but one road to take there is little interest in trying to account for why that road was taken. Modern autobiography is full of byways.

But if Weintraub has it right, if the autobiographical impulse must wait upon an age which offers many roads, imagine what would have been the effect of the anthropologists' questions upon pre-literate American Indians. Not only were these Indians being forced to consider the existence of a culture farther from their own than was Augustine's paganism from his Christianity, they were also being asked to consider as questions matters which they had previously regarded as simple matters of fact. Simply to be asked about the nature of one's god, one's moral system, one's sexual customs, is to be made aware that the universe allows alternatives.

And so hundreds of Indians in the nineteenth and twentieth centuries delivered themselves of narratives in modes to which they were unused, often including topics they regarded as taboo. Sometimes, of course, the Indians were able to work toward their own ends despite, or at least alongside, the inclinations of their editors. Two Leggings (no. 506), for example, seems to have been quite aware that with William Wildschut's mediation he might finally achieve the renown and the glory which his own Crow people had been so reluctant to afford him. Black Hawk (no. 68) and Geronimo (no. 186) sought self-justification in the face of calumny.

Not all Indian autobiographies have been collaborative, of course; indeed, from a surprisingly early date Indians have been writing with full awareness in a variety of autobiographical traditions. We have missionary journals, tales of conversion, and books of confessions--one spiritual autobiography as early as 1829 (no. 14). There are WW II memoirs (e.g., no. 127) and one impressive Osage autobiography after the fashion of Walden (no. 318). And certain characteristic, if not unique, traditions have developed in Indian autobiography as well. (The respective roles of Indians and white questioners in the evolution of these traditions is quite an open question.) Black Elk Speaks, for example, the story of a shaman who feels a responsibility to affect his people's destiny, has established a set of conventions which informs Lame Deer (no. 273), Fools Crow (no. 178), and, probably, the forthcoming To Speak With Our Bodies (no. 131). A much broader autobiographical tradition among the Indians has the narrator recount his personal history along with tribal history and mythic history. Geronimo, for example, begins with a mythic account of the origins of the Aphaches and enough tribal history to allow us to understand Geronimo's sense of who he was and why he acted as he did. Francisco Patencio's two little volumes (nos. 385, 386) move nimbly back and forth between personal history, tribal history, and myth, as do the autobiographies of Dan Kennedy (no. 265), Alma Green (no. 204), John Joseph Mathews (no. 318), Albert Yava (no. 547), and others. Even Simeon Oliver (nos. 375, 376), raised as he was in an orphanage quite apart from his mother's Eskimo culture, wrote that he "found himself" only by going as an adult to live among the Eskimos, to hear their stories and to learn their ways. In this he anticipates N. Scott Momaday, who realized himself only by making his way to Rainy Mountain, by following the path of his Kiowa forebears' tribal migration, by linking, then, his idea of himself to an idea of his people. Momaday's The Way to Rainy Mountain (no. 344) and The Names (no. 345) are two exquisite attempts to remember an Indian past that creates, even as it transcends, the personal.

It is fitting that this walking tour of American Indian autobiography should end with Momaday. It is fitting because, with his Ph.D. and his Pulitzer Prize, Momaday is very much a part of Western culture; we have come far from Black Hawk and Black Elk and Two Leggings. Yet it is fitting as well because no Indian autobiographer before Momaday wrote with such a rich awareness of this Indian autobiographical literature. Whatever uses anthropologists and historians continue to make of the material this bibliography lists, I think that it may be said that Momaday has taken an important step toward transforming this miscellaneous set of anthropological, historical, and literary documents into a living literary tradition.

## What the Bibliography Includes

I have striven to include all printed versions of first-person narratives by North American Indians and Eskimos. I include, then, even very brief narratives, some few being but one page long. The only third-person narratives included are those wherein the autobiographer himself chose to write in the third person (see nos. 46, 338). I have also included a few references to autobiographical materials in manuscript or on tape (only those which seem particularly important or accessible), and a few references to books which have wrongly been listed elsewhere as American Indian autobiographies (e.g., nos. 206, 216, 291).

I include no biographies. I am, of course, fully cognizant that the difference between one of these autobiographies and a biography was sometimes simply the decision of a white editor to cast his data in one mode rather than another. Still it is important to maintain the distinction between autobiography and biography even here, for a narrative which has been cast as an autobiography is at least claiming to be told from the point of view of an Indian, at least claiming either to be written in an Indian's own idiom or in a translation of an Indian's own idiom. A biography makes no such generic claims. A biography may claim to describe an Indian's point of view, but never to embody it. Strangely, as it seems to me, some literary studies of American Indian autobiographies make no distinction between biography and autobiography (see, e.g., O'Brien, 1973, p. 7).

## The Form of the Bibliography

Where a bibliographic entry contains two names before the title, the first is the name of the Indian autobiographer, the second the name of the collaborator-editor-amanuensis. The name in caps is the one under which the book or article is most likely to be listed in card catalogs and indexes. Where there is but one name, it is, then, the name of an autobiographer who had no collaborator. Where the autobiographer's name leaves any doubt as to his/her sex, I include a male/female designation in parentheses.

An (IP) after the title indicates that the item is in print; a (P) indicates the item is in paperback. However, this indicates only that Books in Print and/or Canadian Books in Print listed the item in 1979--and not necessarily in the edition I cite. Each item I cite, on the other hand, I have had in hand and read in the edition I cite, the only exceptions being nos. 131 (not yet in print), 94, 302, 343 (manuscripts), and 564 (a collection of tapes). An asterisk after a title indicates the work's likely appeal to high school students.

Besides the bibliographic reference, I include for each item the following information: autobiographer's birthdate, date of autobiography's composition, autobiographer's tribal affiliation, an account of how the autobiography was composed, and some general remarks about the autobiography.

Anonymous narratives are listed at the end of the bibliography, beginning with no. 564.

## On Naming

The Babel of Indian naming presents something of a problem in the compilation of such a bibliography as this one. The confusion is partly a result of the widespread Indian custom of taking several names during a lifetime; partly it is because many Indians had and have Anglo names as well as Indian names, partly because one anthropologist's phoneticization of an Indian's name might be different from another anthropologist's phoneticization. In yet other cases different parts of a name might be in common use at different times: "thus A.L. Kroeber in 1903 heard 'Arateve,' while George Devereux in 1938 transcribed 'Yarate:va,' whereas in the 1960's Lorraine Sherer heard the whole name 'Eechee yara tav'" (see no. 113, p. x). And then many Indians are known by a translation of their Indian name--Black Elk, Two Leggings, Redsky--while the native language original might also be used. Of course one must also remember that many Indian autobiographers are known to us only by pseudonyms.

In the face of all this, rather than make any attempt to work out what might be the "real" name, I have decided to list that name, or that version of a name, given most prominence in the autobiography. Sometimes I provide alternatives in parentheses, and for Indians whose alternative names are fairly well known I cross reference names (e.g., Crashing Thunder, Big Winnebago, Sam Blowsnake, Gertrude Bonnin, and Sun Chief). Finally, since "Red Sky," "Redsky," "Red-sky," and "Red-Sky" are all possible, I have alphabetized without regard for capitalization, spaces, or hyphens.

## Some Suggestions for Further Reading

Clyde Kluckhohn, The Use of Personal Documents in Anthropological Science (1945), and L.L. Langness, The Life History in Anthropological Science (1965), have provided accounts of the uses to which such "personal documents" as American Indian autobiographies have--and might have--been put. They also included very helpful bibliographies (although there are errors in Langness). Especially Kluckhohn is also important historically, for his essay exercised an influence upon a whole generation of American anthropologists, many of the Indian autobiographies after 1945 showing evidence of Kluckhohn's suggestions about field techniques and editing procedures. John Dollard's attempt to give the use of biographical materials in the social sciences a sound theoretical base, his Criteria for the Life History (1935), is useful in the same way.

What Kluckhohn and Langness did for anthropology, Gordon Allport (1942), Louis Gottschalk (1945), and Robert Angell (1945) have done, respectively, for psychology, history, and sociology. John Garraty (1957) has also written concerning the historian's use of biographical materials. But as is often noted, there have been more abjurations as to the use and proper analysis of personal documents than there have been careful analyses and productive use made of personal documents. David G. Mandelbaum (1973) provides one model of careful analysis, a model which might well be useful to those working with American Indian autobiographies. (Mandelbaum also provides an excellent bibliography on the use of personal documents in the social sciences.) David Aberle's extended commentary (1951) upon Sun Chief is a model of a kind of analysis founded upon more venerable psychological-anthropological assumptions.

I think that those who come to these autobiographies from disciplines other than anthropology might be aided by a sense of the actual practice of field work, by a sense of the dust and the sweat, the habits of mind and the problems of the anthropologists who were spending their hours and their days collecting tales, words, myths, syntax, and autobiographies from American Indians in the first half of this century. For accounts of three anthropologists with widely different temperaments but a single passion, see the following: Carobeth Laird, Encounter with an Angry God (1975), is a remarkable autobiography by the sometime wife of John Peabody Harrington; Theodora Kroeber (1970, 1971), and Julian Steward (1973) provide affectionate accounts of the work of A.L. Kroeber; and Robert H. Lowie has written a self-effacing autobiography (1959). Herbert Passin, "Tarahumara Prevarication: A Problem in Field Method" (1942), can serve as a warning to those who would trust too readily all that is spoken in hogan or tipi. Donald Bahr (1975) provides an exemplary brief history of the transformation of one oral form (Pima and Papago oratory) to written form, along with needful cautions as to the kind and quality of translations from Indian languages. Dennis Tedlock (1977) also offers cautions, particularly as regards transcriptions of oral performances.

Literary scholars have lately turned their attention to American Indian autobiographies. For example, the essays of McClusky (1972) and Castro (1979), mentioned above, Carol T. Holly (1979), and Robert F. Sayre (1971) all deal with Black Elk Speaks. Lynn O'Brien's pamphlet (1973) provides a helpful, if limited, introduction to Plains Indian autobiography. John Leo (1978) has written on S.M. Barrett's Geronimo (no. 186), while H. David Brumble (1980) discusses the history of Anglo attitudes toward, and use of, the sacred materials which are so often a part of these Indian autobiographies. Robert F. Sayre's (1969) is one of the few general treatments of American autobiography which makes mention of Indian autobiography.

Literary studies of autobiography in general are ever more numerous. Given the ways in which the making of autobiography has changed the lives of many Indians, Roy Pascal's suggestion that the "act of writing [autobiography] leaves the man different" (1960, pp. 182-83) seems quite germane to the study of Indian autobiography. Pascal also insists that the study of life and autobiography ought not to be confused--an injunction too little regarded by literary scholars working with Indian autobiography. Robert F. Sayre (1964) and Barrett Mandel (1968) further develop some of the implications of Pascal's position, Sayre arguing that autobiographies are written according to literary forms, Mandel discussing the ways in which autobiographers have created personae, or fictional versions of the self. Passin (1942) can be read as an anthropologist's response to "fiction" in autobiography. Weintraub (1975, 1978), to whom I have already made frequent reference, provides a fine historical overview of Western autobiography up to Goethe, and I find the generic definition attempted by Elizabeth Bruss (1976, pp. 10-11) quite suggestive--especially because of the ways it would have to be altered to take into account such collaborative autobiographies as are listed below. Francis R. Hart (1970) can, I think, be read as an implied argument against making easy distinctions between collaborative and non-collaborative autobiographies. The article is certainly an argument against easy designations of what is "true" autobiography and what is not.

Those interested in early, pietistic Indian autobiographies might find useful Daniel B. Shea, Spiritual Autobiography in Early America (1968), although Shea makes no mention of the Indian works in particular. Sidonie Smith's discussion of black autobiography (1974), although it too makes no mention of Indian autobiography, is interesting for its claim that black autobiographers tend to depict their lives as versions of Ben Franklin's Autobiography or as Horatio Alger stories. Black autobiographers, it seems, characteristically imagine themselves into white society, while Indian autobiographers imagine themselves out.

Since one of the obvious fascinations of especially the early Indian autobiographies is the sense they can give of a life, a culture, a point of view very different from our own, I would like to suggest some treatments of the differences between literate and pre-literate societies. The discussion by Jack Goody and I. Watt (1962-63) of the social, political, and epistemological consequences of literacy is controversial, but is still a good starting place for anyone trying to understand oral cultures. Goody, The Domestication of the Savage Mind (1977), is useful not least for its discussion of the Zunis in relation to these issues. The articles collected in Robin Horton and Ruth Finnegan, Modes of Thought (1973), are all quite helpful, Horton's and Ernst Gellner's essays in particular, since they discuss not only the differences between literate and pre-literate societies, but also contemporary attitudes toward those differences. Many of these scholars are, explicitly or implicitly, answering Claude Lévi-

Strauss's arguments (e.g., 1962) for the complexity of "primitive" thought. See also Lévi-Strauss's (1979, pp. 34-43) brief treatment of folk history.

Finally, O'Brien (1973) includes as a part of her discussion of Plains Indian autobiography references to, and a brief treatment of, Indian pictographs. To her list I would add Amos Bad Heart Bull, A Pictographic History of the Oglala Sioux (1967) and the important recent republication of James Mooney, Calendar History of the Kiowa Indians (1898).

# The Bibliography

1  Abeita, Louise. See no. 169.

2  Adams, Jane. ELIZABETH COLSON. "Autobiography of Jane
   Adams," in Colson, Autobiographies of Three Pomo Women,
   Berkeley:  Archeological Research Facility, Department of
   Anthropology, University of California, 1974 [1956], pp. 195-
   209, 215-16.
      Born, c. 1881; interviewed, 1940-41. Pomo. For each of the
   three main informants in this book Colson provides two kinds of
   autobiographical material: the first is in the form of answers to
   Colson's questions (the questions are included in the text), and
   the second is in each case a brief autobiography, each informant's response to a request for the story of her life. These latter
   are undirected. All three women knew English, and no interpreters were used. Adams's English, as it is here printed with
   very little editing, is quite idiosyncratic. Adams provides a good
   deal of detail about her life of poverty, her hard work, her
   family's profligacy, her lack of schooling, her hop picking, etc.

3  Ah-nen-la-de-ni (Daniel LaFrance). "An Indian Boy's Story," The
   Independent, LV, No. 2852 (July 30, 1903), 1780-87.
      Born, 1879; wrote, c. 1903. Mohawk father, mixed-blood
   mother.  Ah-nen-la-de-ni submitted a typescript to The
   Independent, and the editors there did some rewriting and some
   rearranging. This is one of the better brief autobiographies. We
   are allowed a good sense of the semi-nomadic life of many of
   New York's reservation Indians late in the nineteenth century,
   and there is poignance in Ah-nen-la-de-ni's account of his
   boarding-school years, his sense of loss, for example, when he
   was stripped of his Indian name. But after being trained as a
   nurse, he came to regard the "civilizing" of the Indians as an
   unmixed good, although he hopes that especially the old folks
   (whom he feels to be incapable of change) will be allowed to live
   out their lives as little disturbed as possible.

4   Aknik (M). See no. 203.

5   Akulujuk, Malaya (F).   STUART M. HODGSON.   Narratives by Akulujuk and others to be found in Stories from Pangnirtung (IP).* Edmonton, Alberta: Hurtig Publishers, 1976, 100 pp.
     Born, c. 1913; narrated, 1974.  Pangnirtung Eskimo.  In 1974, a group of Pangnirtung residents interviewed some of the last remaining Pangnirtung Eskimos to have lived the old nomadic way of life.  These interviews were subsequently translated from the Inuktitut and edited into continuous narratives.  The collection was then presented to Hodgson, Commissioner of the Northwest Territories, and subsequently printed.  These Eskimos recall their childhood, training for the hunt, their hunts, relations with whites, matters of diet, and more.  Those whose narratives are autobiographical are as follows:  Markosie Pitsualak (M), born, c. 1893; Jamasie Alivatuk (M), born, c. 1907; Noah Arnaquq, born, c. 1900; Jim Kilabuk, born, c. 1900; Akasyook Etoangat (M), born, c.  1899; Paulosie Qappik (M), born, c. 1909; Josepee Sowloapik (M), born, c. 1909; Katso Eevic (F), born, c. 1896; and Joanasie Kakee (M), born, c. 1907.

6   ALFORD, THOMAS WILDCAT.  Florence Drake.  Civilization, as Told to Florence Drake (IP).* Norman: University of Oklahoma Press, 1936.  203 pp.
     1860-1938; narrated, shortly before 1936.  Shawnee, grandson of Tecumseh.   The nature of the collaboration here is not precisely specified, but it would seem that Alford's form and diction were fairly closely followed.  Alford was well educated, and there was no need for a translator.  The title is, to a certain degree, intended ironically, for Alford has ambivalent feelings about civilization.   Before white contact, there was more of innate, spontaneous morality and fellow-feeling; after white contact, with the coming of civilization, there is rationality, but more of dishonesty.  Before white contact, Indians were guided by "simple courtesy and consideration" in their social intercourse; civilization offers only "meaningless, foolish forms" (p. 53) as the base of social intercourse--but Alford feels himself to have been driven by an "inner voice" to seek a "better way of living than my people knew" (p. 77).  And this something better is civilization, the white man's clothing, schools, dances, toilets, and Christianity.   This is a very interesting book, not least because Alford is not always in control of the ambivalence that is at the heart of the book:  he is a "civilized" Indian yearning with a part of his being for primitive innocence.

7   Alivatuk, Jamasie (M). See no. 5.

8   ALLEN, ELSIE.  Vinson Brown.  Pomo Basketmaking: A Supreme Art for the Weaver (P).*   Healdsburg, Calif.:   Nature

graph Publishers, 1972. 67 pp.

Born, 1899; wrote, c. 1972. Pomo. This is one of the more interesting short autobiographies, largely because Allen talks about the opposition of some of her people to her learning to weave baskets in the traditional ways, their feelings that the art should die out. Allen determined at the age of sixty-two that she would thoroughly relearn the craft, and this she did. She also tells of her youth, of her schooling, of hard times. The autobiography is on pp. 7-15.

9    Ambroise (M). PLINY EARLE GODDARD. "Hunting Experiences--Dunvegan Dialect," in Goddard, Beaver Texts, Anthropological Papers of the American Museum of Natural History, X, Nos. 5,6 (1917), 393-95. Free translations appear in Goddard, Beaver Indians, same journal, X, No. 4 (1916), 290-92.

Born, c. 1850; interviewed, 1913. Beaver. Goddard prints the Beaver language text along with the English translation. Nothing more here than the title promises.

10    Anahareo (Gertrude Bernard). Devil in Deerskins: My Life with Grey Owl.* Don Mills, Ontario: PaperJacks, 1975 [1972]. vii + 190 pp.

Born, 1906; wrote, 1972. Iroquois father. Shortly before WW II a man named Grey Owl, a man who claimed to be half Apache and half Scots, captured the hearts of the English with his book Pilgrims of the Wild. The book told of his conversion from animal-slaughtering trapper to animal-loving conservationist. Shortly after his death, however, it was discovered that this Grey Owl was none other than Archie Belaney--who had in fact been born in England and raised there by his two maiden aunts.

Anahareo was Grey Owl's wife, and she writes here of their years together, from their meeting in 1925 until his death in 1938. She writes, then, of their rather unorthodox courtship, their conservationist work, their arduous journeys through the Canadian wilderness. She tells us a good deal, of course, about her then famous husband, but the book is certainly about Anahareo as well. She was, we find, a resourceful woman quite capable, for example, of making a five hundred-mile canoe trip all on her own. This is a witty and an engaging book.

11    Apache John, Chief (Koon-kah-za-chy). JOSEPH KOSSUTH DIXON. "Chief Apache John," as found in Dixon, The Vanishing Race: The Last Great Indian Council (IP),* Garden City: Doubleday, Page and Co., 1913, pp. 45-47.

Born, 1849; interviewed, 1909. Apache. Apache John and twenty other Indians, fifteen of them chiefs, met with Rodman Wanamaker and Dixon at what Wanamaker and Dixon were pleased to call "the Last Great Indian Council," in the valley of the Little Big Horn, in 1909. Wanamaker and Dixon wanted to preserve as much as possible of the Indians' vanishing way of life. The book cited above was one of the results of that council; and in this book, then, are brief personal accounts from each of the main Indian participants. Evidently such questions as "What was the greatest event of your life?" were asked. Interpreters were used, but in each case, according to Dixon, "the idiom and phrasing and atmosphere of the Indian's speech were faithfully retained" (p. 10). This must be taken with the warning that Dixon's introductory matter and Wanamaker's gorgeous browntone photographs are intensely nostalgic. The book is, in fact, a product of exactly the same assumptions as are at work in Eastman's Indian Boyhood (no. 161), namely, that the real Indians were vanishing, that the only course for such Indians as remained was patriotism and assimilation. For an extreme expression of this book's brand of racial romanticism, see no. 527.

Though Apache John's narrative is quite brief, there is interest. He talks of his whole training as having been centered on warfare--and of how one hour's talk with an official in Washington gave him "other ways of thinking . . . . the new life was better." But then, two sentences later, he says that one of the greatest events in his life was a particularly stirring battle on the banks of the El Paso River.

12  Apauk (M).  JAMES WILLARD SCHULTZ.  Apauk, Caller of Buffalo.* Boston: Houghton Mifflin, 1916.  227 pp.
    1822-c.1882; interviewed in the winter of 1879-80. Piegan. Schultz writes: "I did not, of course, get Apauk's story of his life in the sequence in which it is here laid down. On consecutive evenings he would relate incidents far apart in time, and only by later questioning would I be able to fill in the gaps" (p. 4). Schultz was something of a romantic, but his work was respected by George Bird Grinnell, and he certainly had the confidence of the Indians among whom he lived for many years. Schultz was in the habit of writing down stories that he heard on the evening of their telling; so, while the structure of this book is entirely Schultz's, the episodes are almost certainly authentic. (For more on Schultz's work, see no. 31.)

13  Apekaum, Charles E.  (Charley Charcoal).  WESTON LA BARRE.  The Autobiography of a Kiowa Indian, Microcard Publications of Primary Records in Culture and Personality, ed. Bert Kaplan, II, No. 14, Madison, Wis.: Microcard Foundation, 1957, iii + 184 pp.
    Born, c. 1888; interviewed, 1936.  Kiowa.  This is a transcript of Apekaum's narration, no changes having been made other than the deletion of a few people's names.  Only rarely did La Barre suggest directions, and those few occasions

are indicated in the text.

Since La Barre was doing research on the Peyote Cult at this time, and since Apekaum was both informant and interpreter for that work, it is not surprising that a good deal is said here about peyote experiences, visions, ceremonies, songs, etc. For many readers, however, the book's greatest appeal could rise from the way this gentle, intelligent, and highly acculturated man balances within himself the Kiowa, peyote, and white ways. He tells, for example, of his time in the navy--keeping the ship's log, arresting an AWOL sailor, pitching for the ship's baseball team--and yet he is perfectly willing to cooperate in providing war-related names for Kiowa babies on his return from the service, just as Kiowa warriors had provided names for babies in the previous century. One nephew was named "watching out for the enemy from the bridge [of a ship]" and a cousin's son was named "crossing the ocean" (p. 38). He tells of his extensive education (Haskell, Carlisle, etc.), but he sees this education as leaving him with a responsibility to help his people. This is really quite an appealing book, one whose charm, by the way, is hardly diminished by Apekaum's accounts of his sexual escapades.

14   Apes, William. A Son of the Forest. The Experience of William Apes, a Native of the Forest. Comprising a Notice of the Pequot Tribe of Indians. Written by Himself. N.Y.: Published by the author, 1829. 216 pp.

Born, 1798; wrote, 1829. Pequod. Apes spent most of his youth with white families. He tells of being beaten as a child, of his struggles to find the true Christian faith, and of his conscription into the army, of becoming addicted to rum, swearing, and gambling. He writes of religious persecution and racial prejudice, and of his struggle to make a living at various trades. Eventually he became a preacher. Apes's ambivalence toward his Indianness is very much a part of this book, and the book is one of the few extended Indian autobiographies written before 1850. This book has, however, been neglected, probably because it is thought to be just another book of Christian conversion.

15   Arm-Around-the-Neck (M). See no. 200.

16   Arnaquq, Noah. See no. 5.

17   Ashie Tsosie (M). BRODERICK H. JOHNSON. "Ashie Tsosie," as found in Stories of Traditional Navajo Life and Culture, by Twenty-two Navajo Men and Women (IP),* Tsaile, Ariz.: Navajo Community College Press, 1977, pp. 110-19.

Born, 1912; interviewed, 1976. Navajo. This is one of twenty-two narratives to be found in this volume. The interviewers were Kee Jackson, Leonard Begay, Hoke Denetsosie, and others, evidently, who go unnamed. Since virtually every informant begins with an account of personal clan affiliations, and since virtually every informant provides some account of his or her education, whether formal or traditional or both, it would seem likely that the interviewers asked for such information in particular. All of the informants spoke Navajo during the interviews, though some were fluent speakers of English. The interviewers also spoke Navajo. The interviews were tape-recorded and subsequently translated. The resulting manuscripts were then edited by Johnson to conform fairly closely to the conventions of written standard English. How much cutting and rearranging were done we are not told, though internal evidence suggests that this was minimal. Taken in general these narratives are remarkable for the sense of the vitality of contemporary Navajo culture which they convey.

Ashie Tsosie's is an affecting narrative. The man feels that he has not accomplished what he might have done had his father not refused to allow him to attend school. He talks too of his strong attachment to his own family and of the love his children have each for each.

18 Ashpo, Samuel. JAMES DOW McCALLUM. The letters of Samuel Ashpo in The Letters of Eleazar Wheelock's Indians (P), ed. McCallum, Hanover, N.H.: Dartmouth College Publications, 1932, pp. 33-46.

1718-1795; wrote, 1763-66. Mohegan. This is a very careful edition of letters to, from, and respecting the Indians whom Eleazar Wheelock educated at Dartmouth in the hope that they would become missionaries to the Indians. McCallum prints all letters as they were written, idiosyncratic spellings, vocabulary, and syntax all intact.

To include these letters in this listing is to strain the boundaries of autobiography; however, there are autobiographical elements in many of the letters in this book, the letters in the rich context McCallum supplies are fascinating, and all of this is so early--certainly these are some of the earliest writings by Indians ever published--that I finally decided to include them. Here are letters written by Indians snatched out of a nearly stone-age existence to learn Greek, Latin, English, hygiene, and Calvinism at Wheelock's knee. Perhaps nowhere else in the literature is the clash between two cultures quite as stark as it is here; certainly there are no more unfortunate examples of assimilation than are presented by some of these men and women.

Ashpo, who was frequently in trouble, usually for drunkenness, here writes about his attempts to preach Calvinism to the Indians on the frontier.

19   Asisaro, Lorenzo.  E.S. HARRISON.  "Narrative of a Mission Indian," as found in Harrison, History of Santa Cruz County, California, San Francisco:  Pacific Press Publishing Co., 1892, pp. 45-48.

    Born, 1819; interviewed, 1890.  Asisaro says that his father's "tribe was Jlli, and he belonged to the tribe that lived up the coast.  They lived upon shellfish, which they took from the seacoast, and carried up to the hills, where were their rancherias . . . .  They made their huts of the branches of trees" (p. 47).  Beyond the fact that this narrative was originally taken down in Spanish by E. L. Wilson, we are given no information as to the nature of this collaboration.  Internal evidence suggests, however, that the narrative was prompted along the way by questions, that there was some cutting done, but that there was probably little rearranging of Asisaro's reminiscences.

    This account of life in the Santa Cruz area missions between 1819 and mid-century is quite arresting.  Asisaro tells, for example, of the Christianizing of the Indians by the padres:  "To capture the wild Indian, first were taken the children, and then the parents followed.  The padres would erect a hut, and light the candles to say mass, and the Indians, attracted by the light . . . would approach, and soon be taken.  These would bring in others . . ." (p. 47).  He recalls the severity and guile of the padres in other matters as well.  Asisaro was a witness to the taking of San Francisco by the Americans in 1846.

20   Atsitsina (M).  ADOLF HUNGRY WOLF.  Narratives to be found in Hungry Wolf, The Blood People:  A Division of the Blackfoot Confederacy (IP),*  N.Y.:  Harper and Row, Publishers, 1977, pp. 105-6, 144-47, 163, 221.

    Born, c. 1900; interviewed, 1973.  Blood.  Hungry Wolf is a young white man who has "converted" to the ways of the Blood Indians (see no. 234).  This book is, then, the work of an enthusiast and a romantic, and we are given no suggestion as to the degree of editorial license Hungry Wolf practices upon his informants' narratives.  Internal evidence suggests that Hungry Wolf standardized grammar and did some cutting.  The narratives are so brief that probably there was little or no rearranging.  Atsitsina, a pipemaker, here recalls various experiences relating to ceremonial pipes and traditional dances.  For Atsitsina's father, see nos. 157, 158.

21   Attakai, Ason (F).  See no. 24.

22   Attungoruk (M).  JAMES W. VAN STONE.  "The Autobiography of an Alaska Eskimo," Arctic, X, No. 4 (1957), 195-210.

    Born, 1928; wrote, 1955-56.  Eskimo.  Van Stone asked Attungoruk to write his life story.  What is printed here is the result, unaltered save for spelling, punctuation, and some grammatical editing. Attungoruk was raised to be a hunter, and he continues to support his family largely by his efforts as a hunter, though he has had considerable experience outside the village as a longshoreman, "grease-monkey," and construction worker. He writes a good deal about the stern discipline his father meted out. He also provides a nice account of the way sharing works, and is understood, in an often hard-pressed Eskimo village.

23   Aua (M).   KNUD JOHAN VICTOR RASMUSSEN.   "Aua Is Consecrated to the Spirits," as found in Rasmussen, Intellectual Culture of the Iglulik Eskimos, which is No. 2 of Intellectual Culture of the Hudson Bay Eskimos (IP), which is, in turn, vol. VII of Report of the Fifth Thule Expedition, 1921-24, Copenhagen:   Gyldendalske Boghandel, 1930, pp.   115-20. Reprinted in Joan Halifax, Shamanic Voices:   A Survey of Visionary Narratives (P), N.Y.: E.P. Dutton, 1979, pp. 113-20.
     Born, probably c. 1870; interviewed, c. 1922. Iglulik Eskimo. For the details of this collaboration see no. 50. This is Aua's account of the acquisition of his shamanic powers.

24   Austin, Buck.   RUTH ROESSEL and BRODERICK H. JOHNSON. Narratives by Austin and others in Roessel and Johnson, eds., Navajo Livestock Reduction:  A National Disgrace (IP), Chinle, Ariz.: Navajo Community College Press, 1974,  224 pp.
     The book cited here is a collection of Navajo personal narratives concerning the livestock-reduction program, the federal government's response to drought, erosion, and over-grazing on the Navajo reservation in the early 1940's.  These are "the experiences of those who resisted and were thrown in jail and of those who helped enforce and carry out the program" (p. x).   Most of the Navajos, however, neither accepted nor understood the need for livestock reduction; indeed, many, including some of those who speak to us via these pages, firmly believed, and continue to believe, that the drought and erosion were the result of stock reduction.
     All of these narratives were tape recorded in Navajo and subsequently translated. Those included are:
     Buck Austin, born, 1909. A shaman.
     Eli Gorman, born, c. 1900. A shaman.
     Capiton Benally, born, c. 1910. Recalls that the government promised that jobs would be made available for those who reduced their herds, while in fact few jobs were created.
     Howard W. Gorman, born, c. 1894. Gorman's recollections provide us with a sense of how profoundly two sets of cultural assumptions were in conflict here, the much reviled Indian Commissioner arguing for stock reduction as a response to the drought, the shamans arguing that proper ceremonies could end the drought.

Walter Norcross, born, 1895.
Dan Yazzie, born, c. 1900.
Martin Johnson, born, probably c. 1905.
Mose Denejolie (M), born, c. 1900.
Frank Goldtooth, born, c. 1880.
Tacheadeny Tso Begay (M), born, probably c. 1905. Recalls violent response to the stock-reduction agents and jail for the offending Navajos.
Hosteen Whitewater (M), born, c. 1881.
Henry Zah, born, c. 1900.
Akinabh Burbank (F), born, c. 1882.
Ason Attakai (F), born, c. 1877.
Denah L. Bitsilly (M), born, probably c. 1905.
Curly Tso, born, c. 1884.
Herbert Zahne, born, c. 1907.
Billy Bryant, born, c. 1920.
Hosteen Tsosie Begay (M), born, c. 1905.
Mary Cook, born, c. 1910.
Hoske Yeba Doyah (M), born, c. 1903.
Hascon Benally (M), born, c. 1880.
John Tom, born, c. 1898.
Chee Carol (M), born, c. 1915.
Ernest Nelson, born, c. 1916. A shaman.
Pete Sheen, born, c. 1915.
Curly Mustache, born, c. 1887. A shaman.
Scott Preston, born, c. 1894. A shaman.
Frank Ludi, born, c. 1910.
John Smith, born, c. 1900.
Gyssie Betony (M), born, c. 1910.
Fred Descheene, born, 1909.
Clifford Beck, born, 1905.

25 _____ . BRODERICK H. JOHNSON. "Buck Austin,"* as found in the book cited in no. 17, pp. 135-42.
Born, 1909; interviewed, c. 1976. Navajo. For the details of the collaboration, see no. 17. These are discontinuous reminiscences about folk technology, personal experiences, morality, and tribal history.

26 Badger, Tom (pseudonym). VICTOR BARNOUW. "Reminiscences of a Chippewa Mide Priest," Wisconsin Archeologist, XXXV, No. 4 (1954), 83-112.
Born, c. 1875; interviewed, 1944. Ojibwa. Badger knew some English, but Barnouw worked here with an interpreter. Badger would not answer all of Barnouw's questions and was reluctant to talk about long periods of his life, since he did not want to offend his present wife (who was acting as interpreter) by talking about his relationships with his two former wives. Barnouw not only printed a direct transcription of Badger's

(interpreted) account but also includes his own questions so that the reader has a fairly precise sense of what was spontaneous and what was guided. This is a nice example of one attempt to avoid the problem of the anthropologist's intrusions into what were supposed to be personal documents.

This brief autobiography is also interesting because of Badger's attitude toward the old ways. He sees himself as less powerful than he should be, because he did not persevere in the fasts and other rituals during his youth. Interesting to compare Badger with Radin's Sam Blowsnake (nos. 73, 74) in this regard.

27  Bad Hawk (M). JAMES LARPENTUR LONG (FIRST BOY). A narrative is to be found in Long, The Assiniboines: From the Accounts of the Old Ones, Told to First Boy (James Larpentur Long),* ed. Michael Stephen Kennedy, Norman: University of Oklahoma Press, 1961, pp. 21-22. This book first appeared as Land of Nakoda (1942).

Born, c. 1865; interviewed, 1939. Assiniboine. Part Assiniboine himself, Long was fluent in the language, and he receives high marks from Kennedy for the fidelity of his translations. The book cited here is a sensitive description of Assiniboine ways, and autobiographical fragments by Assiniboines are scattered throughout. Bad Hawk's brief contribution is an account of a humorous incident.

28  Barstow, Rose Mary. JANE B. KATZ. Reminiscences in Katz, I Am the Fire of Time (P),* N.Y.: E. P. Dutton, 1977, pp. 116-18.

Born, 1915; interviewed, 1976. Ojibwa. The book cited contains several excerpts from interviews conducted by Katz and her mother, Blix Ruskay. Though Katz has abridged the interviews, there seems to have been little other editing; some features, for example, of nonstandard English remain. The book also contains excerpts from many of the women's narratives listed in this bibliography. Barstow, a member of the faculty of the University of Minnesota when interviewed, here recalls her early life, her fearful response to schooling, and the humiliation she felt upon learning at school that Indians were "savages."

29  Batter (F). See no. 391.

30  Bear Ghost, Chief. JOSEPH KOSSUTH DIXON. "Chief Bear Ghost,"* as found in the book cited in no. 11, pp. 96-98.

Born, 1856; interviewed, 1909. Yankton Sioux. For the details of the collaboration, see no. 11. A war reminiscence.

31  Bear Head (M). JAMES WILLARD SCHULTZ. "The Baker Massacre (Told by Bear Head, a Survivor)," as found in Schultz, Blackfeet and Buffalo: Memories of Life among the Indians,*

ed. Kieth C. Seele, Norman:   University of Oklahoma Press, 1962, pp. 282-305.

Born, c. 1856; narrated, c. 1935.  Piegan.  Schultz lived among the Blackfeet (of whom the Piegans are a subdivision) for many years, beginning in 1877.  He lived as an Indian, learning their language with fair (if not native) fluency, hunting with them, marrying a Piegan, going on raids with them, making friends among them--and hearing (and telling) many, many tales.  Schultz contributed some Indian articles to George Bird Grinnell's Forest and Stream magazine, but after the death of his wife, after he was forced to realize that the old days were gone, Schultz began to write voluminously--thirty-seven books and many articles.

Schultz was evidently quite careful of facts and dates, and the autobiographical tales in this volume--those by Bear Head as well as those by other Indians--may be taken as genuine (a single exception is noted by Seele in his introduction).  Since, however, Schultz often wrote from notes written down after the original telling--although almost always on the   same evening--we would probably be safest to regard these pieces as careful redactions by a man who lived alongside the lives these tales so vividly describe, a man who knew the language and the narrative patterns of the Blackfeet from the inside.  He is able to provide us with a real sense of how these tales might have been told and enjoyed in a pre-literate culture.  (Much of the above comes from Seele's introduction; see also Schultz's auto-biography, My Life as an Indian, 1907; cf. D.R.  Bedford, 1974, for another appraisal of Schultz's work.)

Bear Head's narrative is well worth the reading.  Before he recalls Major Baker's massacre of the Piegan village (1870), Bear Head tells a good deal about his own youth--including his first participation in a war party at age eight: how, despite his revulsion, he was forced to count coup on a dying warrior, and how his father shamed him into scalping this same warrior, and of the pride he felt once he had so proven himself.

32    Beck, Clifford. See no. 24.

33    Bedonie, Lamar.  KARL W. KLUCKERT.  Autobiographical interview to be found in Kluckert, Navajo Mountain and Rainbow Bridge Religion (P), Flagstaff, Ariz.:   Museum of Northern Arizona, 1977, pp. 143-50.

Born, c. 1907; interviewed, 1976.  Navajo.  The book cited here is an account of the significance of Navajo Mountain and the Rainbow Bridge in Navajo religion.  The book's method is to rely heavily on transcripts of translated interviews with elderly Navajo men who recount, then, personal experiences, doctrines, and ceremonies associated with Navajo Mountain or the Rainbow Bridge.  In addition to Bedonie, those interviewed were

Paul Goodman (born, c. 1880), Long Salt (born, c. 1885), Floyd Laughter (born, c. 1919), Ernest Nelson (born, c. 1908), Buck Navajo (born, c. 1924), and Buster Hastiin Nez (born, c. 1921).

34 Begay, Agnes R. BRODERICK H. JOHNSON. "Agnes R. Begay," as found in Johnson, ed., Navajos and World War II (IP), Tsaile, Ariz.: Navajo Community College Press, 1977, pp. 47-50.

Born, 1913; interviewed, c. 1973. Navajo. This book, like the one cited in no. 17, is a compilation of autobiographical narratives originally collected by Navajo interviewers in Navajo. These interviews were subsequently translated and cut. Some of the interviewer's questions remain. Begay tells about her work in a munitions plant during WW II.

35 Begay, Alberta. EVE BALL. A narrative is to be found in the book cited in no. 138, pp. 248-61. This was first published by Ball as "Massai--Bronco Apache," True West, VI (July-August, 1959).

Born, c. 1896; interviewed, probably c. 1957. Chiricahua Apache. Massai, the "Apache Kid," escaped from the train that was taking him to captivity in Florida in 1886. Begay, Massai's daughter, here tells of his life from this time up until his death and mutilation by a posse, c. 1900. Her account includes her remembrances of her early childhood with her fugitive father in the high Apache country. Probably Ball did more editing and rearranging of this narrative than of the others in her book. For the rest, see no. 138.

36 Begay, Hosteen Tsosie (M). See no. 24.

37 Begay, Keats (M). BRODERICK H. JOHNSON. "Keats Begay," as found in the book cited in no. 34, pp. 11-46.

Born, 1923; interviewed, c. 1973. Navajo. For the details of the collaboration, see no. 34. Begay tells a bit about his childhood and schooling, but this is almost entirely devoted to his WW II experiences. Begay fought in the Pacific and was eventually taken prisoner by the Japanese.

38 Begay, Kenneth. CARL ROSNEK and JOSEPH STACEY. Narrative is to be found in Rosnek and Stacey, Skystone and Silver: The Collector's Book of Southwest Indian Jewelry (IP),* Englewood Cliffs, N.J.: Prentice Hall, Inc., 1976, pp. 115-17.

Born, c. 1920; interviewed, c. 1975. Navajo. The book cited here is a gorgeously illustrated introduction to southwestern Indian jewelers as well as to their jewelry. In addition to Begay's, the authors print edited interviews with the following craftsmen: Phil Navaysa (born, c. 1950; Hopi), Larry Golsh (born, c. 1946; Pala Mission and Cherokee), Johnny and Marlene

Rosetta (born, c. 1950; Hopi), Charles Loloma (born, c. 1950; Hopi), Preston Monongye (born, c. 1920; Mission and Hopi), and Veronica Orr (born, c. 1943; Colville Reservation, Washington). The artists tell about their work, their introduction to silver-smithing, their attitudes toward their own work and the work of others, their early days, their schooling, etc.

39  Begay, Marlene, and Wilson Big, Jerry Gamble, Violet Harvey, Alfred Nelson, Bob Lee Gamble, Carla Willetto, Marvin Yellowhair. ELEANOR VELARDE. Autobiographical narratives are to be found in Velarde, ed., Rough Stones Are Precious Too . . . (P),* Rough Rock, Ariz.: Navajo Curriculum Center, 1978, pp. 70-93.
       All born, c. 1960; all wrote, 1976-77. Navajo. These narratives were all written as high school English assignments. Velarde, the English teacher, writes that she has "done very little 'correcting' (only where a word or the sentence structure confused the meaning)" (p. iii). The narratives have to do with trips to trading posts and sheep and cattle herding.

40  Begay, Myrtle. BRODERICK H. JOHNSON. "Myrtle Begay,"* as found in the book cited in no. 17, pp. 56-72.
       Born, 1912; interviewed, c. 1976. Navajo. For the details of the collaboration, see no. 17. There is much talk here of the value of education and of the teaching of moral principles, along with a sketch of an autobiography.

41  Begay, Tacheadeny Tso (M). See no. 24.

42  Begay, Yazi (pseudonym [M]). EVON Z. VOGT. "Yazi Begay: Life Story," as found in Vogt, Life Histories of Fourteen Navaho Young Men, Microcard Publications of Primary Records in Culture and Personality, ed. Bert Kaplan, I, No. 21, Madison, Wis.: Microcard Foundation, 1956, 253-84. Excerpts from each of these life histories, along with thoroughgoing analyses, are to be found in Vogt, Navaho Veterans: A Study of Changing Values, Papers of the Peabody Museum of American Archaeology and Ethnology, XLI, No. 1 (1951), xix + 223 pp.
       Born, c. 1922; interviewed, 1947. Navajo. All of the autobiographies in this volume were relatively free narratives. Beyond his initial request for a life story, Vogt asked very few questions, and all of these questions are included in the text. The narratives were taken down directly in the words of the informant or the interpreter (in those cases where an interpreter was necessary). Vogt argues in his introduction that these narratives are very much in keeping with the traditions of Navajo storytelling. Since the collecting of these life histories was a part of a large study of Zuni and Navajo WW II veterans (see no. 75), there is a rather surprising range of information

available about these men. See Vogt's references to the results of the psychological testing of these men--Rorschachs, Murray TAT's, and Sentence Completion Tests.

In his work with Begay, Vogt used an interpreter, though the narrative sometimes slips into Begay's own halting English. Begay begins with some charming recollections of his childhood, of his irresponsibility in performing his duties as a shepherd, and of his passion for, and ingenuity in, catching rabbits. Most of the narrative, however, is devoted to his army experiences. He concludes with an account of his feelings upon returning to the reservation.

43  Benally, Capiton. See no. 24.

44  Benally, Dan S. BRODERICK H. JOHNSON. "Dan S. Benally," as found in the book cited in no. 34, pp. 64-85.

Born, 1912; interviewed, c. 1973. Navajo. For the details of the collaboration, see no. 34. After a brief account of his childhood, Benally relates his WW II experiences. He served in Europe and was eventually taken prisoner.

45  Benally, Hascon (M). See no. 24.

46  Bennett, Kay (Kaibah). Kaibah:  Recollection of a Navajo Girlhood.* Los Angeles: Westernlore Press, 1964. 253 pp.

Born, c. 1921; wrote, c. 1964. Navajo. This is a rather artful book, written in the third person. Bennett tells of her years of childhood (1928-35), from the time of the first attempt to take her away to school to the time of her leaving the reservation to live in Los Angeles. She left at a time of sadness, in the midst of the great drought of the 1930's, and during the time of the government's ill-received stock-reduction program. The language of this book is quite simple, but it provides a moving evocation of "an average Navajo family and an average Navajo girl" (p. 8).

47  BENT, GEORGE. George E. Hyde. "Forty Years with the Cheyennes," appeared in six parts, The Frontier: A Magazine of the West, IV, (1905-1906), Oct., 3-7; Nov., 3-5; Dec., 3-7; Jan., 3-6; Feb., 3-7; Mar., 3-8.

1843-1918; wrote, c. 1905. White father, Cheyenne mother. Some have questioned whether Bent or Hyde actually wrote this series, but we can now be fairly certain that the writing is Bent's in fact (see no. 48, p. xvii), with Hyde as editor. This is partly history and partly autobiography, and not simply an abridgment of no. 48; however, most of what is dealt with here is dealt with in no. 48 in much greater detail. Bent was a survivor of the Sand Creek Massacre.

48  Bent, George.  GEORGE E. HYDE.  A Life of George Bent, Written from His Letters (IP), ed. Savoie Lottinville.  Norman: University of Oklahoma Press, 1968.  xxv + 389 pp.

Collaborated, 1905-18.  Hyde corresponded with Bent during the years indicated and assembled this autobiography out of Bent's first-person letters, though the resulting manuscript was to lie idle until it came into the hands of Lottinville. Lottinville kept his own editing to a minimun.  Lottinville, by the way, has worked with the Hyde-Bent letters, and he attests to the authenticity of Hyde's work.

Bent's is a fascinating life.  He fought with the Confederates in the Civil War and so was in danger of being killed by the Union partisans in Colorado upon his return home. His father consequently advised him to join his mother's people for safety, this in 1863.  It was, however, just at this time that the Cheyennes became involved in a bloody war with the U.S. Army, and Bent was cut off from white civilization.  "It is for this period of war, from 1863-1868, that George Bent's information is unique.  He was the only man among the hostiles who could and did set down in writing an account of what he witnessed" (p. ix).  Bent's narrative takes us up to about 1878. Bent writes with the intent of justifying the actions of the Cheyennes, with whom he came to identify himself.

49  Bernard, Gertrude.  See no. 10.

50  Besuk (F).  KNUD JOHAN VICTOR RASMUSSEN.  Three connected narratives are to be found in Rasmussen, The People of the Polar North:  A Record (IP), ed. and trans.  G. Herring, N.Y.:  AMS Press Inc., 1976 [1908], pp. 293-301.

Born, probably before 1865; narrated, 1904.  Eskimo, East Greenland.  Rasmussen was fluent in the native language of the people he presents to us in this remarkable book, which is an account of his travels and of the tales he heard along the way. The translations into Danish were his own.  Sometimes Rasmussen notes a particular narrative is given as a literal translation, and for the rest we may assume that Rasmussen is retelling the narrative.  Rasmussen was, however, evidently quite adept at using native narrative patterns, and so these narratives are probably reasonably authentic.

Besuk tells her macabre recollections of murders and of the consequences of those murders--of a motherless child being taken out onto the rocks to die of cold and starvation, of the fear her tiny community felt at having a maddened murderer in its midst--a man who ate the hearts of his victims.  (For a narrative by this man, Christian, see no. 116.)

51  Betony, Gyssie (M).  See no. 24.

52 BETZINEZ, JASON. Wilber Sturtevant Nye. I Fought with
Geronimo.* Harrisburg, Pa.: The Stackpole Co., 1959. 214 pp.
    Born, c. 1860; wrote shortly before 1959. Apache. Betzinez
wrote his narrative in English, and this was edited by Nye.
Nye's editing included rearranging, changes in phrasing, and the
addition of material collected from Betzinez in conversations,
tape recordings, and correspondence. Betzinez drew maps as
well, and reworkings of his maps are included here.
    Betzinez lived a remarkably various life. We read here of
his childhood, his days as a warrior with Geronimo, his sojourn
at the Carlisle Indian school, his work at a Pennsylvania steel
mill, his struggle for land to call his own, and, in the final
pages, we find him hoping, at the age of ninety-eight, to plant
some tulips and roses for his wife, Anna.

53 Big, Wilson. See no. 39.

54 Big Brave. JAMES WILLARD SCHULTZ. "Gros Ventre
Slaughter,"* as found in the book cited in no. 31, pp. 271-81.
    Born, c. 1853; narrated, c. 1938. Blackfeet. For the details
of the collaboration, see no. 31. Here are Big Brave's remembrances of the outbreak of war between the Gros Ventres and
the Blackfeet--tribes which had previously been allies.

55 Bighead, Kate. THOMAS BAILEY MARQUIS. She Watched
Custer's Last Battle.* Hardin, Montana: Custer Battlefield
Museum (?), 1933. 8 unnumbered pp.
    Born, c. 1847; interviewed, 1927. Cheyenne. For the details
of the collaboration, see no. 484. This narrative is yet another
fruit of Marquis's long-time interest in the Custer battle, and so
this narrative is concerned with but few experiences which are
not related to Custer. The result, however, is unique. I know
of no other sustained account by an Indian woman of Custer
himself. She talks about how attractive he was to her and to
other Cheyenne women and about the prestige her cousin Me-o-
tzi won by consorting with Custer. This pamphlet certainly
deserves reprinting.

56 Big Mouth (M). EVE BALL. Narratives are to be found in the
book cited in no. 138, pp. 198-203, 284-87.
    Born, c. 1860; interviewed, probably c. 1950. Mescalero
Apache. Ball worked through an interpreter here. For the rest
see no. 138. Big Mouth remembers the hard times before the
reservation days--dealing with Kit Carson, the troubles
attendant upon the establishment of Mescalero Reservation
(1873), etc.

57 Big-Ox (M). See no. 200.

58 Big Winnebago (M). See no. 73.

59 Bird Chief (James Bird). JAMES WILLARD SCHULTZ. "The Theft of the Sacred Otter Bow-Case (Told by Bird Chief--James Bird),"* as found in the book cited in no. 31, pp. 179-93.

Born, c. 1813; narrated, probably c. 1880. Blackfeet. For the details of this collaboration, see no. 31. Bird Chief tells about the theft and the recovery of the bow-case (1846), and he has a good deal to say as well about his own and his people's feelings concerning these events.

60 Bissonette, Gladys. THE EDITORIAL COMMITTEE. Narratives by Bisonette and others to be found in Voices from Wounded Knee, 1973: In the Words of the Participants, Rooseveltown, N.Y.: Akwesasne Notes, 1975, 263 pp.

Born, c. 1925; narrated, 1973. Sioux. The book cited here is a running account of the 1973 occupation of Wounded Knee, and its antecedents, as told by the people who were involved. For the most part, the people whose voices we hear are those of the besieged, although an interview with Richard Wilson, the much reviled tribal chairman, is included, and we hear as well from some of the law-enforcement people, clergymen, etc. All of this material was obtained in or near Wounded Knee by five unnamed reporters for The Rest of the News, an underground news organization. Four of these reporters lived with the besieged until the final days. Besides Bissonette--who lost a son, Pedro, during the occupation--we hear from the following (all Sioux, unless otherwise noted): Severt Young Bear, Vern Long, Eddie White Wolf, Pedro Bissonette, Ellen Moves Camp, Richard Wilson, Russell Means, Lorelei DeCora, Duane Camp, Grace Black Elk, Wallace Black Elk, and Stan Holder (Wichita).

61 Bissonette, Pedro. See no. 60.

62 Bitsilly, Denah L. (F). See no. 24.

63 Blackbird, Andrew J. History of the Ottawa and Chippewa Indians of Michigan; a Grammer of Their Language, and Personal Family History of the Author. Ypsilanti, Mich.: Ypsilanti Job Printing House, 1887. 128 pp. Reprinted by Little Traverse Regional Historical Society, Petoskey, Mich., 1979 (P).

Born, c. 1822; wrote, c. 1887. Ottawa. Blackbird tells of his Indian youth, his baptism, and his journey to Ohio to seek an education among the whites. He also tells of his treating with the government for the just treatment of his people, and of being appointed U.S. interpreter in 1861. A Catholic when a youth, Blackbird converted to Protestantism in his teens, and a good deal is said here about religious matters. All of this is woven through his history of the Ottawas and Chippewas.

64     Black Eagle (M). Nez Perce. See no. 509.

65     Black Eagle (M).    WILLIAM WHITMAN.    "Xube, a Ponca Autobiography," Journal of American Folklife, LII (1939), 180-93.

     Born, 1889; interviewed, probably shortly before 1939. Ponca. The presentation here is awkward. Whitman has chosen to edit some of this matter into third person, while the rest is a "verbatim transcription from the dictated life history" (p. 181). This is evidently only a part of a longer autobiography which remains unprinted.

     Whitman says that Black Eagle "is as fearlessly aggressive as he is, in white terms, unmoral. The violence and guile which in other days would have made him a great warrior, have found expression in his pursuit of women" (p. 181). This interpretation closely parallels Radin's interpretation of Sam Blowsnake's behavior (see nos. 73, 74). Even when compared with other Indian autobiographers, Black Eagle describes a life more than usually ruled by cultural contradictions; for example, though his father converted him to Christianity, his father still wanted him to develop his xube, or spiritual powers as traditionally concevied.

66     Black Elk. JOHN G. NEIHARDT. Black Elk Speaks (IP),* with an introduction by Vine Deloria, Jr.   Lincoln: University of Nebraska Press, 1979 [1932].   xix + 299 pp.   Available in paperback from Pocket Books, 1977, xvi + 238 pp.

     1863-1950; narrated, 1931. Oglala Sioux. This narration was accomplished with Black Elk's son as interpreter and Neihardt's daughter as stenographer. The original transcript has been preserved (University of Missouri at Columbia, Western Manuscripts Collection), and two scholars (McClusky, 1972, and Castro, 1979) have made use of this material and an interview with Neihardt to point rather precisely at the changes Neihardt wrought upon Black Elk's narrative. Now the 1979 Nebraska edition of Black Elk Speaks prints two pages of the transcript (for purposes of comparison) and a letter from Neihardt to Black Elk wherein Neihardt suggests the idea of, and makes arrangements for, Black Elk's narrative.

     Evidently, then, Neihardt first met with Black Elk in the hope of getting information about the Ghost Dance movement. By the fall of 1930, however, Neihardt had a larger plan. To quote from Neihardt's letter to Black Elk:

> My idea is to come back to the reservation next spring, probably in April, and have a number of meetings with you and your old friends . . . . I would want you to tell the

story of your life beginning at the beginning and going straight through to Wounded Knee . . . . This would make a complete history of your people since your childhood . . . . I would, of course, expect to pay you well for all the time that you would give me. (Nebraska edition, 1979, pp. 278-79)

This is not quite the sense of the collaboration Neihardt provided in his preface to the 1961 University of Nebraska Press edition of Black Elk Speaks (reprinted in all subsequent editions). There we read that Neihardt played wedding guest to Black Elk's ancient mediciner. The Black Elk of the 1961 preface "seemed to know" that Neihardt was coming to visit him, seemed disinclined to discuss the mundane matters that Neihardt had come to hear about--battles, the Ghost Dance, etc.--"it was increasingly clear that his real interest was in 'the things of the Other World.'" This Black Elk finally says to Neihardt: "'What I know was given to me for men and it is true and it is beautiful. Soon I shall be under the grass and it will be lost. You were sent to save it, and you must come back so that I can teach you.'" Here it is even Black Elk who suggests the time of their meeting: Neihardt was to return "'In the spring when the grass is so high' (indicating the breadth of a hand)."

Now this claim that the writing down of sacred matters was really the Indian's suggestion, not the white collaborator's, that the Indian is eager to have the god-sent white man preserve the Indian's sacred knowledge might have occurred to Neihardt as a result of his reading of Paul Radin's introduction to Crashing Thunder (see no. 129). But for whatever reason Neihardt made this claim, such claims have certainly become one of the conventions of Anglo-assisted American Indian literature (see Brumble, 1980), and Black Elk Speaks has been particularly influential in this regard (see, e.g., no. 178).

Neihardt worked other changes as well. According to Castro (1979), Neihardt placed Black Elk's tragic dimension in bold relief--Black Elk saw the fate of his people as being in his hands; his people's troubles and the woes of all the world's peoples could in large measure have been alleviated had he been able to accomplish the healing that the Grandfathers intended when they bestowed upon him such large powers during his Great Vision. Neihardt exaggerates Black Elk's loneliness, diminishes his pride in his military accomplishments (again, according to Castro).

More generally it may be said that Neihardt cut, rearranged, did some rewording, and even added passages--not least the widely quoted passage about the death of the people's dream (McClusky, 1972). The fact that the three scholars who have compared the transcript with Black Elk Speaks (McClusky, Castro, and Sayre, 1971) nevertheless remain convinced that

Neihardt was essentially faithful to Black Elk's message and intent is a great testimony to Neihardt's skills and sensitivity—and to the power of Black Elk's narrative. Indeed, according to Vine Deloria, Jr., in his introduction to the 1979 edition, "the book has become a North American bible of all tribes" for a whole "generation of young Indians" who look to it "for spiritual guidance, for sociological identity, for political insight, and for affirmation of the continuing substance of Indian tribal life."

But Black Elk Speaks contains much besides the Great Vision which is at its center. Black Elk tells of his life in rich detail, from his childhood to the massacre at Wounded Knee. We read about the acquisition and development of his shamanic powers, his working out of the power of his visions in healing ceremonies and dances, about his travels with Buffalo Bill's Wild West show, his war deeds, including his participation in the Battle of the Little Bighorn, and much else.

67  Black Elk, Grace. See no. 60.

68  BLACK HAWK (M). Antoine LeClaire and John B. Patterson. Black Hawk, an Autobiography (P),* ed. Donald Jackson. Urbana: University of Illinois Press, 1955. 206 pp. Other editions: Life of Ma-ka-tai-me-she-kia-kiak, or Black Hawk (1833, 1834, 1836, 1842, 1847, 1916, 1932) and Autobiography of Ma-ka-tai-me-she-kia-kiak, or Black Hawk (1882, 1912).

C. 1767-1838; narrated, 1833. Sauk. In the introduction to his excellent edition of Black Hawk, Jackson explains the tangled history of this book. The first edition, Jackson argues, is almost certainly authentic, almost certainly Black Hawk's narrative as translated by LeClaire and rendered into manuscript form by Patterson. "The only drawback upon our credence," as an 1835 reviewer put it, "is the intermix of courtly phrases, and the figures of speech, which our novelists are so fond of putting into the mouths of Indians" (quoted by Jackson, p. 32). The 1882 edition, on the other hand, introduces much new material and altered phrasing, all from the mind of Patterson. Jackson's edition, of course, is based on the first edition.

There should be little doubt, then, that this book conveys Black Hawk's intent, which clearly is to present the Sauks' perspective on the Black Hawk War, to show how the Sauks were the persecuted, rather than savage aggressors as they had been depicted. Black Hawk is also concerned to justify himself in his conflicts with his Sauk rivals and enemies.

69  Black-Wolf (M). A.L. KROEBER. "Black-Wolf's Narrative," in Kroeber, Ethnology of the Gros Ventre (IP), Anthropological Papers of the American Museum of Natural History, I, No. 4 (1908), 197-204.

Born, c. 1840; interviewed, 1901. Gros Ventre. "Black-Wolf's Narrative" is one of three personal accounts of war experiences to be found in Ethnology of the Gros Ventre. For the other two, see below, nos. 89 and 515. The details of these interviews are not specified, but I assume that Kroeber worked with an interpreter, though Kroeber did have some knowledge of the native language. Kroeber does say that the three informants were asked "not to describe the engagements and expeditions in which they were involved, but to narrate their personal share in them" (p. 197). Black-Wolf relates events from about 1850 up to 1875. He is limited here to war experiences, but he does talk about his feelings as he engaged in this enterprise and that. This account is of particular interest, however, in that such war narratives would have been much closer to Gros Ventre narrative traditions (e.g., coup tales) than would more typically Western forms of autobiography.

70 Blake, Jeanette. BRODERICK H. JOHNSON. "Jeanette Blake,"* as found in the book cited in no. 17, pp. 201-5.
Born, c. 1902; interviewed, c. 1976. Navajo. For the details of the collaboration, see no. 17. For the most part this narrative consists of Blake's remembrances of her father's trouble with the law and of her own education.

71 Blanco, Johnny (pseudonym). EVON Z. VOGT. "Johnny Blanco: Life Story," as found in the book cited in no. 42, pp. 5-74.
Born, 1921; interviewed, 1947. Navajo. For the details of the collaboration see no. 42. Vogt worked through an interpreter here. This is quite an interesting narrative, filled with detail. Blanco tells of his youth, of his experiences in home-made rodeos, of ceremonials, of a Blessingway Sing that was done for him. He tells of building a hogan for his grandparents. He also talks about his conversion to Christianity and his subsequent "backsliding." And we get an account of Blanco's army experience (WW II) and his response to the reservation upon his return.

72 Blatchford, Paul. BRODERICK H. JOHNSON. "Paul Blatchford,"* as found in the book cited in no. 17, pp. 173-81.
Born, c. 1916; interviewed, c. 1976. White father, Navajo mother. For the details of the collaboration, see no. 17. Blatchford tells of his days at boarding school--and of the rather severe punishments which were meted out, punishments that included belt lines and basement confinement with ball and chain.

73 Blowsnake, Sam (Big Winnebago, pseudonym: Crashing Thunder. For an account of these names see no. 74). PAUL RADIN. The Autobiography of a Winnebago Indian (P).* N.Y.: Dover

Publications, Inc., 1963. 91 pp. This is an unaltered reprint of
the work first published in University of California Publications
in American Archaeology and Ethnology, XVI, No. 7 (1920), 381-
473. An edition of part I of The Autobiography is in The
Portable North American Indian Reader (P), ed. Frederick W.
Turner III, N.Y.: The Viking Press, 1973, pp. 378-454. The 1920
edition (and thus the Dover reprint) contains two parts, the first
being the autobiography proper, the second being twenty-three
pages entitled "My Father's Teachings." The Portable edition
deletes this second part.

Born, c. 1875; wrote, c. 1917. Winnebago. Blowsnake wrote
his autobiography in a syllabary then commonly in use among
the Winnebagos. Radin translated this text, with the aid of his
native interpreter, Oliver Lamere, and prints it without alterations of any kind. Radin claims that "no attempt of any kind
was made to influence [Blowsnake] in the selection of the
particular facts of his life which he chose to present" (p. 2);
however, Radin mentions, in a footnote late in the book, that he
did suggest that Blowsnake might want to write in order to
convince later generations of the errors of the old ways--
Blowsnake being a recent convert to the Peyote Cult, and Radin
needing some means of motivating Blowsnake to write. The
result is what must be called a book of confessions. Blowsnake
tells us about his fasting for a vision, about his participation in
the medicine dance, but he assures us that it was all false, that
there was no power there to be had. Real visions are finally
possible to him as a participant in the Peyote Cult.

The faults he recalls have to do with his personal failings as
well as the failings of the Winnebago religion. He had been a
womanizer, a drunkard, and now he is a changed man. The
fascination of this book, however, lies in the ways in which
Blowsnake's traditional Winnebago moral and religious assumptions are woven through his new faith in the peyote church, the
ways in which he embraced the Peyote Cult because it fulfilled
so many of the expectations which his traditional culture had
built up within him, the ways in which his participation in the
cult is shaped by his personality, shaped as it had been in turn
by traditional Winnebago culture.

This a very important autobiography, not only for the
quality of the work itself, but for all that it tells us about the
relationship of the informant and the anthropologist.
Blowsnake is the brother of Crashing Thunder (no. 129) and
Mountain Wolf Woman (no. 349).

74 _____ . _____ . Crashing Thunder: The Autobiography
of a Winnebago Indian.* N.Y.: Appleton and Co., 1926. xxv +
203 pp.

This is an expanded version of no. 73, Radin adding more
than a third again to the length of the original by fitting

excerpts from other material he had collected from Blowsnake over the years. Where, for example, Blowsnake wrote in the 1920 edition that he prayed to the spirits, Radin here interpolates an appropriate prayer to the spirits, which he had at some other time taken down from Blowsnake's dictation. Radin also did some rearranging. The "Teachings of My Father" are no longer a separate part at the end of the book, for another example, but rather are worked in along the way. Radin also deletes here a good deal of the annotation that accompanied the 1920 edition.

Finally, something must be said about all of Blowsnake's names. Because of his desire for anonymity, Sam Blowsnake was known as S.B. in the 1920 edition. But when Radin decided to publish this edition of 1926, he had a more popular audience in mind, and he wanted an Indian name for his autobiographer. As Nancy Lurie explains, however, Big Winnebago, the English version of Blowsnake's Indian name, seemed "amusingly inappropriate. As the title of a book it is somehow evocative of the 'heap big Indian' school of fiction," but by "1926 the real Crashing Thunder [Blowsnake's brother; see no. 129] had died, and since he had been an even more important informant than Big Winnebago, and a considerably less controversial figure, Radin calculated that a book by Crashing Thunder would not evoke undue curiosity among the Winnebago generally" (no. 349, pp. 97-98).

75  Bob.  JOHN ADAIR.  "Life History of Bob," as found in Adair, Life Histories of Six Zuni Young Men, Microcard Publications of Primary Records in Culture and Personality, ed. Bert Kaplan, I, No. 23, Madison, Wis.: Microcard Foundation, 1956, 108-25.

Born, 1920; interviewed, 1947. Zuni. The six life histories contained in the volume cited are important, among other reasons, because they are some of the relatively few autobiographies by young Indians. Adair publishes the transcript of the interview in each case, including his own questions. Features of nonstandard English are left unedited. This collection is a part of a large study of Navajo and Zuni WW II veterans (see no. 42). Consequently, a rather surprising range of information is available about these men. See Adair's references to the results of their psychological testing--Rorschachs, Murray TAT's, and Sentence Completion Tests. (See Vogt and Albert, 1966, pp. 299-305, for a bibliography of publications resulting from this whole "Comparative Study of Values in Five Cultures" project.)

Bob tells of his schooling, his army experience, his courting, and his marital troubles. Perhaps the most interesting aspect of this autobiography is Bob's account of what it was like to return to Zuni after having been in the army. He talks about the sense of confinement he feels at Zuni, of his desire to "get out someplace where I can be free" (p. 111)--free, for example, to speak English without being chastised.

76  Bogoutin, Howard.  BRODERICK H. JOHNSON.  "Howard Bogoutin,"* as found in the book cited in no. 17, pp. 280-84.
      Born, 1890; interviewed, 1976. Navajo. For the details of the collaboration, see no. 17. Bogoutin tells here of his formal education at trade school and his traditional education.

77  Bonnin, Gertrude. See no. 562.

78  Boulanger, Tom.  An Indian Remembers (P).*  Winnipeg, Manitoba: Peguis Publishers Ltd., 1971. 90 pp.
      Born, 1901; wrote, 1967-68. Cree. Boulanger's spelling has been regularized, but otherwise his felicitously idiosyncratic English is printed intact. "I am writing a few news from that time of my life, when I remember about six or seven years' old and the people I knew" (p. 1). Boulanger writes as a Christian but also as a Cree with some remnants of the old ways adhering. For the most part, however, Boulanger tells of his life as a trapper and woodsman.

79  Brown, Catherine. RUFUS ANDERSON. Memoir of Catherine Brown, a Christian Indian of the Cherokee Nation. Philadelphia: American Sunday School Union, 1832. 138 pp.
      Born, c. 1800; wrote, 1821. Cherokee and white. This book is biography, but Anderson does include a few (edited) pages of Brown's journal (pp. 65-76) and letters (pp. 81-93). This book offers little to others than those interested in early Indian pietism.

80  Brown, Charlie.  BRODERICK H. JOHNSON.  "Charlie Brown,"* as found in the book cited in no. 17, pp. 143-48.
      Born, c. 1902; interviewed, c. 1976. Navajo. For the details of this collaboration, see no. 17.  These are discontinuous reminiscences of religion, personal experiences, and folk traditions, by a man without formal education, and who prefers the Navajo religion.

81  Brown, Cozy Stanley.  BRODERICK H. JOHNSON.  "Cozy Stanley Brown," as found in the book cited in no. 34, pp. 51-63.
      Born, c. 1925; interviewed, c. 1973. Navajo. For the details of the collaboration, see no. 34.  Two pages are devoted to Brown's childhood and youth; the rest is devoted to his WW II experiences.  Brown was one of the Navajo Code-Talkers; that is, he was one of those Navajos whom the army relied upon to communicate messages in code, in Navajo.

82  Brown, Fanny. See no. 107.

83  Brown, Mable.   ELIZABETH COLSON.   "Autobiography of Mable Brown," as found in the book cited in no. 2, pp. 99-107.
    Born, c. 1849; interviewed, 1939. Pomo. Taken in halting English and printed here with a minimum of editing, this is a directed narrative, and most of Colson's questions are included. See no. 2 for further details of the collaboration.   Minor rearranging. This is a curious one, since Brown was well along the road to senility at the time Colson worked with her. She was, however, still an important member of her community and highly regarded for her one-time abilities as a dancer. This is the mother of Sophie Martinez (no. 316).

84  Bryant, Billy. See no. 24.

85  Buck, Neil.   GRENVILLE GOODWIN.   Narratives are to be found in The Social Organization of the Western Apache, Tucson: University of Arizona Press, 1969, pp. 206, 467, 486-96, 550.
    Born, c. 1863; interviewed, 1930's. Apache. In the book cited Goodwin proceeds by interspersing his own description and analysis with illustrative quotations from his informants. Some of these are identified (see nos. 406, 430) and many are not. Buck, who would have worked with Goodwin through an interpreter, tells about his childhood, his joking relationship with an aunt, games, and his experience of institutionalized giving.

86  Buckanga, Gertrude.   JANE B. KATZ.   Reminiscences* in the book cited in no. 28, pp. 94-95, 122.
    Born, c. 1925; interviewed, 1976. For the details of the collaboration, see no. 28. Here are fond memories of the primitive life on the reservation at Pine Point, Minnesota, by a member of the faculty at St. Catherine's College.

87  Buffalo Child Long Lance (M). See no. 291.

88  Bullheart, Johnny.   EDWARD SAPIR and LESLIE SPIER.   A narrative to be found in Sapir and Spier, Wishram Ethnography (IP), University of Washington Publications in Ethnography, III, No. 3 (1930), pp. 222-23, 233-35.
    Born, c. 1836; interviewed, 1908. Shasta-Molala, but raised by the Klickitats and Wishrams. I presume that Bullheart spoke through an interpreter. Bullheart here recounts his capture by the Klickitats, c. 1842. He was subsequently sold to Wishram Indians, with whom he lived quite happily. Bullheart is even able to tell of having gone to war (at the age of sixteen) with his adopted tribe.

89  Bull-Robe (M). A.L. KROEBER.   "Bull-Robe's Narrative," as found in the book cited in no. 69, pp. 204-16.

Born, c. 1840; interviewed, 1901. Gros Ventre. For further detail, see no. 69.

90 Bull Snake (M). JOSEPH KOSSUTH DIXON. "Bull Snake,"* as found in the book cited in no. 11, pp. 101-4.

Born, c. 1844; interviewed, 1909. Crow. For the details of this collaboration, see no. 11. Bull Snake tells of receiving a crippling wound while fighting for General Crook and of never receiving the pension to which his wound entitled him.

91 Burbank, Akinabh (F). See no. 24.

92 Burson, Fred. T.D. ALLEN. "Why Not? It's New Years!" in Arrows Four: Prose and Poetry by Young American Indians, N.Y.: Washington Square Press, 1974, pp. 115-20.

Born, c. 1954; wrote c. 1971. Ute. The book cited here is a collection of narratives and poems written by Indian school children. Many of these pieces are autobiographical. All have been edited toward standard English. Burson recalls meeting a derelict in Salt Lake City while on his way to spend New Year's with his sister. Burson relates this experience to his own coming of age.

93 Burton, Jimalee Chitwood (Ho-chee-nee [F]). Indian Heritage, Indian Pride: Stories That Touched My Life (IP).* Norman: University of Oklahoma Press, 1974. xvi + 176 pp.

Born, c. 1920; wrote, 1967-73. Cherokee and white. This book combines a sentimental folk history and folk ethnography with nostalgia-sweetened personal reminiscences about growing up in Oklahoma, travel, etc. Burton is an artist, and this book is liberally illustrated with her work.

94 Bushotter, George. JAMES OWEN DORSEY. "George Bushotter's Autobiography," as found in "Lakota Texts by George Bushotter," trans. and ed. Dorsey, National Anthropological Archives, Smithsonian Institution, MS. No. 4800, no. 101, 117 pp. Brief excerpts from this autobiography are included in Raymond J. DeMallie (1978), pp. 90-102.

1864-92; wrote, 1887. Teton Sioux. This autobiography is but one of 259 Lakota texts--totaling some 3,500 pages of text and interlinear translation--which Bushotter supplied to Dorsey. In the autobiography, Bushotter tells about the life he lived before he learned the ways of the white man and something about his schooling (Hampton) as well. This is interesting material that seems to be well worth the editing and publication which DeMallie says he hopes to accomplish. In the meantime we must be content with Ella C. Deloria's free translations of Bushotter's texts, which are available in the Library of the American Philosophical Society, Philadelphia.

95   Caballo, Sam (pseudonym). EVON Z. VOGT. "Life History: Sam Caballo," as found in the book cited in no. 42, pp. 75-91.

    Born, c. 1920; interviewed, 1948. Navajo. For the details of the collaboration, see no. 42. Vogt worked with an interpreter here, though Caballo knew some English. As with many other Navajo autobiographies, this one begins with sheepherding. As is also quite often the case, Caballo recalls the fear he had to contend with as a child out there all alone with the sheep. He goes on to tell of small-scale farming, his relationship with girls, and his travels.

96   Cadman, William. BRODERICK H. JOHNSON. "William Cadman,"* as found in the book cited in no. 17, pp. 206-19.

    Born, 1916; interviewed, c. 1976. Navajo. For the details of this collaboration, see no. 17. Cadman talks about his traditional and his boarding school education. He also tells of being one of the Navajo Code-Talkers who worked in the Pacific during WW II; that is, he was one of the Navajos assigned to send and receive radio messages in code in Navajo--"the enemy forces were absolutely stunned, and they never figured out what we were talking about" (p. 213). Cadman went to work in the schools and eventually become president of a Navajo savings and loan bank in Window Rock.

97   CALF ROBE, BENJAMIN AUGUSTINE. Adolf and Beverly Hungry Wolf. Siksika: A Blackfoot Narrative (P).* Invermere, B.C.: Good Medicine Books, 1979. xvi + 107 pp.

    Born, 1890; collaborated, 1976-78. Siksika Blackfeet. According to Hungry Wolf, Calf Robe sought him out because Calf Robe wanted to tell his stories and his life experiences to someone who could write them down and preserve them for "the future generations" (p. x). For the most part, Calf Robe spoke English during the resultant tape-recorded interviews, but some tales he preferred to tell in Blackfeet. These were translated by Calf Robe and Beverly Hungry Wolf. Although the nature of the collaboration is not further specified, it would seem that Adolf Hungry Wolf did some cutting and rearranging of passages, but probably did little rephrasing and probably added virtually nothing. This is a valuable book for those interested in the transition from the old ways to the new. Calf Robe began his schooling around 1900 and later graduated from a Calgary technical school, but his interest in the old ways did not flag. He relates his remembrances of the oral history of his tribe with relish, and he is eager as well to recall the history of the Sun Dance among the Siksika--down to the recent filming of an entire Sun Dance and its attendant ceremonies (a project in which Calf Robe was largely instrumental). Calf Robe worked as a printer, a tribal policeman, and a farmer.

98 Callihoo, Victoria. "Our Buffalo Hunts,"* <u>Alberta Historical Review</u>, VIII, No. 1 (1960), 24-25.

   Born, c. 1865; wrote, 1948. Cree, Iroquois, and white. Callihoo recalls the first buffalo hunt in which she participated (age, thirteen). She includes some homely details of camp life, recalling, for example, how slow they all were to light their fires of a morning, each waiting for another to go to the trouble of lighting fire from flint and birch punk-- whereupon there would be a general rush to borrow fire from the first tipi that showed smoke.

99 Calvin, Hezekiah. JAMES DOW McCALLUM. Letters to be found in the book cited in no. 18, 47-67.

   Born, c. 1749; wrote, 1766-68. Delaware. For the details of the writing and the editing of these letters see no. 18. These letters reveal Calvin to be a troubled young man. In one letter he writes of his plans for proselytizing and his longing for home; in another he confesses his sins and begs forgiveness; in another he plans marriage; in another he writes of his work and begs leave to go home; in another he confesses to drunkenness and "horrible crimes" (p. 62); and again he implores Wheelock to allow him to go home--all of this before the age of twenty. Eventually he was jailed for forgery.

100 Camp, Duane. See no. 60.

101 Campbell, Maria. <u>Halfbreed</u> (P).* Toronto: McCelland and Stewart-Bantam, Ltd., 1973. 184 pp.

   Born, 1940; wrote shortly before 1973. Métis ("Halfbreed") from the area north of Prince Albert, Saskatchewan. Campbell asks us to see her life in the larger context of her family's history, and so she begins with an account of the troubles of Saskatchewan Métis which led, ultimately, to rebellion under the leadership of Louis Riel in 1884. Campbell sees her own life, her struggles, as a continuation of that rebellion, until, in the final pages, she tells of her realization that armed rebellion will not and should not come. She feels, finally, that Métis and whites must work together, if not for love, then out of need.

102 Carol, Chee (M). See no. 24.

103 Cedric. JOHN ADAIR. "Life History," as found in the book cited in no. 75, pp. 269-84.

   Born, c. 1908; interviewed, 1947. Zuni. For the details of this collaboration, see no. 75. Much of this is devoted to the problems of learning to cope with witches.

104 Ch'ahadiniini Binali (M). BRODERICK H. JOHNSON.

"Ch'ahadiniini Binali,"* as found in the book cited in no. 17, pp. 220-29.

Born, c. 1882; interviewed, 1976. Navajo tribal affiliation, but his father was Hopi. For the details of this collaboration, see no. 17. Personal reminiscence interwoven with tribal history and talk about education.

105 Chamiso, Haske (pseudonym [M]). EVON Z. VOGT. "Haske Chamiso: Life History," as found in the book cited in no. 42, pp. 175-98.

Born, c. 1920; interviewed, 1947. Navajo. Vogt worked through an interpreter here. For further details of the collaboration, see no. 42. There are childhood reminiscences here, and reminiscences of sings done for his ailing wife, but Chamiso's response to military life (WW II) is the most interesting part of this narrative--the response of a man who had had a very narrow range of experience to the complexity and mechanization of army life.

106 Chamiso, Ted (pseudonym). EVON Z. VOGT. "Ted Chamiso: Life History," as found in the book cited in no. 42, pp. 112-26.

Born, probably c. 1920; interviewed, 1948. Navajo. Vogt worked with an interpreter here. For further details of the collaboration, see no. 42. Chamiso tells of his youth and his work. The most interesting part of the narrative has to do with his journey into Utah to look for work in 1942. He spoke no English. The final few pages are devoted to questions and answers, and here we find that Chamiso has seen a ghost, that he knows nothing about condoms, etc. Chamiso led a culturally confined life. It would be interesting to systematic-ally compare those men in Vogt's study who speak English with those who do not.

107 Charles, Nels. CORA DuBOIS. An autobiography is to be found in DuBois, Wintu Ethnography, California University Publications in American Archeology and Ethnography, XXXVI (1935), 95-97.

Born, c. 1888; interviewed, c. 1934. Wintu. Charles spoke English, and his narrative has been printed with a minimum of editing, including some rearranging. Though the events of his childhood are mentioned, the narrative has mainly to do with the acquisition and exercise of shamanistic powers. Other personal accounts of Wintu shamans, Fanny Brown, Wash Fan (M), Tilly Griffen, Kate Luckie, and Jake Cornish are also to be found in the book cited above, pp. 88-112.

108 Charley. EDWARD SAPIR. A narrative is to be found in the book cited in no. 88, pp. 252-53.

Born, c. 1840; interviewed, c. 1909. Wishram. Sapir

worked through an interpreter. Charley tells of having "died,"
c. 1860, and of the wonders he witnessed during his three days
"high up in the air." This experience allowed him to become a
"preacher" in the Smohallah cult (evidently Ghost Dance-
related).

109  Chee, Peggy Jane. BRODERICK H. JOHNSON. "Peggy Jane
Chee," as found in the book cited in no. 34, pp. 116-22.
Born, c. 1920; interviewed, c. 1973. Navajo. For the
details of the collaboration, see no. 34. Chee tells a bit about
her childhood and then goes on to tell about her WW II
experiences as a member of the Women's Army Corps.

110  Chelooyeen (M). See no. 509.

111  Chihuahua, Eugene. EVE BALL. Narratives are to be found in
the book cited in no. 138, passim.
Born, c. 1875; narrated, probably c. 1965. Chiricahua
Apache. These interviews were conducted in English. For the
rest, see no. 138. Chihuahua recalls his father's experiences as
one of the Chiricahua scouts who served with the army in the
pacification of the Apaches, and he has a good deal else to say
about life in pre- and early reservation days. He was a
member, for a time, of one of the small bands which fled the
reservation, but finally he was shipped, along with the rest of
his family, off to the Florida prison camps. We read about the
Apaches' response to the camps, their enforced change of diet,
their oppression by the humid heat and insects. He recalls,
too, the last days of Geronimo.

112  Chona, Maria. RUTH UNDERHILL. The Autobiography of a
Papago Woman (P), Memoirs of the American Anthropological
Association, No. 46 (1936). 64 pp. Reprinted as pt. II of
Underhill, Papago Woman, N.Y.: Holt, Rinehart and Winston,
1979.
Born, c. 1846; interviewed, 1931-35. Papago. Though
Chona knew some Spanish and Underhill some Papago, an
interpreter was used during these interviews. The text as we
have it is close to a literal translation. Underhill did
rearrange and edit, deleting repetitions and "insignificant"
detail, putting the whole into chronological order. Underhill
does warn the reader where there are deletions.
This is a beautifully evocative autobiography, telling of
cactus fruit gathering, singing, composing songs, and visions--
of life in the desert. Chona is a woman proud of her
accomplishments. One is reminded of Mountain Wolf Woman's
autobiography (no. 349) and of Nancy Lurie's suggestion in the
introduction to that work that the transition from the old ways
to the new was easier for the women than the men.

113 Chooksa homar (Jo Nelson [M]). A.L. and CLIFTON B. KROEBER. A Mohave War Reminiscence, 1854-1880, University of California Publications in Anthropology, X (1973), x + 97 pp.

Born, c. 1840; interviewed, 1903. Mohave. A.L. Kroeber, working through an interpreter, asked Chooksa homar to tell of his war experiences. Kroeber did ask questions in order to fill in names and for clarification, but otherwise this is not a guided narrative. No attempt was made to reshape the narrative in the course of editing. A.L. Kroeber provides anthropological annotations, while Clifton B. provides historical annotations. Chooksa homar provides little other than the accounts of fighting which the title promises.

114 Chopari, John. MORRIS EDWARD OPLER. Childhood and Youth in Jicarilla Apache Society (IP), Publications of the Frederick Webb Hodge Anniversary Publications Fund, V (1946), 48, 56, 58, 60, 142-47, 151-52, 162.

Born, before 1890; interviewed, 1934-35. Jicarilla Apache. The plan of the book cited here is to make its explanations with the aid of frequent extended quotations from native informants. While they are not individually attributed, probably each of the autobiographical passages on the pages cited above is by one of Opler's two main informants, Chopari or Alasco Tisnado (M). Opler worked through an interpreter, and it would seem that he did little or no tampering with these short narratives, each of which would have been elicited by Opler's questioning. Much the most interesting of these brief narratives is the one which recalls the narrator's first war experience--his ritual preparation, etc. (pp. 142-47).

115 Chris (pseudonym [M]). MORRIS EDWARD OPLER. Apache Odyssey: A Journey between Two Worlds (IP). N.Y.: Holt, Rinehart and Winston, 1969. xvi + 301 pp.

Born, c. 1880; interviewed, 1933-36. Chiricahua Apache, Mescalero Apache upbringing. Chris spoke English, and Opler could converse, though at this time not fluently, in Apache. No mention is made of an interpreter, and I assume the interviews to have been largely in English. Opler allowed Chris to emphasize, embellish, and ignore as he chose. Opler presents it all "as it was told" though it is obvious that there has been some editing of the kind necessary to fit spoken language to the conventions of written English. Opler has done some rearranging as well, in order to fit the text to the conventions of chronological presentation. And he has added superb notes and introduction.

This is one of the very good Indian autobiographies. Chris was taken off to the East for incarceration with the Apaches, but his family was allowed to return after only two years--

twenty-five years before the rest were allowed to return. Chris is also interesting in that he is a partial believer. He subscribes to the large articles of Apache belief, but not to the small--he feels free, for example, to eat the meat of a deer slain by an eagle. For this and other reasons, Chris was not a comfortably accepted member of his tribe. He is a classic instance of the Indian caught between two cultures, fully accepted by neither, completely comfortable in neither.

One of the unusual and rewarding sections of this book is that devoted to Chris' account of his children. Love of children is no unusual feature in Indian autobiographies, but the kind of detailed, perceptive account of children that Chris provides is.

116 Christian (Autaruta). KNUD JOHAN VICTOR RASMUSSEN. A narrative is to be found in the book cited in no. 50, pp. 305-8. This narrative is reprinted in the second book cited in no. 202, pp. 107-10.

Born, probably before 1855; narrated, 1904. Eskimo, East Greenland. For the details of the collaboration, see no. 50. This is an account of the acquisition of shamanic powers by the man who committed the most grisly of the (cannibalistic) murders recounted in no. 50. By the time he spoke with Rasmussen he had been baptized a Christian.

117 Chuslum MoxMox (M). See no. 509.

118 Clani, Thomas. BRODERICK H. JOHNSON. "Thomas Clani,"* as found in the book cited in no. 17, pp. 243-55.

Born, c. 1902; interviewed, c. 1976. Navajo. For the details of the collaboration, see no. 17. Not much of this piece is autobiographical. For the most part it consists of miscellaneous thoughts on tribal history, education, etc.

119 Clara. DOROTHEA LEIGHTON and JOHN ADAIR. "Story of Myself," as found in, People of the Middle Place: A Study of the Zuni Indians (IP),* New Haven: Behavior Science Monographs, 1966 [1963], pp. 127-28.

Born, c. 1932; wrote, c. 1942. Zuni. Leighton elicited several written autobiographies from Zuni school children during 1942 and '43. In addition to Clara's, then, there is one by Frank (born, c. 1925), pp. 136-38, and another by Angela (born, c. 1926), pp. 133-35. There is not much here, though it is interesting to see how favorably Frank regards the Zuni virtues of restraint and obedience.

120 Cloud, Reverend Henry Roe. "From Wigwam to Pulpit: A Red Man's Own Story of His Progress from Darkness to Light," Missionary Review, XXXVIII (May, 1915), 328-39.

Born, 1884; wrote, c. 1915. Winnebago. Cloud tells of his childhood, his education in the sacred songs of the Winnebagos, his school years, conversion, and years at Yale (beginning 1906). He ends by pronouncing his devotion to his ministry and his determination to work for interdenominational Indian education.

121 COCHISE, CIYE "NINO." A. Kinney Griffith. The First Hundred Years of Nino Cochise.* London: Abelard-Schuman, 1971. 346 pp.

Born, 1874; collaborated, 1969. Cochise claims to be Chiricahua Apache and the grandson of the famous Apache chief Cochise. "Some authorities, however, regard this book as spurious. ... several will not even grant that [Nino Cochise] is an Apache" (Melody, 1977, pp. 15-16). Griffith provides no account of the nature of this collaboration, but one assumes that he did considerable editing and rearranging of material obtained from Cochise in interviews.

Whatever the validity of Cochise's account of his early years as a member of a "family clan" which "fled south into Sonora, disappearing into legendry," and none of whose members' names were ever again to appear on "any reservation list" (p. 4), the book does provide a spirited account of a footloose Indian man earning his living as he could. Cochise acted in Hollywood movies in the 1920's, tried off and on to make a paying museum out of his personal collection of artifacts, and even learned to fly an airplane for a cropdusting firm in his seventies. But, of course, the question of veracity lingers, as does the question of the degree of Cochise's participation in the writing of the book.

122 Comock (M). ROBERT FLAHERTY. The Story of Comock the Eskimo (P),* ed. Edmund Carpenter. N.Y.: Simon and Schuster, 1968. 95 pp.

Born, probably c. 1870; narrated, 1912. Eskimo, from the northeastern shores of Hudson Bay. Though little information is provided as to the details of this collaboration, it would seem that Comock spoke to Flaherty in his native language. Flaherty first retold this story over the BBC during the winter of 1949-50. We must assume that the phrasing is largely Flaherty's. Carpenter evidently worked from the text of that broadcast. Carpenter also supplies introductory material.

This is an amazing account of the journey of Comock and his family across the ice to an uninhabited Hudson Bay island many miles from the mainland. In the course of their journey the ice splits, and the group is cut in half--and Comock and one of his two wives and their children must go on, alone, with only a few dogs, one ivory knife, and their "fire stones." The narrative tells of their eventual arrival at the island, of their waxing there, and, when their oldest son reaches manhood, of their eventual decision to return across that same deathly expanse of ice to the mainland. As Carpenter says, this is an account "of human life reduced to a man, a woman, fire-making stones, and the will to perpetuate life" (p. 8).

123   Cook, Mary. See no. 24.

124   Copway, George (Kah-ge-ga-gah-bowh). The Life, History, and Travels of Kah-ge-ga-gah-bowh. Albany: Weed and Parsons, 1847. vii + 224 pp. Later editions are entitled The Life, Letters, and Speeches of Kah-ge-ga-gah-bowh, N.Y., 1850, and Recollections of a Forest Life, London, 1850.
     C. 1818-67; wrote, 1846. Ojibwa. This is one of the few Indian autobiographies written before 1850, and it is one of several Indian autobiographies designed to demonstrate the glories of Christianity (see nos. 14, 128, 192, 443). Copway, however, tends to see the moral training he received as a child as being consonant with Christian morality. Like Alford (no. 6) and Eastman (no. 161), then, he can be at once nostalgic and thankful for the Christian revelation, at once proud of his heritage and happy to have escaped it.

125   _____. The Traditional History and Characteristic Sketches of the Ojibway Nation. London: Charles Gilpin, 1850. xii + 298 pp. A later edition is entitled Indian Life and Indian History . . . (IP), Boston, 1860 (reprinted, N.Y.: AMS Press, n.d.).
     Copway mixes a generous helping of personal anecdotes into this history of the Ojibwas. In his descriptions of their original territory, for example, he includes his own remembrances of his responses to certain scenes (pp. 11, 14); he recalls his exploits as a hunter (pp. 28-35), his training as a warrior (p. 129), etc.

126   Cornish, Jake. See no. 107.

127   Courchene, Richard M. Hell, Love and Fun. Wolf Point, Montana: published by the author, 1969. 138 pp.
     Born, c. 1916. Assiniboine. In a handwritten note on the inside cover of Harvard Library's copy of this book, Courchene says that he had worked at the book "off and on" since 1943. Courchene first describes himself as a "small town Montana youth" (p. 1). It is not until p. 6 that Courchene mentions that "home" is a Montana reservation. He does not even mention his tribal affiliation. The book is a collection of memoirs of army life and the war in the Pacific, by a man who happens to be Indian. The tone and contents may be inferred from the title.

128 Craig, John Freeman (Chief White Eagle). Fifty Years on the Warpath. Kansas City, Mo.: Nease Printing Co., 1930. 88 pp.

Born, 1865; wrote, 1930 or very shortly before. Indian mother of unspecified tribe, white father. Craig, who was made a chief of the Winnebagos in 1882, writes of his life as a Christian zealot and orator on patriotic topics. The book also contains disconnected sub-sections on such topics as the state of Mexico and the erring ways of the Christian Scientists.

129 Crashing Thunder (M). PAUL RADIN. "Personal Reminiscences of a Winnebago Indian," Journal of American Folklore, XXVI (1913), 293-318.

Born, c. 1865; narrated, c. 1913. Winnebago. For an account of the tangled relationship between Crashing Thunder and Sam Blowsnake (Big Winnebago; pseudonym: Crashing Thunder), see no. 74. Radin told Crashing Thunder that he "wanted something about his beliefs and about the people he had met; but beyond that [Radin] did not guide him in any respect" (pp. 293-94), although it should be remembered that, as Radin wrote elsewhere, Crashing Thunder wove Radin into "the whole fabric of his life. [Radin] was the pre-ordained one who had sensed what was the proper time to come among the Winnebago" (no. 74, p. x).

Radin wrote down the Winnebago original, and this is printed along with the English translation which Radin worked out, with the aid of a native interpreter, in the presence of Crashing Thunder. These reminiscences are quite disconnected. Crashing Thunder tells, for example, of an ancestor's vision quest and of his brother-in-law's experiences as a shaman in addition to recalling his own childhood, his participation in the Medicine Dance, etc. Like that of his brother, Sam Blowsnake (nos. 73, 74), Crashing Thunder's account of his life is colored by his conversion to the Peyote Cult. He looks back upon the Medicine Dance, for example, as being "untrue."

130 Crashing Thunder (pseudonym [M]). See nos. 73, 74

131 CROW DOG, LEONARD. Richard Erdoes. To Speak with Our Bodies. New York: Harper and Row, forthcoming. Excerpts from this book have appeared in the second book cited in no. 202, pp. 76-86.

Born, c. 1940; interviewed, mid 1970's. Sioux. Crow Dog was educated in the old way, rather than in the schools. He is, then, illiterate, and so Erdoes works here from taped interviews. Crow Dog tells about his childhood, his training as a shaman, and his eventual involvement as the spiritual leader of the American Indian Movement. The book includes Crow Dog's account of the 1973 occupation of Wounded Knee.

132    Crow King. W. A. GRAHAM. Narratives by Crow King and others are to be found in The Custer Myth: A Source Book of Custeriana, Harrisburg, Pa.: The Stackpole Co., 1953, pp. 7-112.

All were born before 1860; collected from the 1870's to the 1920's. The book cited is, as the title indicates, a source book of accounts of the Custer battle, its antecedents, and its aftermath. The attraction of this book for Custerphiles and Custerphobes is obvious, but students of Indian autobiographies should consult this book as well: some very early interviews with Indians are printed here, and the attitudes of some of the interviewers and their concerns come through quite clearly in some cases; and then this book offers us some very good examples of how Indian interests were sometimes shaped and fashioned by white interests.

The narrators (except where noted, the references to other numbers in the bibliography are to other narratives by the Indian named): White-Man-Runs-Him (Crow; see no. 528), Curley (Crow; see no. 137), Goes Ahead (Crow; see no. 189), Hairy Moccasin (Crow), Red Star (Arikara; this is an abridgment of no. 423), Kill Eagle (Sioux), Red Horse (Sioux; some pictographs by Red Horse are included), Sitting Bull (Hunkpapa Sioux), Low Dog (Sioux), Crow King (Hunkpapa Sioux), Hump (Minneconjou Sioux), Iron Thunder (Minneconjou Sioux), Gall (Hunkpapa Sioux), Feather Earring (Minneconjou Sioux), Two Moon (Northern Cheyenne; this is a reprint of no. 507), Wooden Leg (Cheyenne; this is an abridgment of no. 545), Waterman (Arapaho), and Left Hand (Arapaho; see no. 282).

133    Crying Wind (F). Crying Wind.* Chicago: Moody Press, 1977. 189 pp.

Born, c. 1950; wrote, c. 1976. Kickapoo mother, white father. Crying Wind recalls a difficult life in order to emphasize the peace she attained by her conversion to Christianity. A "halfbreed," deserted by both parents, she felt neglected even on the reservation growing up under the care of her grandmother. When, at the age of fifteen, she was forced to move to the city and go it alone, her sense of isolation was acute. At her nadir she comes in contact with a pastor, and eventually she converts to Christianity--but only after a struggle between her traditional Indian religion and her new faith. The narrative includes some remembrances of Kickapoo oral history and Crying Wind's responses to the Peyote Cult and the 1973 occupation of Wounded Knee.

134    Cuero, Delfina. FLORENCE SHIPEK. The Autobiography of Delfina Cuero.* Morongo Indian Reservation, Calif.: Malki Museum Press, 1970 (1968). 67 pp.

Born, c. 1900; interviewed, 1965. Diegueno. Shipek

worked through an interpreter. There is no indication as to how much direction was given to the autobiographer, but it would seem that the book is the result of questioning and subsequent selection and ordering. Cuero lived a life on the cusp of the old ways. She did not experience the initiation ceremonies, but she did live the life of a hunter-gatherer for many years. She includes much folklore and folk wisdom.

135   Cuffe, Paul. SHELDON H. HARRIS. "The Journal," and "The Letters," as found in Harris, Paul Cuffe: Black American and the African Return (P). N.Y.: Simon and Schuster, 1972, pp. 77-262.
       1759-1817; wrote, 1810-17. Black father, Wampanoag mother. Insofar as may be judged from these materials, Cuffe identified himself entirely with his father's people rather than his mother's. These are, however, fascinating documents. Cuffe was an important figure in the back-to-Africa movement. He was a mariner and a wealthy man as well. This is the father of Paul Cuffe (no. 136).

136   Cuffe, Paul. Narrative of the Life and Adventures of Paul Cuffe, Pequot Indian: During Thirty Years Spent at Sea, and in Travelling in Foreign Lands.* Vernon: Horace N. Bill, 1839. 21 pp.
       Born, c. 1796; wrote, 1839. Wampanoag grandmother. This little narrative reads a bit like a ship's log, covering the travels of Cuffe from the time of his first sailing with his father, Paul Cuffe (no. 135), to the time of his return to Stockbridge in 1838. Cuffe sailed aboard whalers, freighters, and fishing ships. He shot polar bears, saw Eskimos, lived with the natives in Central America, steamed to Detroit, Chicago, and Cleveland--a lot of watery life in twenty-one pages.

137   Curley (M). JOSEPH KOSSUTH DIXON. "Curley,"* as found in the book cited in no. 11, pp. 140-45, 159-64.
       Born, c. 1856; interviewed, 1909. Crow. For the details of the collaboration, see the book cited in no. 11. Reminiscences of boyhood, war, and work as a Custer scout. For another Curley narrative, see no. 132.

138   Daklugie, Asa. EVE BALL. Narratives by Daklugie and others are to be found in Indeh: An Apache Odyssey (IP), Provo, Utah: Brigham Young University Press, 1980, passim.
       C. 1870-1955; narrated, c. 1954-55. Nednhi Apache. At the time of Ball's association of Daklugie he was "the dominant patriarch of the Mescalero reservation" (p. xv), and certainly his is the most dominant voice--and the most frequently heard--in this volume. It took Ball four years to overcome his haughty reluctance to speak with her. When she

did manage to break through his reserve, she found that his English was quite fluent (indeed, Daklugie had served as interpreter for Barrett in his work with Geronimo; see no. 186). Ball did a fair amount of editing at the sentence level, but the individual narratives are probably otherwise very close to their oral originals.

The book tells the story of the dark years of white-Apache warfare, of capture and surrender, the years in the prison camps of the East, and, finally, the return home to Apache country. Ball alternates her own historical accounts--pieced together largely from interviews with some 120 individuals, Apache and white--with long quotations from Daklugie and the other major informants. The anger that burned so fiercely during the Apache wars, that smoldered during the twenty-three years of imprisonment in the East, this anger is still hot in these pages.

For his part, Daklugie seems to have been motivated to collaborate with Ball for many of the reasons that moved his uncle Geronimo to collaborate with Barrett--vindication of the Apaches, "setting the record straight." He tells Apache history (from about 1860 to 1923) and recalls a wide range of personal experience--his training as a warrior, his raids, his marriage, his relations with, and feelings toward, Apache leaders. He tells about his schooling at Carlisle and his marriage. And he provides a real sense of the assumptions, the fears, and the perspective of the Apaches during the eastern exile. Along the way he talks about the Ghost Dance, Apache religion (sees no conflicts with Christianity), the Native American Church, and a good deal else. This is a unique voice well recorded.

139 Daniel (pseudonym). MARGARET LANTIS. Narrative to be found in Eskimo Childhood and Interpersonal Relationships: Nunivak Biographies and Genealogies, Seattle: University of Washington Press, 1960, pp. 153-59.

Lantis's method in the book cited here is to describe Eskimo childhood and interpersonal relationships by printing brief autobiographical narratives along with extensive notes and commentary. Her method in eliciting the narratives was to ask her informants to tell about their lives from their earliest memory on, however far they would like to go. She made do with a minimum of questions and tried to ask questions only when the narrative flow halted, and then only to get her informant talking again. She emphasizes in her introduction that this whole enterprise was quite outside the normal range of experience for these Eskimos: it must be remembered that extensive outside contact came so late to the Nunivakers that many of the childhoods recalled here were lived out in the period of cultural isolation. Lantis provides us with the results of psychological testing performed upon these people, and her commentary in general is often quite revealing; however, the narratives themselves are only rarely more than recitations of deeds done or events witnessed.

Since all of Lantis's Eskimos are known to us only by pseudonyms, they are all listed here rather than individually. All are Nunivak Eskimos. All were interviewed in 1946.

Daniel, pp. 3-26. Born, c. 1866. Lantis worked here through an interpreter. Daniel tells about his childhood, seal hunting, feasts, and a good deal more, but perhaps the most interesting parts of Daniel's narrative have to do with his first contacts with white men, as when, for example, he tells of letting crackers mold because he did not know that they were food.

Christine Gregory, pp. 27-42. Born, c. 1910. Lantis worked here through an interpreter. Some small sense of Gregory's high spirits and forceful personality show through here. She recalls shamans, her childhood, the use and storage of a beached whale, and more. This is the sister of Paul Scott (below).

Zachary, pp. 43-48. Born, probably c. 1890. Lantis worked here through an interpreter. Childhood, feasts, singing, hunting.

Nu-san (M), pp. 49-51. Born, probably c. 1890. Lantis worked through an interpreter here. Childhood, remembrances of the old trading ships.

Paul Scott, pp. 52-62. Born, c. 1913. No interpreter here. Lantis prints Scott's nonstandard English with very little editing. Childhood, hunting, trapping, attitudes toward his children, fasting, ceremonies.

Edwin Larson, pp. 65-69. Born, c. 1880. Lantis used an interpreter here. Childhood, hunting, spirits, dealings with shamans.

Luther Norton, pp. 70-73. Born, c. 1910. Interpreter. Norton recalls his first song--"a big event"--ceremonies, hunting, family.

Oliver, pp. 83-90. Born, c. 1913. Lantis used an interpreter here. Oliver talks about his adoption, hunting, ceremonies.

Ethan, pp. 91-97. Born, c. 1910. An interpreter here. When asked to relate his remembrances of his early life he responded with this narrative which is entirely about hunting.

Richard Chappel, pp. 111-27. Born, c. 1910. Interpreter here. Chappel was a sometime shaman who ceased his practice after the missionaries came. "I became a Christian and tried to forget my dreams and spirits. But for three years I saw spirits."

Helene Stephens, pp. 131-38. Born, c. 1900. An interpreter here. One of the last three practicing shamans on the

Island, Stephens would help the hunters by attracting seals to the hunting grounds with her drumming. She recounts some of her visions here.

Rachel, pp. 139-42. Born, c. 1910. An interpreter here. Ceremonies, giving children for adoption, and more.

Lydia, pp. 143-47. Born, c. 1916. Interpreter here. Family remembrances, particularly of her father's practice as a shaman.

Nicholas, pp. 148-50. Born, c. 1910. Lantis worked through an interpreter here. Hunting, ritual feasting, and a bit more.

Virginia Cannon, pp. 153-59. Born, c. 1927. Lantis worked here without an interpreter, but she prints no more than a paraphrase of the original--probably because Cannon's English was so far from standard that it would have been impractical to do otherwise. This is the "bad girl" of the community, having been made pregnant by a white man, and that outside of wedlock. Cannon talks about marriage, scandal, and gossip.

140 Davis, Rosie. ADOLPH HUNGRY WOLF. "Mrs. Rosie Davis,"* as found in the book cited in no. 20, pp. 342-43.

Born, c. 1874; interviewed, c. 1972. Blood. For the details of the collaboration, see no. 20. Very little here.

141 DeCora, Lorelei. See no. 60.

142 Deloria, Vine, Sr. "The Standing Rock Reservation: A Personal Reminiscence,"* as found in American Indian II, ed. John Milton, Vermillion: University of South Dakota Press, 1971, pp. 167-95. The contents of this volume are the same as South Dakota Review, IX, No. 2 (1971).

Born, 1901; wrote, shortly before 1971. Mixed blood Hunkpapa Sioux. Deloria, an Episcopal minister and the father of Vine Deloria, Jr. (author of Custer Died for Your Sins), here fondly recalls the early days of the Standing Rock Reservation, a time when there were no fences. He also writes, however, of the fencing of the land, of its slipping away from the Indians by leasing, etc. The piece is critical of the government's handling of Indian affairs.

143 Denejolie, Mose (M). See no. 24.

144 Denetsosie, Hoke (M). BRODERICK H. JOHNSON. "Hoke Denetsosie,"* as found in the book cited in no. 17, pp. 73-104.

Born, 1920; interviewed, 1976. Navajo. For the details of the collaboration, see no. 17. Denetsosie tells here of his experiences at boarding school, of becoming a professional artist, of being chosen to illustrate the first bilingual readers for Navajo school children.

145 Deric. JOHN ADAIR. "Autobiography," as found in the book
cited in no. 75, pp. 239-46.
Born, c. 1924; wrote, 1947. Zuni. Deric wrote his own
autobiography, and Adair does no editing or correcting, but see
no. 75. Deric writes for the most part about his schooling and
army experience (WW II). He recollects that he was often
surprised that the whites were not so universally rich and well
educated as he had assumed. He also expresses shock at the
level of morality he discovered in the army, but this is not a
dour narrative.

146 Descheene, Fred. See no. 24.

147 Dick, John. BRODERICK H. JOHNSON. "John Dick,"* as
found in the book cited in no. 17, pp. 182-200.
Born, c. 1908; interviewed, 1976. Navajo. For the details
of the collaboration, see no. 17. Dick does provide some
autobiographical fragments here, but for the most part he is
concerned to talk about education and his duties as a teacher
in the Rough Rock Demonstration School and as president of
the Rough Rock school board.

148 DION, JOSEPH F. Hugh A. Dempsey. My Tribe, the Crees
(IP). Calgary, Alberta: Glenbow Museum, 1979. x + 194 pp.
1888-1960; wrote, during the 1950's. Cree. Dion was at
work on this book when he died. He had "worked on his
manuscript periodically, rather than constantly," and so "his
material came out as a series of unrelated articles, rather
than as a cohesive book." Accordingly, Dempsey did considerable editing "to eliminate repetition," and to "provide a
general chronological flow" (p. vii). Very little editing was
done to the phrasing, however. The book as we have it is a
history of the Crees and the Métis, an account of the
contemporary social situation of these peoples, and a plea for
understanding and better treatment. In the later chapters all
of this merges neatly into autobiography. Given Dion's compassion for the people he writes of, this is quite a balanced
account.
Dion himself we find to have been a school teacher,
farmer, writer, and an important political leader among the
Crees and the Métis. He provides a good deal of detail here
about his childhood, his Catholic schooling (for which he was
very grateful), and his young manhood. It is interesting to
note that Dion, like Deloria (no. 142), sees the early reservation days (around the turn of the century) as, if not quite a
golden age, at least a happy age of unity and fellow-feeling, a
time much to be preferred to the dissolution of the 1920's and
1930's.

149 Domingo, Jim (pseudonym). EVON Z. VOGT. "Jim Domingo: Life History," as found in the book cited in no. 42, pp. 285-314.

Born, c. 1920; interviewed, 1948. Navajo. Vogt worked through an interpreter here. For further details of the collaboration, see no. 42. This narrative is dominated to a rather remarkable degree by Domingo's concern for his live-stock--how much they sold for in which year, how many were lost by his careless wife, how much wool they produced, and so forth. Along the way he provides some interesting material on the relationships among the white traders, the government agents, and the Navajos. Domingo does talk about his induction into the army (WW II) and his early release. As Vogt suggests, Domingo seems to have readjusted to reservation life with remarkable ease--as though his mind had never left his sheep. Sally Yazi (no. 550) is Domingo's second wife.

150 Dominguez, Chona (F). H. SEILER. "Bygone Days," in Seiler, ed., Cahuilla Texts, with an Introduction (P), Bloomington: Indiana University Press, 1970, pp. 148-53.

C. 1855-1960; narrated, 1955. Cahuilla. This is a verbatim transcription of Dominguez's native-language narration, with a literal translation on facing pages. Disconnected reminiscences.

151 Downing, Linda. T.D. ALLEN. "Day of Confusion,"* as found in the book cited in no. 92, pp. 57-59.

Born, c. 1952; wrote, c. 1969. Cherokee. For the details of the collaboration, see no. 92. Downing recalls her life of poverty with her father--and her father's commiting her to an orphanage.

152 Doyah, Hoske Yeba (M). See no. 24.

153 Duck (M). JAMES LARPENTUR LONG. Autobiographical fragments are to be found in the book cited in no. 27, pp. 43-46, 52-56, 109-11, 170-72.

Born, c. 1860; interviewed, 1939. Assiniboine. For the details of the collaboration, see no. 27. Duck tells of mad dogs, the hunt, and war.

154 Dutchman, Charles (Nehtsiwihtuk). LEONARD BLOOMFIELD. Narratives to be found in Bloomfield, Menomini Texts (IP), Publications of the American Ethnological Society, XII (1928), 30-43.

Born, probably before 1870; narrated, 1920-21. Menomini. These are complete, though brief, narratives, with the formalities of Menomini story-telling observed. Bloomfield, who relied here on an interpreter, prints the native-language text on facing pages with a free translation. Dutchman recounts a visionary experience, hunting experiences, and a wonderful eating story.

155 Dutchman, Louise (Maskwawanahkwatok). LEONARD BLOOMFIELD. Narratives to be found in the book cited in no. 154, pp. 22-25, 42-49.

Born, probably before 1870; narrated, 1920-21. Menomini. See no. 154 (Louise's husband) for the details of the collaboration. Dutchman tells of her husband's goodhearted prodigality and goes into considerable detail about her child-hood--her naming, hard times, work, schooling, etc. She mentions, for example, that her teacher "spoke Ojibwa; she spoke no English at all; and that was all the children learned to understand. To be sure, we read the [Bible in Ojibwa translation] in school, but we did not understand what that book said" (p. 49).

156 E. (M). J.S. SLOTKIN. A Case Study and Autobiography of a Menomini Indian Paranoid Schizophrenic Man, with a Rorschach Analysis by George D. Spindler, Microcard Publications of Primary Records in Culture and Personality, ed. Bert Kaplan, III, No. 6, Madison, Wis.: Microcard Foundation, 1956, 94 pp.

Born, 1927; interviewed, 1950-51. Menomini. E. knew English, and so no interpreter was necessary. Slotkin asked E. to tell him "something about his life" so that they could "become better acquainted . . . . No prompting or questions occurred during these sessions, and a complete transcript is given" (p. 49). Slotkin does not edit toward standard English, and so there are many, many sentence fragments, false starts, etc. Slotkin provides psychoanalytic as well as anthropological annotations.

E. tells of his troubled childhood (Oedipal problems, according to Slotkin), and of his childish triumphs (many of these are evidently wishful fantasies). He goes on to tell of his father's murder and his family's conversion to the Peyote Cult (quite a bit is said here about the rituals and affairs of the cult). E. does talk briefly about his mental breakdown but not at all about the time he spent in a mental hospital.

157 Eagle Plume (Natosina [M]). JAMES WILLARD SCHULTZ and JESSIE LOUISE DONALDSON. A narrative is to be found in The Sun God's Children,* Boston: Houghton Mifflin Co., 1930, pp. 217-36.

Born, probably before 1860; narrated, c. 1927. Blackfeet. Schultz lived for many years among the Blackfeet and the Cheyenne during the 1870's and '80's. He learned their languages, he learned their ways, and he made many friends.

54

During the summer of 1927 or '28, as Schultz put it, "a number of us old ones repaired to Waterton Lakes National Park [Alberta], there to camp together for a time . . . and, around our lodge fires recall our adventures in the days before the whites swarmed upon our plains" (p. 167). Tourists stopped by to hear these tales, an interpreter being provided for their benefit. Schultz recorded these tales. For more about Schultz's work and methods, see no. 31. Eagle Plume tells his war deeds here. For Eagle Plume's son, see no. 20.

158       . JAMES WILLARD SCHULTZ. "Eagle Plume,"* as found in the book cited in no. 20, pp. 256-63.
    Narrated sometime in the 1920's. Adolf Hungry Wolf says that Eagle Plume's son, Atsitsina (no. 20), recognizes this narrative as "a good version of the way his dad used to relate this adventure" (p. 256). Schultz knew the native language. See no. 31 for further information about Schultz's work. This is a narrative about a raid on the Crows.

159 Eagle-ribs (M). PLINY EARLE GODDARD. Various narratives are to be found in Goddard, Sarsi Texts, University of California Publications in American Archeology and Ethnology, XI, No. 3 (1915), 222-23, 232-35, 238-45, 268-72.
    Born, c. 1840; interviewed, 1905. Sarsi. Goddard worked with an interpreter. A literal translation is printed here on facing pages with a transcription of the native-language text. This is one of many such texts printed for linguistic rather than ethnological or literary purposes. The present narratives are discontinuous, but they are more interesting than most such texts because Eagle-ribs tells of attaining his powers from the rock and the squirrel, and of the military feats which the rock and the squirrel predicted for him and prepared him to accomplish. These feats, in turn, allowed him to become a chief.

160     .     . Coup narratives are to be found in "Notes on the Sun Dance of the Sarsi," Anthropological Papers of the American Museum of Natural History, XVI, pt. 4 (1919), 281-82.
    Narrated, 1905. Goddard worked through an interpreter, but otherwise these coup narratives are, according to Goddard, "probably in the form in which [Eagle-ribs] was accustomed to recite them in the Sun Dance lodge." The events of Eagle-ribs's war deeds probably took place during the time of the Cree rebellion of 1884-85.

161 Eastman, Charles Alexander. Indian Boyhood (P).* Boston: Little Brown and Co., 1922 [1902]. viii + 289 pp.
    1858-1939; wrote, shortly before 1902. Santee Sioux.

According to some, Eastman relied on his wife, Elaine Goodale Eastman, to put his manuscripts into final form (David R. Miller, 1978, p. 66). According to Eastman's daughter, however, Mrs. Eastman did no more than copy-edit her husband's finished manuscripts (Kay Graber, personal communication).

This book is an account of Eastman's first fifteen years as a prelapsarian Indian, written from the perspective of a well-educated (Dartmouth and Boston University Medical School) participant in modern civilization. In the front matter Eastman wrote: "The North American Indian was the highest type of pagan and uncivilized man. He possessed not only a superb physique but a remarkable mind. But the Indian no longer exists as a natural and free man. Those remnants which now dwell upon the reservations present only a fictitious copy of the past."

Distinctions are thus to be made, according to Eastman, between pagans and civilized men, between lower pagans and the pre-reservation Indians--and even between higher and lower pre-reservation Indians (p. 87). Eastman's people, the Santee Sioux, were the highest type of Indian. Implicit in all of this is Eastman's belief that he himself represented the very embodiment of social Darwinism. His people were the highest type of Indians--indeed, his mother had "every feature of Caucasian descent with the exception of her luxuriant black hair and deep black eyes" (p. 5; Eastman's mother was, in fact, half white, the daughter of the western artist Seth Eastman)--while he himself went on to become a highly educated member of the most advanced civilization.

In what might be said to be the second volume of his autobiography, From the Deep Woods to Civilization (no. 162), published some fourteen difficult years after Indian Boyhood, Eastman writes of his disillusionment with white civilization. But Indian Boyhood gives voice to no such doubts. Alford (no. 6) is perhaps the nearest analogy.

Indian Boyhood is also remarkable for its elaborately polite prose, prose very like that of the Horatio Alger novels. Eastman, who was writing for the same youthful audience as Alger, was capable of having an Indian child explain that the eagle best shows its "judgment in caring for its young" by choosing to bring its young "up under the spell of the grandest scenes," and by inspiring its young "with lofty feelings and bravery" (p. 79). Eastman obviously invents many such dialogues, and many situations as well, in order to provide narrative contexts for the exposition of his romantic conception of pre-reservation Indians. (See nos. 11, 399, and 527 for Indian romanticism.)

162 _____. From the Deep Woods to Civilization: Chapters in

the Autobiography of an Indian (P),* with an introduction by Raymond Wilson. Lincoln: University of Nebraska Press, 1977 [1916]. xxii + 206 pp.

Wrote, c. 1916. This book takes up where Indian Boyhood (no. 161) leaves off, which is to say that it begins with Eastman's journey, literally, from the deep woods where he had lived with his uncle as a pre-reservation Santee, to such civilization as the Dakota territory offered in 1875. Here he was to live with his newly Christianized father, and here he was to begin the seventeen years of schooling which ended with his graduation from Boston University Medical School.

This book is different from Indian Boyhood in many important ways. Eastman does much less romanticizing of the old ways here, and real sympathy for the reservation Indians is now evident. Eastman, who was the doctor in attendance upon those wounded during the massacre at Wounded Knee, allows his feelings toward civilization to structure the book. He tells of his initial distrust, of his later wholehearted acceptance of the white man's ways and religion, and of his partial disillusionment. Finally, his views seem close to those of Alford (no. 6) and Standing Bear (nos. 469, 470, 471): he accepts the precepts of Christianity, though he recognizes the manifest failures of many Christians. "Civilization," then, comes to have ironic intent, for there are many ways in which Eastman, along with Alford and Standing Bear, views the aboriginal Indian as having been more civilized--more decent, more just, more honest--than many so-called civilized individuals and institutions.

163 Edwards, Jim (pseudonym). ROBERT N. RAPOPORT. "Jim Edwards' Account," and "Jim Edwards--a Doubtful Galilean (Conflictful Type)," in Rapoport, Changing Navaho Religious Values: A Study of Christian Missions to the Rimrock Navahos, Papers of the Peabody Museum of American Archaeology and Ethnology, XLI, No. 2 (1954), pp. 83-108, 125-29.

Born, 1914; interviewed, 1948. Navajo. Rapoport writes that Edwards "was a man with an unusual memory . . . . His detailed accuracy was beyond cavil and almost beyond belief. His account was non-directively rendered for the most part and recorded verbatim on a typewriter" (p. 14). The only changes made were some minor editing toward standard English and massive cutting--the account here is but one fifth of Edwards's narrative--though Rapoport assures us that most of what was deleted was redundant material, mostly dialogue.

This is a detailed account of Edwards's work as a missionary and interpreter for the fundamentalist Galilean church, from 1945 to 1948. He tells of the church's struggle with the traditional Navajo ways and with the Mormons. A good deal is said about individual Navajos' responses to the two religions. In 1948 Edwards left the employ of the church.

The second section cited above is a life history, but it is mostly written by Rapoport with excerpts from Edwards's first-person narration included along the way. He tells of a hard life, of not recognizing his parents after a six-year stay at the Fort Wingate boarding school. He tells too of his motivation for wanting to become a shaman (economic) and of becoming a paid interpreter.

164    Eevic, Katso (F). See no. 5.

165    En-me-gah-bowh (John Johnson). En-me-gah-bowh's Story: An Account of the Disturbances of the Chippewa Indians at Gull Lake in 1857 and 1862 and Their Removal in 1868. Minneapolis: Women's Auxiliary, St. Barnabas Hospital, 1904. 56 pp.

1816-1902; wrote, 1902. Ojibwa. En-me-gah-bowh was educated by missionaries to serve as their interpreter, and he continued to work in various mediatory capacities throughout his life. This narrative deals almost entirely with his role in the "disturbances" of 1847-62 and the removal of his people in 1868. Throughout, the book is never far from anguish. En-me-gah-bowh felt keenly that injustices were done his people, and yet, despite his bitterness toward the government, he found himself all too often forced to collaborate with the whites. His life was consequently many times endangered by resentful members of his tribe. The book is also interesting for the pan-Indian sentiments it expresses. The author was a staunch Christian.

166    Ennou, Jean Baptiste. PLINY EARLE GODDARD. Two narratives are to be found in Goddard, Chipewyan Texts, Anthropological Papers of the American Museum of Natural History, X, No. 1 (1912), 43-45, 64-65.

Born, c. 1876; interviewed, 1911. Ojibwa. Goddard prints the Chippewan and the English translation. A hunting narrative and a brief moralizing account of a villager's death.

167    Enote (M). THE ZUNI PEOPLE. Two narratives by Enote are in The Zunis: Self-portrayals by the Zuni People (P),* N.Y.: New American Library, 1974, pp. 35-36, 54-55.

Born, probably c. 1900; interviewed, c. 1965. Zuni. Enote's brief narratives are a part of the Zunis' effort, beginning in 1965, to record their oral literature. "The major storytellers of the tribe were gathered and asked to relate on tape the legends, myths, and history of the pueblo" (p. v). The recording was managed by Quincy Panteah. These materials were translated, and then edited by Virginia Lewis, though the final choices were approved by the governor and council of the pueblo. Enote tells first about the early days of nearly constant hunger, and of the prosperity of these modern times in the pueblo. The second narrative is about Enote's trip to the spirit world of the Zunis.

168 Etoangat, Akasyook (M). See no. 5.

169 E-Yeh-Shure (Louise Abeita). I Am a Pueblo Indian Girl. Eau Claire, Wisc.: E.M. Hale and Co., 1939. 23 unnumbered pp.
Born, probably before 1920; wrote, c. 1939. Hopi. This book could best be described as a beautifully illustrated Hopi ethnography written for children. Abeita provides very little autobiographical detail, except insofar as she tells how "we" baked bread, cared for horses, etc.

170 Fan, Wash (M). See no. 107.

171 FaSiSo47A (With thanks, this is a pseudonym [M]). JOHN M. ROBERTS. "Autobiographical Statements by FaSiSo47A," as found in Roberts, Zuni Daily Life (P), Human Relations Area Files Press, 1965 [1956] pp. 100-107.
Born, 1904; interviewed, 1951. Zuni. "The statements were made freely and were not the products of focused interviews. The material has been edited slightly in the interests of brevity and clarity" (p. 100). The narrator learned English as a second language (his uncle needed someone to interpret for him in his trading with the whites), and the narrative retains a strong nonstandard flavor. FaSiSo47A tells of his schooling and his training for, and life as, a sheepman.

172 Feather Earring (M). See no. 132.

173 Fergusson, Hattie. "Employment of Native Teachers," in National Conference on Indian and Northern Education, Saskatoon, 1967, ed. Mary Anne La Vallee, Saskatoon, Saskatchewan Society for Indian and Northern Education and Extension Division, University of Saskatchewan, pp. 35-39.
Born, probably c. 1925; wrote, c. 1967. Tsimshian. Fergusson tells of her experiences as a teacher in a boarding school and an integrated high school.

174 FILOMENA, ISIDORA (PRINCESS SOLANO). Hubert Howe Bancroft. "My Years with Chief Solano," trans. Nellie Van de Grift, Touring Topics, XXII (Feb., 1930), 39, 52.
Born, c. 1784; narrated, 1874. Chuructos, married into the Suisuns. This is one of the very interesting brief autobiographies. Filomena dictated her memoirs for Bancroft in "simple and broken Spanish" and this was finally translated

and published, complete, by Van de Grift. Filomena tells of being captured by, and then married to, Solano, chief of the Suisun Indians and "an important ally and aid to General M.G. Vallejo, in keeping the Indians of North Central California in subjection." She recalls the time of plenty before the coming of the white man and the changes that have come about after contact with such "cheating" white men as John Sutter.

175 FINE DAY (M). Adolf Hungry Wolf. My Cree People (P).* Invermere, B.C.: Good Medicine Books, 1973. 63 pp. Much of this material appeared originally in David G. Mandelbaum, The Plains Cree (IP), Anthropological Papers of the American Museum of Natural History, XXXVII, pt. 2 (1940), particularly pp. 198, 224-26, 253, 256, 278, 301-6, 313-16.

Born, c. 1853; interviewed, 1934. Cree. Fine Day was Mandelbaum's principal informant in his work with the Crees. Mandelbaum includes many (translated) extended quotations from Fine Day on a wide variety of topics, but the longest narratives have to do with Fine Day's battle deeds and his vision quest and dreams. This is finely detailed material, and quite enough to allow us a good sense of this man--and a remarkable man he was. He led the Plains Crees in their rebellion against the Canadian government forces in 1885, and he was, according to Mandelbaum, the most renowned Cree warrior alive in 1934. He also enjoyed a considerable reputation as a shaman. (It is interesting to note, given the reservations that so many Indians have had about revealing sacred matters to the anthropologists, that Fine Day was willing to divulge sacred matters not because he had less belief than some in the dangers of telling secrets--but rather because he had more courage to face those dangers! See Mandelbaum, p. 163.)

Hungry Wolf came upon Mandelbaum's field notes at the New York Museum of Natural History, and My Cree People is, says Hungry Wolf, the result of his "copying down many pages of anecdotes and quotes" (p. 3). Actually, Hungry Wolf made some changes in the text, mainly lexical--"uncle" for Mandelbaum's more precise "mother's brother," "our people" for Mandelbaum's "we," and so forth. Hungry Wolf prints a good deal of material that Mandelbaum does not, and again, this is finely detailed--dogs, marriage, horses, hunting, sacred bundles, etc.--but finally we get a better sense of Fine Day by piecing together bits from Mandelbaum's monograph than we do from My Cree People, since Hungry Wolf, with his characteristic emphasis on the homely and the sacred, edits out virtually everything Fine Day has to say about his war deeds.

176 First Rider, George. ADOLF HUNGRY WOLF. Narratives* are to be found in the book cited in no. 20, pp. 211-13, 232-35.

Born, 1904; interviewed, early 1970's. Blood. Hungry Wolf is not careful to distinguish between materials he himself collected and those he reprints from other sources, but I infer that First Rider spoke through an interpreter, and that Hungry Wolf got this material from the Alberta Provincial Museum. Dave Melting Tallow was evidently the man who recorded First Rider. First Rider here recalls his participation in Horn Society ceremonies and narrates a brief autobiography, telling of his traditional upbringing, his lapses into drunken, "bad" living, and his eventual conversion to Christianity.

177 Flying Hawk (M). M.I. McCREIGHT. Firewater and Forked Tongues: A Sioux Chief Interprets U.S. History. Pasadena, Cal.: Trail's End Publishing Co., Inc. 1947. xxiv + 180 pp. Excerpts appeared in McCreight, Chief Flying Hawk's Tales, N.Y.: Alliance, 1936, and The Wigwam--Puffs from the Peace Pipe, Sykesville, Pa.: Nupp, 1943.

1852-1931; interviewed, in the late 1920's. Oglala Sioux. McCreight worked through an interpreter. After the material was translated and edited, it was "read back to Flying Hawk for his correction and approval" (pp. xiv-xv). Autobiographical details are scattered through the book, but there is a brief autobiography proper, pp 1-14. Flying Hawk tells of some of his war experiences, of having been made a chief at the age of thirty-two, and something of his wives and two of his relatives, Crazy Horse and Sitting Bull.

178 FOOLS CROW, FRANK. Thomas E. Mails. Fools Crow (IP).* Garden City, N.Y.: Doubleday and Co., Inc., 1979. 278 pp.

Born, c. 1891; collaborated, beginning 1974. Teton Sioux. Fools Crow knew some English, but for the most part Mails and Fools Crow worked through an interpreter. These interviews were directed by Mails, and Mails was, according to his own account, especially persistent in overcoming Fools Crow's reluctance to relate the details of his visionary and other spiritual experiences. Mails cut, edited, and rewrote the resulting material into a chronological narrative. In all of this Mails quite evidently sees himself as playing Neihardt to Fools Crow's Black Elk (no. 66): like Black Elk, Fools Crow was told by Wakan-Tanka that "'the time had come for him to tell certain things about himself and his Teton people to a person who would be made known to him'" (p. 4). Needless to say, that person turns out to be Mails, Neihardt redux. In fact, Mails's presense in the book is a bit cloying.

Fools Crow tells of the early reservation days, and of the sometimes trying, but for Fools Crow almost always interesting, adaptations his people had to make to reservation life-- learning to use scissors, stoves, automobiles, and the rest; indeed, Fools Crow speaks with real nostalgia of this time, particularly the years from 1908 to 1928. For the rest, he tells of vision quests, hard work, ceremonies, and his work and concern for his people. He was appointed ceremonial chief of the Teton Sioux, served as a negotiator in disputes with the government, and long worked as a spokesman for his people's grievances. Fools Crow also has a good deal to say here about the trouble at Wounded Knee in 1973. Altogether, this is a lively portrait of a singular man, a man who speaks articulately (albeit via an interpreter and Mails) about the history and present circumstances of the Sioux.

179   Fornsby, John.   JUNE M. COLLINS.   "John Forsby:   The Personal Document of a Coast Salish Indian," in Marian W. Smith, ed., Indians of the Urban Northwest, N.Y.:   Columbia University Press, 1949, pp. 287-341.
      Born, 1855; interviewed, 1942 and 1947.   Coast Salish. Collins interviewed Fornsby in the hope of getting information on Salish religion and kinship systems, but Fornsby so frequently disregarded her questions or simply allowed her questions to serve as springboards for personal reminiscences, that it occurred to Collins to arrange the material in chronological order, delete myths and some ethnographical detail, translate the Salish words that peppered Fornsby's English, and publish it as a life history. Fornsby remembers a time before the coming of the white man, and as he relates his life history he is still a believer in power dreams, some of which he relates here. He was a highly regarded shaman.

180   Fowler, David. JAMES DOW McCALLUM. Letters are to be found in the book cited in no. 18, pp. 85-113.
      1735-1807; wrote, 1764-68. Montauk. For the details of the writing and the editing of these letters, see no. 18. Fowler's letters include confessions of sins, some expression of indignation at the way he is treated by a trader and by Wheelock, and fairly extensive accounts of the Indians, the "lazy and sordid wretches" (p. 96), among whom he labored. Fowler was one of Wheelock's very few Indian successes.

181   Frank. JOHN ADAIR. "Frank's Life History," as found in the book cited in no. 75, pp. 126-238.
      Born, c. 1924; interviewed, 1947. Zuni. For the details of the collaboration, see no. 75. Frank tells, with very few questions asked of him, about his life and loves (thirty-three women, by his own count). He also talks about his silversmithing and his university education. This is, however, mainly devoted to his army experiences (WW II). At the end of this narrative Adair adds a long section devoted to questions and answers concerning witchcraft, curing, sexual experiences, etc.

182    Gamble, Bob Lee. See no. 39.

183    Gamble, Jerry. See no. 39.

184    George, Phil.   JOHN R. MILTON.   "My Indian Name,"*   in
       Milton, ed., The American Indian Speaks (P), Vermillion, S.D.:
       University of South Dakota Press, 1969, pp. 142-47.   This
       volume is identical with South Dakota Review, VII, No. 2
       (1969).
           Born, c. 1945; wrote, c. 1968.  Nez Perce.  George writes
       his remembrances of his naming ceremony, which took place
       when he was eight years old.

185    Gerard, Mary Ann.   T. D. ALLEN.   "It's My Rock,"* in the
       book cited in no. 92, pp. 31-39.
           Born, c. 1953; wrote, c. 1968.  Blackfeet.  For the details
       of the collaboration, see no. 92.  Gerard recalls her loneliness
       and a related drug experience.

186    GERONIMO (M).  S.M. Barrett.  Geronimo's Story of His Life
       (IP).*  N.Y.: Duffield and Co., 1906.  xxvii + 216 pp.
           1829-1909; collaborated, 1905-1906.  Apache.  This work
       was done, according to Barrett, at the insistence of Geronimo.
       On each day of their collaboration Geronimo would tell what
       he had decided that day to tell, and would not expand or
       respond to questions.   Once the work was in manuscript
       (Apache), however, he did consent to listen to a reading of the
       transcription, and at this time he also consented to respond to
       questions and to amplify where Barrett was able to convince
       him that such was necessary.  All of this was done through an
       interpreter.  We are left to guess at how much editing Barrett
       did, but Geronimo's own purpose in setting down the story of
       his life is obvious.  As a prisoner of war, as an Apache Indian
       who felt that his people had been wronged, Geronimo wrote to
       win for his people leniency and understanding.  The book is
       thus one of those Indian autobiographies wherein the Indian has
       guided the narrative toward his own ends.
           Barrett's   account   of   the   collaboration   should   not
       necessarily be swallowed whole, however.  See the account by
       Daklugie, Geronimo's interpreter and nephew, in the book
       cited in no. 138:  "Barrett . . . wished to write a book about my
       uncle.  And strangely, to me, Geronimo consented."  Daklugie
       goes on to recall some of their fears about working with
       Barrett:  Barrett might be "a spy and the book a device for
       getting information not obtainable by other means."  Then, in
       a footnote, "There are many errors in that book.   And
       Geronimo was far too wise to tell all he knew" (pp. 173-74).
           Geronimo had been a prisoner of war for twenty years by
       the time he undertook this work, and Barrett was at first

denied permission to take down Geronimo's autobiography by the officer in charge of the military reservation. Eventually Barrett received permission from President Theodore Roosevelt to proceed, and Geronimo consequently dedicates the book to Roosevelt. The book begins with Geronimo's account of the mythological origins and the historical past of the Apaches.

187 Giago, Tim A., Jr. The Aboriginal Sin: Reflections on the Holy Rosary Indian Mission School (Red Cloud Indian School) (P).* San Francisco: The Indian Historian Press, 1978. ix + 83 pp.
　　Born, 1934; wrote, c. 1977. Oglala Sioux. Except for a brief autobiographical introduction in prose, Giago's book is autobiographical poetry, devoted in the main to resentful and yet nostalgic accounts of life at a Catholic boarding school.

188 Gladstone, Senator James. "School Days," Alberta Historical Review, XV, No. 1 (1967), 18-24. An abridgment appeared as "Akainah-Mukah, the Senator," in Kent Gooderham, ed., I Am an Indian (P),* Toronto: J.M. Dent and Sons, Ltd., 1969, pp. 48-50.
　　C. 1887-1971; wrote, c. 1967. Blood. Gladstone tells of his school days at St. Paul's Anglican boarding school.

189 Goes-Ahead (M). JOSEPH KOSSUTH DIXON. "Goes-Ahead,"* as found in the book cited in no. 11, pp. 145-49, 164-68.
　　Born, c. 1850; interviewed, 1909. Crow. For details of the collaboration, see no. 11. These are war reminiscences, including a brief account of Goes-Ahead's work as a Custer scout. For another narrative by Goes-Ahead, see no. 132.

190 Goldtooth, Frank. See no. 24.

191 Golsh, Larry. See no. 38.

192 Goodbird (M). GILBERT L. WILSON. Goodbird the Indian: His Story, Told by Himself to Gilbert L. Wilson.* N.Y.: Fleming H. Revell Co., 1914. 80 pp.
　　Born, 1869; interviewed, 1913. Hidatsa. Goodbird is the son of Maxidiwiac (nos. 319, 320, 321) and the nephew of Wolf-Chief (nos. 541, 542), and he served as Wilson's interpreter throughout the course of Wilson's work with both uncle and mother. Internal evidence suggests that Wilson has done some rearranging of Goodbird's material. Wilson also put "Goodbird's Indian English into common idiom." This is an account of Goodbird's partial assimilation and of his conversion to Christianity.

193    Goodman, Paul. See no. 34.

194    Good Shot, Oscar. THOMAS B. MARQUIS. "Oscar Good Shot,
       a Sioux Farmer," as found in Cheyenne and Sioux: The
       Reminiscences of Four Indians and a White Soldier (IP),
       compiled by Marquis, ed. Ronald H. Limbaugh, Stockton, Cal.:
       Pacific Center for Western Historical Studies, 1973, pp. 60-72.
       A condensed version of this narrative was published as "The
       Autobiography of a Sioux," Century Magazine, CXIII (1926),
       182-88.
         Born, 1900; interviewed, 1926. Oglala Sioux. Limbaugh
       provides us with Marquis's original text, which had lain in
       manuscript since Marquis's death in 1935. "Marquis's original
       narrative style was retained consistent with clarity and
       grammar" (p. 4). Good Shot knew English, and this interview
       almost certainly was conducted in English. This narrative
       shows Good Shot to be a young man caught between two
       cultures, white-educated, but fully accepted by neither Indians
       nor whites.

195    Gordo, Louis (pseudonym). EVON Z. VOGT. "Louis Gordo:
       Life History," as found in the book cited in no. 42, pp. 218-26.
         Born, c. 1920; interviewed, 1947. Navajo. Gordo spoke
       English, and there was, then, no need for an interpreter here.
       For the further details of the collaboration, see no. 42. Gordo
       provides scattered reminiscences of childhood, boarding
       school, the army (WW II). Not much here.

196    Gorman, Eli. See no. 24.

197    Gorman, Howard W. See no. 24.

198    Grasshopper, Pat (M). PLINY EARLE GODDARD. Narratives
       to be found in the book cited in no. 159, pp. 236-38, 272-77.
         Born, probably about 1850; interviewed, 1905. Sarsi. For
       the details of the collaboration, see no. 159. Grasshopper tells
       about his vision quest and a buffalo-hunting experience.

199    Gray-bull (M). ROBERT H. LOWIE. Narrative to be found in
       Lowie, Social Life of the Crow Indians (IP), Anthropological
       Papers of the American Museum of Natural History, IX, pt. 2
       (1912), 233-35.
         Born, probably, c. 1845; interviewed, c. 1910. Crow.
       Lowie worked through an interpreter. This is a war
       reminiscence.

200    Gray-Bull and his contemporaries, One-Blue-Bead, Scratches-
       Face, Arm-Around-the-Neck, Lone Tree, White Arm, and Big-
       Ox. ROBERT H. LOWIE. Narratives to be found in Lowie,

The Religion of the Crow Indians (IP), Anthropological Papers of the American Museum of Natural History, XXV, pt. 2 (1922), 324-83.

Born, previous to reservation days; interviewed, 1907-16. Crow. Lowie had a fair command of the native language, but he worked with an interpreter--carefully, sometimes checking one interpreter against another. Autobiographical narratives having to do with vision quests and other supernatural experiences are scattered throughout the pages cited.

201 Gray-Bull and his contemporaries, Hillside, Scratches-Face, and Young-Jackrabbit. ROBERT H. LOWIE. Narratives to be found in Lowie, The Crow Indians (P), N.Y.: Farrar and Rinehart, Inc., 1935, pp. 177-78, 214, 223-25, 241.

Born, previous to reservation days; interviewed, 1907 and 1933. Crow. For the details of the collaboration, see no. 200. These are brief narratives having to do with men's society activities, war, and the seeking of visions.

202 Green, Joe. WILLARD ZERBE PARK. Narratives in Park, Shamanism in Western North America (IP), N.Y.: Cooper Square Publishers, Inc., 1975 [1938], pp. 16, 17, 19, 21, 22, 24-25, 30, 58-59, 60. Some of this is reprinted in Joan Halifax, Shamanic Voices (P),* N.Y.: E.P. Dutton, 1979, pp. 102-4.

Born, before 1885; interviewed, 1934-36. Paviosto. The interviews were conducted in English, a second language for Green. Park edited Green's narratives into standard English. Green talks here about how he won, used, and lost his shamanic powers.

203 GREEN, PAUL (AKNIK). Abbe Abbott. I Am Eskimo--Aknik My Name (P).* Juneau, Alaska: Alaska Northwest Publishing Co., 1959. x + 86 pp.

Born, 1901; wrote, c. 1959. Alaska Eskimo. Knowing Green to be a fine teller of tales, Abbott urged him to write some of his stories down (c. 1956). Rather to her surprise, a couple of years later Green gave her a thick handwritten manuscript. She has printed his stories (with illustrations by George Ahgupuk, an Eskimo artist of some renown) with little alteration. Green's nonstandard English survives, as does the flavor of oral storytelling--there is, for example, little order here: an account of the origin of nose-rubbing follows Green's remembrances of the old-time foods; folk tales, autobiographical tales, folk technology, and hunting lore intermingle. This is quite an engaging book. We get a clear sense of both Green and his conception of his people.

204 Greene, Alma (Gah-wohn-nos-doh [F]). Forbidden Voice: Reflections of a Mohawk Indian. London: Hamlyn Publishing

Group, n.d. [c. 1971]. 157 pp. Excerpts are published in the book cited in no. 188, pp. 169-74.

Born, c. 1895; wrote, c. 1968. Mohawk. This book is like Momaday's Way to Rainy Mountain (no. 344), in that Greene gathers together mythic tales and personal, tribal, and family history in an attempt to define both herself and her people. Until the last few pages, the autobiographical passages are in the third person.

205 Gregorio (pseudonym, Jaime another pseudonym). ALEXANDER H. and DOROTHEA C. LEIGHTON. Gregorio, the Hand-Trembler: A Psychobiological Personality Study of a Navaho Indian. Papers of the Peabody Museum of American Archeology and Ethnology, XL, No. 1 (1949), xiv + 177 pp. An abridged version is to be found in Leighton and Leighton, The Navaho Door (IP), Cambridge: Harvard University Press, 1944, pp. 95-109, where the hand-trembler's pseudonym is Jaime.

Born, c. 1902; interviewed, 1940. Navajo. The first book cited here is a full-scale study of a single Navajo man. For an autobiography proper, Gregorio's response to the Leightons' request for a life story, see pp. 46-81. His narrative is printed as it came from the interpreter, with few emendations--deletion of a very few passages whose meaning was unclear, grammatical alterations where necessary to clarify meaning (the narrative retains a strong oral, colloquial flavor), and the use of pseudonyms throughout. All questions asked by the Leightons are included in the text.

Gregorio accepts the traditional assumptions of his people without question, his accounts of the cures effected upon him and by him being as matter-of-fact as are his accounts of his sheepherding. Gregorio talks particularly (though reticently) about the Hand-trembling Way, a ceremony in which he is adept. This ceremony is "often used to treat the Hand-trembling sickness, paralysis, nervousness, mental disturbance" (p. 57). Gregorio's account of his first marriage, a marriage sprung upon him without a day's notice, is also of considerable interest. He good-naturedly tells about the frustrations of having to acquaint himself with this woman whom he had never before met, having to teach her how to cook, having to deal with his in-laws, etc.

The worth of this narrative is considerably enhanced by the wealth of biographical and cultural material which fills the rest of this book to overflowing.

206 Grey Owl (Archie Belany). See no. 10.

207 Griffen, Tilly. See no. 107.

208 Griffis, Joseph K. (Tahan). Tahan: Out of Savagery, into

Civilization. N.Y.: George H. Doran, Co., 1915. 263 pp.

Born, c. 1854; wrote, c. 1915. Griffis's parentage is not entirely certain, but it is likely that his mother was Osage. As a child, however, Griffis was captured and raised by the Kiowas--until he was fourteen, at which time he was "rescued" by whites who assumed that he was a white child in the clutches of the Kiowas. Later he managed to return to live with a band of Indians for a time.

Griffis recounts a remarkable life. Like Eastman (no. 161), Griffis finally sees himself as something of an embodiment of social Darwinism: he sees himself as having progressed from being a leader of savages to being "the friend of the scientist and the literary critic" (p. 8).

209 GRISDALE, ALEX. Nan Shipley. "Alex Grisdale's Story," as found in Grisdale, Wild Drums: Tales and Legends of the Plains Indians, ed. Shipley, Winnipeg: Peguis Publishers Ltd., 1974, pp. 72-78.

Born, 1895; wrote, 1972. Ojibwa. The autobiography cited here is an addendum to Grisdale's collection of tales. Shipley does little editing. Working from Grisdale's handwritten manuscript, she allows his language to retain many of its nonstandard features. The result is a rather discontinuous narrative, Grisdale telling of his childhood, work as a logger-- and of his determination to write down the Indian tales he loved so well.

210 GROS-LOUIS, MAX. Marcel Bellier. Max Gros-Louis, First Among the Hurons (P),* trans. from French by Sheila Fischman. Montreal: Harvest House Ltd., 1973. 151 pp.

Born, 1931; wrote, shortly before 1973. Huron. The nature of the collaboration is not specified, but Gros-Louis is a literate and forceful man, and one cannot but feel that he was in control of the writing of this book which so thoroughly intertwines autobiography with Indian rights and Huron history. Gros-Louis tells of his life in such a way as to suggest to other Indians how they best might organize and educate themselves in order to have a better chance of gaining their due. Not an assimilationist, Gros-Louis has been a successful Indian leader during the years of his chieftainship.

211 Hadley, Tillman. BRODERICK H. JOHNSON. "Tillman Hadley,"* as found in the book cited in no. 17, pp. 285-98.

Born, 1896; interviewed, c. 1976. Navajo. For the details of the collaboration, see no. 17. Little here beyond education and occupations.

212 Hairy Moccasin (Isapi-Wishish [M]). JOSEPH KOSSUTH DIXON. "Hairy Moccasin,"* as found in the book cited in no.

11, pp. 138-40.

Born, c. 1848; interviewed, 1909. Crow. For the details of the collaboration, see no. 11. This is Hairy Moccasin's account of his work as a government scout. For another narrative by Hairy Moccasin, see no. 132.

213  Hanley, Max. BRODERICK H. JOHNSON. "Max Hanley,"* as found in the book cited in no. 17, pp. 16-55.

Born, 1898; interviewed, c. 1976. Navajo. For the details of the collaboration, see no. 17. Hanley tells of growing up, learning to tend sheep at the age of five, going off to begin his schooling at the age of eighteen, and of becoming a baker and finally an interpreter for anthropologists.

214  Hanna, Mark. RICHARD G. EMERICK. "Man of the Canyon: Excerpts from a Life in a Time--in a Place--in a Culture," Emerick, ed., Readings in Introductory Anthropology, vol. II, Berkeley, Calif.: McCutchan Publishing Co., 1970, pp. 267-92.

Born, 1882; interviewed, 1953. Havasupai. Hanna had been one of Leslie Spier's interpreters in the 1920's. There was, then, virtually no need for translation during the course of these interviews. The interviews were accomplished with very little direction from Emerick. He did do some abridging and some rearranging in order to preserve chronology, but "grammatical correction of Mark's narrative has been done only where the more gross errors would have made reading difficult" (p. 273). This tolerance has allowed such pleasant stuff as the following to survive: "Supai Charley bought me some marbles in the store and I played with those boys. I never played marbles before and I lost all those marbles" (p. 282). And upon seeing Theodore Roosevelt at the Grand Canyon: "I sure was glad to see that president. He looked like a good fellow and I was glad I was seeing him" (p. 287).

The autobiography is remarkably lacking in bitterness. Hanna tells, for example, of visiting a city dump at Williams-- on his first trip to the city. He tells of finding overalls there, and shoes, and a shirt: "and I sure was glad when I put that stuff on" (p. 282). It is only at the very end of the piece that Hanna begins to talk in a way that reminds us of the theme of the fallen state of the post-contact world.

> The land used to be good but now it's not good no more. That Bermuda grass has strong roots and it kills those crops. There didn't used to be Bermuda grass down here but now it's all over here and there's no way we can kill it. We tried to kill it but we can't do it. It's too hard and the land isn't good now. (p. 291)

The severe discipline, sexual inhibition, and generally tight restrictions imposed upon Hanna as a child invite comparisons with <u>Sun Chief</u> (no. 483).

215 Harris, George William.  GEORGE ANCOMA.  "George William Harris," in Ancoma, ed., <u>Growing Older</u> (IP), N.Y.: E.P. Dutton, 1978, 2 unnumbered pp.

Born, 1912; interviewed, c. 1977.  Sauk and Fox.  Ancoma taped interviews with many aged Americans.  The book cited here is a collection of miscellaneous autobiographical excerpts from these interviews.  Two are by Indians, Harris and Ann Shadlow, a Cheyenne from the Pine Ridge Reservation.

216 Harsha, William Justin.  <u>Ploughed Under: The Story of an Indian Chief, Told by Himself.</u>  N.Y.:  Fords, Howard, and Hulbert, 1881.  268 pp.

Although this is sometimes listed as autobiography, it is fiction, published anonymously by Harsha, who was not an Indian.

217 Harvey, Violet.  See no. 39.

218 Hatch, Claude.  BRODERICK H. JOHNSON.  "Claude Hatch," as found in the book cited in no. 34, pp. 123-28.

Born, 1912; interviewed, c. 1973.  Navajo.  For the details of the collaboration, see no. 34.  Hatch recounts his WW II army experiences, including his capture and detention by the Japanese.

219 Heavy Eyes (M).  JAMES WILLARD SCHULTZ.  Narratives are to be found in <u>Friends of My Life as an Indian,</u>*  Boston: Houghton Mifflin Co., 1923, pp. 18-23, 58-75, 190-202.

Born, probably c. 1835; narrated, 1922.  Piegan mother, white father.  In the summer of 1922 Schultz sent a messenger to several of the Blackfeet Indians whom he had known so well during the 1870's and '80's, asking them to camp with him and to recall, with him, the old days.  The tales in this book, then, are close redactions of the tales told around the camp fire in the fall of 1922.  For more about Schultz's methods, see no. 31.  Heavy Eyes' first narrative is about a bear hunt which he embarked upon contrary to the dictates of his vision.  He was wounded terribly.  In the second he recalls some of the more exciting events of his life:  trapping with his father, Hugh Monroe (born, 1798--probably the first white man among the Blackfeet), particularly their fight with hostile Indians.  In the third narrative we get an account of what Heavy Eyes claims was the last "buffalo trap" (i.e., running buffalo over a cliff) accomplished by the Blackfeet (c. 1842).

220 Heavy Head (M).  JOHN C. EWERS.  A Sun Dance narrative is

to be found in Ewers, <u>The Blackfeet, Raiders on the Northwestern Plains</u> (IP), Norman: University of Oklahoma Press, 1958, pp. 181-83.

Born, c. 1870; narrated, 1947. Blackfeet. Heavy Head, one of the last Blackfeet to submit to self-torture in the Sun Dance, here recalls his experience. This is one of the very few first-person accounts of such Sun Dance self-torture.

221 Herman, Jake. JEANNETTE HENRY. "Pine Ridge,"* in Henry, ed., <u>The American Indian Reader, Book III: Literature</u> (IP), San Francisco: The Indian historian Press, Inc., 1973, pp. 130-34.

Born, c. 1892; wrote, 1965. Oglala Sioux. This witty narrative is devoted mainly to Herman's years as a rodeo cowboy and clown. Pp. 134-47, by the way, include poetry and brief bits of Oglala folklore and history, all originally written by Herman for the journal <u>The Indian Historian</u> in the 1960's.

222 Hightower, James. <u>Happy Hunting Grounds</u>.* Colorado Springs: published for the author, 1910. 151 pp.

Born, c. 1855; wrote c. 1910. Cherokee father. Hightower, white-educated, tells of his youth spent as a member of a "band of Indian trappers" (p. 7). Hunting, trapping, woods lore. He is similar to Eastman (no. 161) in his romantic depiction of the woodland life, but his language is not similarly inflated.

223 Hillside (M). See no. 201.

224 Hiparopai (F). NATALIE CURTIS. "The Words of Hiparopai: A Leaf from a Traveler's Diary, Showing the Indian's Outlook upon the Transition Period," <u>The Craftsman</u>, XIII (1907), 293-97.

Born, before 1850; interviewed, c. 1906. Yuma. There is no mention of an interpreter here, but there could well have been one. Curtis includes some of her questions as well as Hiparopai's responses. Curtis's romantic assumptions are evident throughout. This is not so much a continuous narrative as a sheaf of reminiscences about the evil that has befallen the Yumas as a result of white contact—most specifically the injustice of white insistence upon assimilation.

225 Ho-chee-nee (F). See no. 93.

226 Hoffman, Joseph. GRENVILLE GOODWIN. "Joseph Hoffman," as found in <u>Western Apache Raiding and Warfare from the Notes of Grenville Goodwin</u> (P), ed. Keith Basso, Tucson: University of Arizona Press, 1971, pp. 72-91.

C. 1847-1936; interviewed, 1932. Cibecue Apache.

Goodwin had considerable knowledge of the Athapaskan dialects, but he worked with an interpreter in his interviews with Hoffman and the other informants in this volume. All of this material would have come in response to particular questions put by Goodwin. The resultant notes were edited by Basso in 1969, some twenty-eight years after Goodwin's death at the age of thirty-three. Hoffman begins with his childhood, but this narrative is mainly devoted to his remembrances of intertribal warfare, raiding, victory dances, and the like.

227 Holder, Stan. See no. 60.

228 Hollow Horn (M). JAMES WILLARD SCHULTZ. "To Old Mexico," as found in Schultz, Why Gone Those Times (IP),* ed. E.L. Silliman, Norman: University of Oklahoma Press, 1974, pp. 53-59.
   Born, late eighteenth century; told his tale, c. 1870. Blackfeet. This is a tale of Hollow Horn's participation in a Blackfeet raiding party that reached Mexico. Schultz knew the native language, and there would have been no interpreter. Originally written and published in 1900. For further information as to how Schultz worked, see no. 31.

229 Hopkins, Sarah Winnemucca. "The Pah-Utes," The Californian, VI, No. 33 (1882), 252-56. Reprinted as "An Ethnographic Sketch of the Paviotso in 1882," ed. Robert F. Heizer, Contributions of the University of California Archeological Research Facility, No. 7 (1970), pp. 55-63.
   1844 (or 1848)-1891; wrote, c. 1882. Piute. Some of this material is repeated in Life among the Piutes (no. 230), and there is not much autobiographical material here, but anyone interested in Hopkins or her work ought to look at her account of the Piute mode of life.

230 _____. Mrs. Horace Mann. Life Among the Piutes: Their Wrongs and Claims (P).* Bishop, Cal.: Sierra Media, Inc., 1969 [1883]. 268 pp.
   Wrote, c. 1882. Hopkins wrote the book. Mann's editing was limited to corrections of spelling and other "occasional emendations" at Hopkins's request. This is one of the very good autobiographies. As Mann recognized, Hopkins's writing evinces an "extraordinary colloquial command of the English language," and we owe Mann a debt of thanks for tampering so little with Hopkins's "fervid eloquence" (p. 3).
   Hopkins writes of her life in such a way as to provide a defense of the character and the claims of the Piutes. She remembers her band's first contact with the white man, she remembers her grandfather's eagerness and anticipation as he went forth to meet these new men, and she remembers their

cold rebuff. This is very much a pattern for the book. She describes her people as acting in simple good faith, only to receive dishonesty or violence in return.

She tells of a life which qualified her to speak on the wrongs her people had endured: she was an important member of many missions to seek submission from hostile groups of her people, and acted often and well as an interpreter and intermediary. She was an early advocate of pan-Indianism. This is the first Indian autobiography to play ironically with "civilization"--the "civilized" white men, or the "civilized" Yakima Indians, steal from the honest and trusting "savages," and so forth. Alford (no. 6), Eastman (no. 162), and many others were later to develop the same ironic point.

231   Hubbard, Chester. BRODERICK H. JOHNSON. "Chester Hubbard," as found in the book cited in no. 34, pp. 134-43.

Born, 1927; interviewed, c. 1973. Navajo. For the details of the collaboration, see no. 34. Hubbard tells about his youth and his work as a Navajo tribal judge.

232   Hudson, Peter. "Recollections of Peter Hudson," Chronicles of Oklahoma, X (1932), 501-19.

Born, 1861; wrote, probably c. 1931. Choctaw. These are rather impersonal, seemingly randomly ordered recollections of childhood, schools, and local and Choctaw history. Hudson was an Indian educator, the superintendent, for example, of the Tushkahoma Female Seminary for some years.

233   Hump (M). See no. 132.

234   Hungry Wolf, Beverly. The Ways of My Grandmothers. New York: William Morrow and Co., 1980. 256 pp.

Born, 1950; wrote, beginning c. 1975. Blood. Hungry Wolf writes: "It was not until I married my husband, Adolf Hungry Wolf, that I began to learn the ways of my grandmothers. Although he was born in Europe, my husband knew more about being a traditional Indian than I or any of my generation at that time. He encouraged me to find pride and meaning in my ancestry" (p. 16). The result is this book, part autobiography, part family history, part tribal history--with a good deal of folk technology (recipes, how to tan, make dresses, do bead-work . . .) as well. Hungry Wolf is a good example of the phenomenon of the young, white-educated Indian very self-consciously returning to an approximation of the old ways. What Momaday does in his imagination (see nos. 344, 345), Hungry Wolf and her husband are trying to do in fact.

235   Hunting Deer, Henry. THE ZUNI PEOPLE. "Henry Hunting Deer,"* as found in the book cited in no. 167, pp. 7-10.

Born, probably c. 1900; interviewed, c. 1965. Zuni. For the details of the collaboration, see no. 167. This is a narrative about Hunting Deer's deer hunting.

236 HUNTINGTON, JAMES. Lawrence Elliott. On the Edge of Nowhere.* N.Y.: Crown Publishers, Inc., 1966. vi + 183 pp.
Born, c. 1912; collaborated, c. 1964. Athapascan mother, white father. According to the dust jacket, Elliott "kept as close as possible to James Huntington's own words," though internal evidence suggests that there was, as usual, rearranging--and some embellishment of the prose. This is very much a book of adventure, of man against nature in the far north, of ferocious battles with bears and the elements.

237 Igjugarjuk (M). KNUD JOHAN VICTOR RASMUSSEN. Narrative is to be found in Intellectual Culture of the Caribou Eskimos, which is No. 2 of Intellectual Culture of the Hudson's Bay Eskimos (IP), which is vol. VII of Report of the Fifth Thule Expedition, 1921-24, Copenhagen: Gyldendalske Boghandel, 1930, pp. 51-55. This narrative is reprinted in the second book cited in no. 202, pp. 65-70.
Born, probably before 1875; interviewed, c. 1922. Caribou Eskimo. Rasmussen was able to take this narrative down word for word. For further details of the collaboration, see no. 50. This is a fantastic account of Igjugarjuk's acquisition and exercise of shamanic powers--ordeals, visions, etc.

238 Iron Teeth (F). THOMAS B. MARQUIS. "Iron Teeth, Cheyenne Old Woman," as found in the book cited in no. 194, pp. 4-26. A condensed version of this narrative was published as "Red Pipe's Squaw," Century Magazine, CXVIII (1929), 201-9.
Born, c. 1834; interviewed, 1929. Cheyenne. Marquis worked through an interpreter here, though he was fluent in sign language. For other details of the collaboration, see no. 194. This is a remarkable narrative. Iron Teeth claims to remember her people's taking up the nomadic way of life which the horse made possible. This is one of the most interesting of the brief autobiographies, full of incidents not found elsewhere. Iron Teeth talks, for example, of being given a white girl, a captive, to raise as her own child.

239 Iron Thunder (M). See no. 132.

240 Issuth-Gweks (F). "An Excerpt from My Memoirs," The Peak, V, No. 15 (Wed., April 5, 1967), 11.
Born, probably before 1937; wrote, c. 1967. Skeena, Kispiox Band. Reminiscences of life in the Indian village of Kispiox, B.C., for the most part having to do with the Potlach. She also comments on the unfortunate contemporary situation

of the Indian in Canada.

241 Jacobs, Peter (Pah-Tah-Se-Ga). Journal of the Reverend Peter Jacobs, Indian Wesleyan Missionary from Rice Lake to the Hudson's Bay Territory, and Returning, Commencing May, 1852. With a Brief Account of His Life . . . . N.Y.: Published for the author, 1857. 96 pp.
Born, before 1810; wrote, 1852-57. Ojibwa. An autobiography proper is on pp. 2-6; the rest is Jacobs's missionary journal for the spring and summer of 1852. Autobiographical sections are scattered throughout. Jacobs tells of his own conversion and says a good deal about the vile limitations of Indian religion, and a good deal as well in appreciation of various wonders of nature, quite in the manner we might expect from one who, like Jacobs, had been educated in England during the first half of the nineteenth century.

242 Jaime (pseudonym). See no. 205.

243 JAMES, ALLEN. Ann M. Connor. Chief of the Pomos: Life Story of Allen James (P). Santa Rosa, Cal.: Ann M. Connor, 1972. 144 pp.
Born, 1904; wrote, c. 1966. Kashia Pomo. Evidently Connor did only minor editing; many irregularities of spelling, etc., remain. This is an engaging autobiography. James was motivated to write, he tells us, by his desire that the traditions of his people might be remembered, and indeed, he does relate some traditional tales and recount traditional methods of cooking buckeyes and making poisons and medicines. But James also takes considerable pleasure in recalling the good times and the triumphs of his years at school and his career as a logger, a career in which he was determined to excel by ingenuity more than by muscle and speed. He can describe, then, a time when his forefathers lived in wigwams made of the bark of the redwoods, while he is also quite capable of yearning for the glory years of unrestrained logging in California. His account leaves off at about 1933.

244 Jerry. JOHN ADAIR. "My Life Story," as found in the book cited in no. 75, pp. 247-68.
Born, c. 1925; wrote, 1947. Zuni. Jerry wrote his own autobiography, and Adair did no editing or correcting. See no. 75 for further detail. There are some light-hearted childhood recollections here, but for the most part this narrative is devoted to his army experiences (WW II). He does write briefly about his hopes and goals upon his return from the army to the reservation.

245 Joab (pseudonym). DOROTHY EGGAN. "Joab's Comments on

His Life," in Eggan, Hopi Dreams and a Life History Sketch, Microcard Publications of Primary Records in Culture and Personality, ed. Bert Kaplan, II, No. 16, Madison, Wis.: Microcard Foundation, 1957, 24-37.

Born, c. 1886; interviewed, 1939. Hopi. Joab knew some English, but Eggan worked through an interpreter. The translation is printed here with very little editing, other than the substantial cutting (about two-thirds of the narrative) which was necessary to preserve Joab's anonymity. Eggan's questions are included in the transcript.

Joab talks about his impoverished, hungry childhood--his earliest memory is of hunger--and his family, his work, his hunting, etc.; but perhaps the most interesting portion of the narrative is the brief section devoted to the split at Old Oraibi. Joab was a member of the group that went to Hotevilla. Many of Joab's dreams are recorded in the pages that follow the autobiography.

246    John, Martha. T. D. ALLEN. "Writing in the Wind,"* as found in the book cited in no. 92, pp. 146-48.

Born, c. 1955; wrote, c. 1972. Navajo. For the details of the collaboration, see no. 92. John recalls the events associated with her uncle's death.

247    Johnson, Frances. EDWARD SAPIR. "Frances Johnson Is Cured by a Medicine-Woman," in Sapir, Takelma Texts, Anthropological Publications of the University of Pennsylvania Museum, II, No. 1 (1909), 184-89.

Born, c. 1850; interviewed, 1906. Takelma. Sapir prints this narrative in Takelma and in free English translation. Johnson here describes a cure which was performed upon her by a female shaman. She offers this experience and mentions others in order to prove the efficacy of the native healers, in the face of the doubts of the younger generation of Indians.

248    Johnson, Joseph. JAMES DOW McCALLUM. Letters are to be found in the book cited in no. 18, pp. 121-53, 172-90.

1751-76; wrote, 1767-74. Mohegan. For the details of the writing and the editing of these letters, see no. 18. Johnson writes of his labors among the Senecas and the Onandagas, confesses his sins (Wheelock eventually cast him off as a drunkard and an apostate) and searches his soul. He also writes about his conversion and his miserable poverty.

249    Johnson, Martin. See no. 24.

250    Jones, Jeff. WALTER GOLDSCHMIDT. "Autobiography of Jeff Jones," as found in Goldschmidt, Nomlaki Ethnography, University of California Publications in American Archeology

and Ethnography, XLII, No. 4 (1952), 433-34.

Born, 1865; interviewed, 1936.   Nomlaki.   Jones was Goldschmidt's chief informant for Nomlaki Ethnography, and so this brief autobiography is included as an appendix to that work.  The English is Jones's nonstandard English.  Jones has cut himself off from the old ways, though he is respected by other Indians for his knowledge of the old ways.

251   JONES, REV. PETER.  Wesleyan Missionary Committee.  Life and Journals of Kah-ke-wa-quo-na-by:  (Rev. Peter Jones), Wesleyan Missionary.  Toronto:  Anton Green, 1860.  xi + 424 pp.

1802-56.  Jones wrote the brief autobiography which constitutes the first chapter of this book shortly before his death; the journal which follows covers the years 1825 to 1856. Welsh father, Ojibwa mother.    The Wesleyan Missionary Committee which edited this material did a good deal of cutting; however, they did strive to maintain something of the flavor of Jones's prose:  "the presence of our dear brother was never  forgotten;  hence  there  are  sufficient  pecularities sprinkled through the Journal to give internal evidence of the idiosyncracy of his mind" (p. iv).

Jones was raised by his mother until his fourteenth year and thus was taught "the superstitions of her father" (p. 2).  At his father's urging, Jones converted to Wesleyan Christianity in  1822,  and  by  1824  he  was  keeping  a  day  school  and preaching.  He began his missionary labors among the Indians in 1825.  His account accentuates the physical hardships and the spiritual desolation of pre-Christian Ojibwa life--but Jones says that he was at first reluctant to be baptized because of the drunkenness and depravity of the Christian Indians (Mohawks) whom he knew.  The journal contains much of  the  standard  stuff  of  missionary  journals--conversions, backslidings, and the proselytizer's hopes.

252   _____ .  History  of  the  Ojebway  Indians  with  Especial Reference to Their Conversion to Christianity . . . with a Brief Memoir of the Writer . . . .  London:  A.W. Bennet, 1861.  viii + 278 pp.

Wrote, c. 1843.  There is a first-person account of Jones's conversion to Christianity on pp. 5-9, but this book is also included here because Jones often relates the history of his people in terms of what he saw and what he remembers about witchcraft, about the old tales, about keeping time, playing games, and much else.  This is really quite an interesting work by a man who felt the plight of his people keenly.

253   Joseph, Chief.  "An Indian's View of Indian Affairs,"* with an introduction by William H. Hare, North American Review,

CXXVIII (April, 1879), 412-33. This was reprinted in Cyrus Townsend Brady, Indian Fights and Fighters (P), Lincoln: University of Nebraska Press, 1971 [1909], and reprinted again as Chief Joseph's Own Story (P),* with a foreword by Donald MacRae, Seattle, Wash.: Shorey Book Store, 1975, 31 pp. An abridgment is in Jane B. Katz, ed., Let Me Be a Free Man (IP),* Minneapolis, Minn.: Lerner Publications Co., 1975, pp. 48-76.

   1832-1904; narrated, 1879. Nez Perce. We are told nothing about the details of this collaboration, other than that Chief Joseph told his story to a reporter from the Review. This is a moving account of the Nez Perce war, which ended in 1877, and the events which precipitated the conflict.

254   Josie. RUTH LANDES. Josie's life history is in Landes, The Ojibwa Woman (P), N.Y.: Columbia University Press, 1938, pp. 239-47.

   Born, probably before 1860; narrated, shortly before 1936. Ojibwa. Evidently Landes had an Ojibwa interpreter collect many life histories for her (see Kluckhohn, 1945, p. 89). Three of these are printed here. The narratives appear not to be guided by questions, and though there are excisions, there seems to be little other editing. All three are quite good.

   Josie's narrative is unusual in that it deals almost exclusively with the problems she encountered in matters of love, of being forced to marry a man she did not love, rather than the man she did love, of parting from her husband, and of other related vicissitudes. Finally she tells of being happily married to a man with whom she remained into her old age.

   All three of Landes's autobiographies are so narrowly concerned with the problems of matrimony that one must assume that she edited these narratives in order to bring out precisely these qualities, allowing other chapters in the book to tell about other aspects of Ojibwa life.

255   Jude (pseudonym). PAMELA HARRIS. Narrative to be found in Another Way of Being: Photographs of Spence Bay, N.W.T. (P),* Toronto: Impressions, 1976, pp. 7-10.

   Born, c. 1945; interviewed, c. 1975. Eskimo. No interpreter was involved here, and Harris marks all elisions and allows many nonstandard features of Jude's language to remain. This brief autobiographical narrative, part of the introductory matter for this book, is intended to give us a sense of Eskimo life. Jude talks about his childhood, schooling, his hunting, and his feelings about being an Eskimo.

256   KABOTIE, FRED. Bill Belknap. Fred Kabotie: Hopi Indian Artist (P).* Flagstaff, Ariz.: Museum of Northern Arizona with Northland Press, 1977. xv + 149 pp.

C. 1900; interviewed, c. 1976. Hopi. No information is given as to the nature of the collaboration here, but it would seem likely that Belknap, a long-time friend of Kabotie, taped Kabotie's narrative, asking questions along the way, and then did the usual cutting, rearranging, and editing toward standard English.

Kabotie was six at the time of the strife between the Hostiles and Friendlies--that is, those who opposed and those who favored white ways, particularly white schooling. He is able to tell us of his family's sorrow upon being forced, along with the rest of the Hostiles, to leave their homes in Shungopavi; indeed, Kabotie's account of this whole troubled period is insightful and fairly detailed. But he manages as well to convey what was his own childish understanding of those events. He remembers, for example, his delight in entertaining the soldiers with his somersaults, the same soldiers who had just forced the Hostiles to leave their newly settled Hotevilla, the same soldiers who were soon to arrest most of the adult male Hostiles, including Kabotie's own father and several uncles.

This somersaulting boy went on to become an artist of some renown and an important figure in Indian educational and cultural affairs. As Belknap says in his introduction, even the present extremes of Kabotie's life are "hard to believe. Today . . . he might be sweating in his desert cornfield . . . tomorrow he could be jetting to New York" helping to decide "who will receive fine arts grants, and joining distinguished colleagues for dinner at the Century Club" (p. xv). He still takes part in the traditional Hopi religious life.

Perhaps a single anecdote will serve to indicate how distinct and engaging a personality emerges from these pages. When Kabotie was about thirteen, his uncle returned from the Carlisle Indian school full of ambition. The two decided to raise cattle. In order to get the money necessary to buy the beginnings of a herd, they decided to make jewelry, turquoise and shell necklaces:

> It was slow, tedious work and we needed help with the drilling. Here's where my marble-playing came in--and my big bag of marbles. We could get boys to drill all day for five marbles. My job was to pay off the workers and win back our capital. (p. 16)

The book is lavishly illustrated with color reproductions of Kabotie's exquisite paintings of Hopi ceremonies, and Kabotie has a good deal to say about his arts--music, painting, silversmithing, and weaving.

257   Kaibah (F). See no. 46.

258 Kakee, Joanasie (M). See no. 5.

259 Kakianak, Nathan (pseudonym). CHARLES C. HUGHES. Eskimo Boyhood: An Autobiography in Psychosocial Perspective (IP). Lexington: University Press of Kentucky, 1974. 429 pp.
Born, c. 1935; wrote, c. 1958. Eskimo. Hughes writes:

> [This] life story was written (in English) at my request and mostly under conditions conducive to recalling nostalgic personal memories, for much of the first part was set down while [Kakianak] was hospitalized with an advanced case of tuberculosis. The autobiography is presented almost in its entirety; only a few sections have been deleted to shorten the document and minor editorial revisions and grammatical alterations made for easier reading. It is important ... to reaffirm the authenticity of the phraseology ... for Nathan had only a fourth-grade education .... (pp. 3-4)

Kakianak writes of his childhood and adolescence. He tells of hard winters and what we recognize as many aspects of the transition from the old ways to the new. Hard winters, seal hunting, and schooling. The language is colloquial.

260 Kansaswood, Lee. BRODERICK H. JOHNSON. "Lee Kansaswood,"* as found in the book cited in no. 17, pp. 273-79.
Born, c. 1905; interviewed, c. 1976. Navajo. For the details of the collaboration, see no. 17. Kansaswood tells about his education, his years of work, and a bit of tribal history.

261 Kanseah, Jasper. EVE BALL. Narratives are to be found in the book cited in no. 138, pp. 104-5, 109-10, 112, 131-33.
Born, c. 1870; interviewed, probably during the 1950's. Chiricahua Apache. No interpreter was necessary here. For the rest see no. 138. This nephew of Geronimo recalls the sad early days on the reservation, his life with Geronimo, his exile in the East with the other Apaches, Geronimo's last days, etc.

262 KAYWAYKLA, JAMES. Eve Ball. "I Survived the Massacre of Tres Castillos,"* True West, VIII, No. 6 (1961), 22, 38.
C. 1875-1963; interviewed, c. 1961. Apache. Kaywaykla spoke English. Ball edited and rearranged the material elicited during her interview with him. Some space is devoted here to Kaywaykla's own remembrances of the massacre of Victorio's band of Warm Springs Apaches, of which Kaywaykla was a five-year-old member. For the most part, however, this

narrative is devoted to Kaywaykla's recollections of his grand-mother's experiences as one of the Apache prisoners of war in the East.

263 _____. _____. In the Days of Victorio: Recollections of a Warm Springs Apache (P).* Tucson: University of Arizona Press, 1970. xv + 222 pp.

Interviewed, c. 1956-63. Beyond a statement that she interviewed Kaywaykla innumerable times "over a period of seven years," Ball provides no account of the nature of her collaboration with the narrator. Internal evidence suggests that Ball determined the book's order and interpolated some material from sources other than Kaywaykla; a good deal of the phrasing is almost certainly Ball's as well. There seems no reason to doubt, however, that this book is faithful to Kaywaykla's conception of the history of this period and his point of view. He cooperated with Ball so that, as he says, Apaches of later generations might "know of the courage and resourcefulness of their ancestors." He hopes as well that his "account may bring about a better understanding of the Apaches among white Americans" (p. xv).

We read about Kaywaykla's childhood, lived in the days of the Apache wars of Nana, Victorio, and Geronimo. Kaywaykla was among those Apaches shipped to detention camps in Florida, and he speaks bitterly of that confinement and of the white man's treatment of his people generally. Finally, he provides an account of his schooling at Carlisle, another unhappy experience.

264 KEGG, MAUDE (NAAWAKAMIGOOKWE). John Nichols. Gabekanaansing /At the End of the Trail: Memories of Chippewa Childhood in Minnesota, with Texts in Ojibwa and English, Occasional Publications in Anthropology, Linguistic Series (P), No. 4 (1978), x + 85 pp. Seven of the tales printed here were privately printed as Gii-ikwezensiwiyaan / When I - Was a Little Girl, Onamia, Minn., 1976.

Born, 1904; narrated, 1971-77. Ojibwa. Nichols transcribed and edited these Ojibwa language reminiscences. This book includes the native text, an interlinear translation, and a free translation. The final text was submitted to Kegg for alterations and emendations. The result is quite an attractive collection of disconnected childhood reminiscences and tales. Kegg tells of maple-sugaring, fasting experiences, moving, harvesting wild rice, and a good deal else.

265 KENNEDY, DAN (OCHANKUGAHE). James R. Stevens. Recollections of an Assiniboine Chief (IP). Toronto: McClelland and Stewart, 1972. 160 pp.

Born, c. 1870; wrote, 1920's and '30's. Assiniboine.

Kennedy's writings came to Stevens as a mass of typewritten material, some of which had been published as magazine and newspaper stories. Stevens did a good deal of editing to turn Kennedy's disconnected reminiscences into a less miscellaneous form. Stevens also did some cutting; for example, "Kennedy . . . wrote with favor in regard to European transformation of the plains. Phrases that were overly complimentary were edited out" (Stevens, personal communication. All information regarding Stevens's work on the Kennedy manuscript comes from this letter). Kennedy, who did live to see his work published, was evidently quite proud of the book in its final form.

The book is rather like Momaday's Way to Rainy Mountain (no. 344), in that it combines personal, tribal, and legendary history. The most important autobiographical material here has to do with Kennedy's childhood and his enforced schooling.

266  Kenoi, Samuel E.  MORRIS E. OPLER.  "A Chiricahua Apache's Account of the Geronimo Campaign of 1886," New Mexico Historical Review, XIII, No. 4 (1938), 360-86.

Born, 1875; interviewed, 1932. Chiricahua Apache. This and no. 267 are sections of a long autobiography taken down by Opler. The rest is unpublished. Opler could converse in the native language, but he used an interpreter here. It would seem a safe assumption that Opler proceeded here as he did at about this same time with another autobiographer, Chris (see no. 115). If so, Kenoi was allowed to embellish, expand, leave out as he chose.

Only part of this account is autobiographical. Kenoi does, however, tell of being taken off, as a child of eleven, with the other Chiricahuas to their prison camp in the East, and of his eventual release along with the other Chiricahuas--some after twenty-seven years of incarceration. Kenoi's is a most unflattering account of Geronimo.

267  _____. _____. "A Description of a Tonkawa Peyote Meeting Held in 1902," American Anthropologist, XLI (1939), 433-39.

Kenoi describes a Peyote Cult meeting he attended. For the rest, see no. 266.

268  Kilabuk, Jim. See no. 5.

269  Kill Eagle (M). See no. 132.

270  Kiyaani, Mike.  DAVID F. ABERLE.  Narratives are to be found in The Peyote Religion among the Navaho, Viking Fund Publications in Anthropology, No. 42 (1966).

Born, probably before 1915; interviewed, 1954-57. Navajo.

Aberle provides accounts by Kiyaani and other Navajos (many known only by pseudonyms) about peyote. Some speak favorably, some unfavorably. Kiyaani provides a detailed account of his version of the peyote ritual. Some of these interviews, at least, were done with the aid of interpreters. Aberle evidently prints the narratives with little change. His own questions, and sometimes even his own motivations for asking certain questions, are included in the text.

271 La Flesche, Francis. The Middle Five: Indian Schoolboys of the Omaha Tribe,* Foreward by David A. Baerreis. Madison: University of Wisconsin Press, 1963. xxiii + 152 pp. Reprinted, Lincoln: University of Nebraska Press, 1978 (P). Originally, The Middle Five: Indian Boys at School (1900).

1857-1932; wrote, shortly before 1900. Omaha. La Flesche, who went on to become a professional anthropologist, reminisces here about his years as a student at a Presbyterian mission school, c. 1864-75. This is a perceptive book, written quite self-consciously as an attempt to better the Indian in the eyes of the white man. In this respect the book is like those of Alford (no. 6), Eastman (no. 162), Standing Bear (nos. 469, 470), and Hopkins (no. 230).

272 LaFrance, Daniel. See no. 3.

273 LAME DEER, JOHN (FIRE). Richard Erdoes. Lame Deer: Seeker of Visions (P).* N.Y.: Simon and Schuster, 1972. 288 pp.

Born, c. 1900; collaborated, c. 1966-70. Sioux. We are told nothing about the details of the collaboration, though internal evidence suggests that Erdoes took a lot of notes, edited the language into standard written English with a colloquial flavor, and did a lot of rearranging and some cutting. Lame Deer was fluent in English.

Lame Deer was only intermittently a seeker of visions, devoting the rest of his time to a rather remarkable range of pursuits; he was at one time or another, soldier, drunkard, hippie, tribal policeman, sign painter, farmhand, jail inmate, and shaman. One of the irritating aspects of this autobiography is the way in which Erdoes includes himself in the book. Lame Deer's constant references to Erdoes seem designed mainly to show us all how wonderfully Erdoes was accepted as friend to the Indians. This book is often polemical and wittily bitter.

274 LaMonte, Agnes. ROXANNE DUNBAR ORTIZ. Narratives by LaMonte and others are found in Ortiz, ed., The Great Sioux Nation: Sitting in Judgment on America (P), Berkeley: Moon Books, 1977, 224 pp.

Born, probably c. 1925; narrated, 1974. Oglala Sioux. The book cited here is a collection of excerpts from the "Sioux Treaty Hearing" which was held before Federal Judge Warren Urbom at Lincoln, Nebraska, 1974. This hearing was an attempt to annul the charges made against various of the participants in the siege at Wounded Knee, 1973, the argument being that the Sioux were an independent nation, and so the Federal law enforcement officers who made the arrests at Wounded Knee had no jurisdiction there. The judge's decision went against the defendants. The book cited here is a collection of court transcripts, heavily edited: virtually none of the testimony hostile to the defendants' case is included; virtually all of the questions posed by attorneys are excluded; some of the attorneys' questions were worked into the witnesses' testimony; some of the testimony was reworked into verse form; and much of the testimony has been translated from the Lakota.

Since the defendants' lawyer, Larry Leventhal, was trying, among other things, to convince the court of the validity of oral history in deciding such cases, there is a good deal said here by various witnesses about oral history itself, and it is instructive to compare the conception of oral history presented here with that of Goody and Watt (1962-63). The book is also of value for its presentation of the militants' sense of the siege at Wounded Knee.

La Monte, who lost a son during the siege, provides the most extended account of Wounded Knee, but the book also includes first-person accounts by Leonard Crow Dog (see no. 131) and Russell Means, both of the American Indian Movement.

275 Lansing, David.   BRODERICK H. JOHNSON.   "David Lansing,"* as found in the book cited in no. 17, pp. 105-109.

Born, 1905; interviewed, c. 1976. Navajo. For the details of the collaboration, see no. 17. Memories of growing up and caring for a family along with talk about the importance of education.

276 Last (M).  JAMES LARPENTUR LONG.  Autobiographical fragments are to be found in the book cited in no. 27, pp. 38-39, 79-80, 177.

Born, c. 1853; interviewed, 1939. Assiniboine. For the details of the collaboration, see no. 27. Last recalls various experiences, including hunting and camp cooking.

277 Last Gun (M).  ADOLF HUNGRY WOLF.  "The Last Real War Party,"* as found in the book cited in no. 20, pp. 287-300.

Born, c. 1857 (the date is provided by Hungry Wolf, who is in this, and much else, determinedly credulous); interviewed,

c. 1972. Piegan. Last Gun evidently spoke English. Internal evidence suggests that Hungry Wolf edited for standard English. Last Gun tells here of the last Blood war party, a month-long raid into Montana (1889).

278 Laughter, Floyd. See no. 33.

279 Leaning-Over-Butchering (M). JAMES WILLARD SCHULTZ and JESSIE LOUISE DONALDSON. A narrative* is to be found in the book cited in no. 157, pp. 193-216.

Born, probably before 1850; narrated, c. 1927. Blackfeet. For the details of the collaboration, see no. 157. These are tales of war.

280 LEE, BOBBI (F). Don Barnett and Rick Sterling. Bobbi Lee, Indian Rebel: Struggles of a Native Canadian Woman (P), vol. I. Richmond, B.C.: Liberation Support Movement Information Center, 1975. 120 pp.

Born, 1950; narrated, 1972. Métis (Cree and white). Barnett and Sterling tape-recorded this life history and printed the transcript with little editing. Lee recounts the events of her troubled childhood and adolescence--parental problems, racism, drugs, physical problems--and goes on to show how a growing acquaintance with communism, socialism, and the Black Panthers allowed her to understand herself and her people's predicament. Lee's account of her move from the reservation to the city gives the reader a very real sense of the problems faced by so many urban Indians.

281 Leevier, Annette. Psychic Experiences of an Indian Princess. Los Angeles: The Austin Publishing Co., 1920. 32 unnumbered pp.

Born, c. 1856; wrote, c. 1920. Ojibwa father, French mother. This is a strange one. Leevier was brought up according to the dictates of her mother's Catholic faith, was, for example, early sent to live in a nunnery. But her life was finally to be determined by "spirit guides"--her dead father, Sitting Bull, Abraham Lincoln, Martin Luther, Mrs. Bennette (who had been a resident of Cleveland during her material existence), and Longfellow.

Students of linguistic parapsychology might be interested to know that while Martin Luther was capable of communicating with Leevier in perfectly grammatical English verse, Leevier's poor Indian father, even in his spirit existence, could manage no better than "Muche Heape Good Man . . . ."

282 LEFT-HAND (M). F.L. King. Chief Left-Hand: His Life Story, as Told by Himself. N.Y.: The Americans Baptist Home Mission Society, n.d. [c. 1910]. 15 pp. The American

Indian: Chief Left Hand's Life. The American Baptist Home Mission Society, n.d. [c. 1910], 4 unnumbered pages, is an abridged republication.

Born, c. 1838; interviewed, 1907. Arapaho. King was a missionary, and he asked Left-Hand for his life story because "a number of Christian people are anxious to hear of his life," and to tell his life story would thus be "really a work for Jesus" (p. 2). Left-Hand spoke through an interpreter. Left-Hand tells of his youth and his years as a warrior. He concludes with an account of his conversion. A second "talk" delivered by Left-Hand on the subject of his conversion is included here. For another narrative by Left-Hand, see no. 132.

283 Left Handed (M). WALTER DYK. Son of Old Man Hat. A Navaho Autobiography. N.Y.: Harcourt Brace, 1938. xiv + 378 pp. Reprinted, Lincoln: University of Nebraska Press, 1967 (P).

Born, 1868; interviewed, 1934. Navajo. Left Handed knew no English. Dyk worked through an interpreter. The resulting text "differs in no essentials from that first telling," aside from some rearranging (particularly of the early episodes) for a more nearly chronological presentation, and some cutting of recurring episodes (p. xii). Once Left Handed's account reached his fourteenth year, however, the chronological sequence is evidently his own. This narrative was guided, in part, by questions, and so, as Clyde Kluckhohn (1945, p. 92) cautions, we cannot assume that the freedom with which Left Handed talks about sexual matters, for example, is necessarily an indication of his own lack of inhibitions. It might simply, or at least partly, be a result of Dyk's prodding. But a person is revealed in these pages to a degree that is wonderful. Left Handed tells of his family, of his growing up with the sheep and the lice; he tells of his fears, his triumphs, and his courting, and of the hopes that bind him.

284 Lincoln, Murray. BRODERICK H. JOHNSON. "Murray Lincoln," as found in the book cited in no. 34, pp. 145-53.

Born, 1911; interviewed, c. 1973. Navajo. For the details of the collaboration, see no. 34. Lincoln tells about his youth, schooling, and his work as a Navajo tribal judge.

285 Little Finger (M). PLINY EARLE GODDARD. "A Captive of the Navajo," as found in Goddard, White Mountain Apache Texts (IP), Anthropological Papers of the American Museum of Natural History, XXIV, pt. 4 (1920), pp. 504-9.

Born, probably c. 1850; narrated, 1910. White Mountain Apache. The native language text is printed on facing pages with a literal translation. Little Finger tells of being taken captive by the Navajos and of his escape.

286 Little Owl (F). RUTH LANDES. Narrative to be found in the book cited in no. 254, pp. 227-33.

    Born, probably before 1865; narrated, shortly before 1936. Ojibwa. For the details of the collaboration, see no. 254. Little Owl recalls the trials of her married life.

287 Loloma, Charles. See no. 38.

288 LONE DOG, LOUISE. Vinson Brown. Strange Journey: The Vision Life of a Psychic Indian Woman. Healdsburg, Calif.: Naturegraph Publishers, 1964. 64 pp.

    Born, c. 1915; wrote, c. 1964. Mohawk and Delaware. No account is given of the nature of Vinson's editing, but it would seem to have been minimal. The book is an earnest blend of psychic mysticism, Christianity, health-foodism, and autobiography, written by a woman who considers her spiritual gifts and practices to be very much in keeping with the traditions of the Mohawks and the Delawares.

289 Lone-tree (M). ROBERT H. LOWIE. Narrative to be found in the book cited in no. 199, pp. 239-41. For another brief narrative by Lone-tree, see no. 200.

    Born, probably c. 1845; interviewed, c. 1910. Crow. This includes the native-language text, an interlinear translation, and a free translation. This is a war experience.

290 _____. _____. A narrative is to be found in The Sun Dance of the Crow Indians (IP), Anthropological Papers of the American Museum of Natural History, XVI (1915), p. 41.

    Narrated, c. 1907. This is Lone-tree's relation of his ceremonial preparations for war, and of his "war captain's vision." Lowie worked through an interpreter. Probably Lowie did no cutting or rearranging here.

291 Long, Sylvester (Buffalo Child Long Lance). Long Lance: The Autobiography of a Blackfoot Indian Chief.* N.Y.: Cosmopolitan Book Corporation, 1928. xv + 278 pp.

    1891-1932; wrote, 1928. Croatan and black, adopted Blackfeet. This is not really an autobiography. As Long wrote in a letter to a friend:

> My publishers asked me last year for a "Boys' Book" on the Indian . . . . lots of adventure and a goodly amount of Indian customs. I connected up my own experiences and those of many other Indians I know and made a running story out of it. . . . But when they received the copy

they thought it was "too good for a boys' book," and forthwith they decided to run it as a straight book. (As found in Dempsey, 1978, p. 202)

292 Long, Vern. See no. 60.

293 Long Lance (M). See no. 291.

294 Long Salt. See no. 33.

295 Longstreet, David (Nalte). GRENVILLE GOODWIN. "David Longstreet," as found in the book cited in no. 226, pp. 186-203.
Born, c. 1855; interviewed, 1931. White Mountain Apache. See no. 226 for the details of the collaboration. "Longstreet's recollections begin around 1865," but for the most part his narrative deals with "the capture of his mother by troops stationed at Tucson and his own experiences as a scout on Crook's famous expedition into Sonora, Mexico" (p. 187).

296 Louis, Sammy. WILLIAM C. SAYRES. Sammy Louis: The Life History of a Young Micmac. New Haven: The Compass Publishing Co., 1956. lix + 285 ppp.
Born, 1923, interviewed, 1950. Micmac. Louis's native language was English, and the interviews were in English, taken down verbatim with speed writing, then typed out the following day. Questions were asked of Louis, but once he began talking he was generally not interrupted. Sayres edited the material into chronological order but provided a complete account at the end of the book as to which day which paragraph was elicited. Most of the nonstandard features of Louis's dialect have been retained. Louis was chosen as an informant because he was thought not to have been a very remararkable individual. He was a soldier in WW II, though he never fired a shot; he had in-law troubles; and he had a mental breakdown.

297 LOW CLOUD, CHARLES ROUND. William Leslie Clark and Walker D. Wyman. Charles Round Low Cloud: Voice of the Winnebago. River Falls: University of Wisconsin -River Falls Press, 1973. vii + 93 pp.
1872-1949. Winnebago. This book contains selections from a column Low Cloud wrote for the Black River Falls Banner-Journal, 1932-49. Some of the pieces are personal anecdotes--all are in nonstandard, unedited English.

298 Low Dog (M). See no. 132.

299 Lowry, Annie. LALLA SCOTT. Karnee: A Paiute Narrative.

Reno: University of Nevada Press, 1966. xviii + 139 pp.

1867-1943; interviewed, 1936. Piute mother, white father. Scott first interviewed Lowry simply in the hope of gaining ethnographic information, but soon the two women began to talk more personally about a wide range of topics. It was only years later that it occurred to Scott that all of the resultant material could be shaped into a single narrative. The book as we have it falls into two parts, the first telling something of the history of the Piutes in general and of Lowry's mother in particular, the second part telling Lowry's own life history. The first part is largely synthetic, Scott's arranging and blending of material from a wide range of primary and secondary sources besides the Lowry material. The second section is almost entirely in the first person, and according to Charles R. Craig's introduction, Scott here "worked almost entirely from her notes, transcribing them with a minimum of revision." In this second part she interpolates some material, usually "originating from local Indians, but these instances are few and brief" (p. xvii).

Lowry was raised largely by her Piute mother, although she talks at some length here about the conflict between her parents' two cultures (eventually she chose to live among her mother's people), and so we read, for example, of her white education as well as of her experiences with shamans. This is good reading for those interested in the problem of the Indian caught between two cultures.

300 Luckie, Kate. See no. 107.

301 Ludi, Frank. See no. 24.

302 Luiseno. J. Cesar. "Cosas de Indios de California." MS. in Bancroft Library, University of California, Berkeley, 1879.

According to Robert F. Heizer (1977), this is a "verbatim life history of Luiseno [who was] born at Mission San Luis Rey in 1824."

303 Mahwee, Dick. WILLARD ZERBE PARK. Narratives in the first book cited in no. 202, pp. 17, 27-28, 54. Much of this is reprinted in the second book cited in no. 202, pp. 180-83.

Born, sometime before 1885; interviewed, 1934-36. Paviosto. Park worked through an interpreter, but Mahwee knew enough English to be able to check the translation, and this he did, evidently, with some care. Mahwee talks about the acquisition and the use of his shamanic powers.

304 Manitowabi, Edna. "An Ojibwa Girl in the City,"* This Magazine Is about Schools, IV, No. 4 (1970), 8-24. This was reprinted, with few changes, as An Indian Girl in the City,

Buffalo, N.Y.: Friends of Malatesta, n.d. [c. 1971], 17 pp.

Born, c. 1945; wrote, 1969. Ojibwa. Manitowabi writes a penetrating account of the effect her Catholic boarding school experience had on her later life, of the feelings of inadequacy and the fear which resulted from not being allowed to speak her own language, from being unable to understand her teacher's English. She writes too of how all of this led to the severance of her ties to her family. Eventually she went to Toronto, where the evils of the city beset her, and where she attempted suicide and eventually received psychiatric help. She writes, however, as one who is finally at peace with herself. She has come to terms with her Indian past, and she looks forward to working with her people.

305 Many Big Ears (M). JAMES WILLARD SCHULTZ and JESSIE LOUISE DONALDSON. A narrative* and pictograph are to be found in the book cited in no. 157, pp. 244-49.

Born, probably before 1855; narrated, c. 1927. Blackfeet. For the details of the collaboration, see no. 157. Many Big Ears relates some of his war and hunting experiences by explaining the details of one of his pictographs.

306 Manychildren, Selena. T.D. ALLEN. "My Mother,"* in the book cited in no. 92, pp. 50-54.

Born, c. 1953; wrote, c. 1970. Navajo. For the details of the collaboration, see no. 92. Manychildren recalls her childhood, with fond remembrance, especially, of her mother.

307 Many Mules (M). JAMES WILLARD SCHULTZ. "Many Mules,"* as found in the book cited in no. 20, pp. 276-77.

Born, c. 1860; narrated, in the 1920's. Blood. For the details of the collaboration, see no. 20. This is a war reminiscence.

308 Many Tail Feathers (M). JAMES WILLARD SCHULTZ. A narrative* is to be found in the book cited in no. 219, pp. 223-54.

Born, 1845; narrated, 1922. Piegan. For the details of the collaboration, see no. 219. Many Tail Feathers tells of his vow--imposed upon him by his mother--to kill the Assiniboine warrior who had killed his father. It took him nearly thirty years to accomplish his vow, and his revenge was terrible. The Assiniboine was scalped alive. Besides being a ripping good tale, this narrative is valuable for its account of the mechanics, customs, and assumptions of a Piegan war party.

309 Many Wounds (M). See no. 509.

310 Marchand, Leonard S. KENT GOODERHAM. "The Honourable

Member for Kamloops-Cariboo,"* as found in the book cited in no. 188, pp. 40-44.

Born, c. 1933; wrote, 1968. From the Kamloops Indian Reserve, Okanagan band. Marchand tells about his life in such a way as to explain how he came to be the first Indian elected to the Canadian House of Commons.

311    Marcos (pseudonym). ROBERT N. RAPOPORT. "Marcos--a Strong Mormon," in the book cited in no. 163, pp. 129-33.

Born, c. 1896; interviewed, 1949. Navajo. Probably Rapoport worked through an interpreter here. This life history is in Rapoport's words, with long excerpts from Marcos's undirected narrative interspersed. Marcos tells of a hard childhood, his dislike for the boarding school, his passage to manhood and drinking, and his eventual conversion to the Mormon church. This is the brother of Nanabah (no. 353) and the half-brother of Moustache (no. 350).

312    Maria, Casa (M). PLINY EARLE GODDARD. Narratives are to be found in Goddard, Jicarilla Apache Texts (IP), Anthropological Papers of the American Museum of Natural History, XVIII (1911), 144-69, 250-60.

Born, c. 1840; interviewed, 1909. Jicarilla Apache. The native language text is printed with an interlinear literal translation (pp. 144-69) and also in free translation (pp. 250-60). Goddard worked through an interpreter. These are reminiscences about war and hunting.

313    Mario, Eddie (pseudonym). EVON Z. VOGT. "Eddie Mario: Life History," as found in the book cited in no. 42, pp. 315-67.

Born, c. 1920; interviewed, 1947. Navajo. No interpreter was necessary here, since Mario spoke English. For further details of the collaboration, see no. 42. Mario talks of his school days at some length, of his early childhood experiences and fears, and of sheepherding. There is an account of WW II experiences here. Mario seems to have had little trouble readjusting to life on the reservation.

314    Martin, Mrs. Bob. BRODERICK H. JOHNSON. "Mrs. Bob Martin,"* as found in the book cited in no. 17, pp. 120-34.

Born, 1892; interviewed, c. 1976. Navajo. For the details of this collaboration, see no. 17. The daughter of a medicine man, Martin continues to depend on the Navajo prayers despite her school education. This narrative is largely devoted to memories of boarding school and to recipes and folk technology.

315    Martinez, Elaine. ELIZABETH COLSON. "Autobiography of Elaine Martinez," as found in the book cited in no. 2, pp. 98-

99.
Born, c. 1930; narrated, 1941. Pomo. Elaine, the grand-daughter of Sophie Martinez (no. 316), asked if she could tell her own life story, after hearing hours of Colson's interviewing her grandmother. Colson consented, and the result is printed here with virtually no editing. This was, then, an unrequested as well as unguided autobiography. There is very little here, unfortunately.

316 Martinez, Sophie. ELIZABETH COLSON. "Life History of Sophie Martinez," as found in the book cited in no. 2, pp. 34-94, 95-97.
Born, c. 1874; interviewed, 1939-41. Pomo. Martinez had a command of English barely sufficient for these interviews, and her narratives needed more editing than those of the other women in this volume. Still, Colson allows a strongly idiomatic flavor to remain. For further details of the collaboration, see no. 2. This interesting pair of documents follows Martinez through the years of culture contact and change. She includes much detail about her adolescence, puberty, fears of poisoning, familial relations, hop-picking, etc.

317 Mason, Billy. RONALD L. OLSON. Narratives to be found in Olson, The Quinault Indians, University of Washington Publications in Anthropology, VI, No. 1 (1936), 155-58, 169.
Born, c. 1860; interviewed, 1925-26. Quinault. It would seem that Mason knew English, and no interpreter was necessary here. Olson edits for standard English, but probably there is little other emendation. Mason tells of the acquisition and the exercise of his shamanic powers.

318 Mathews, John Joseph. Talking to the Moon. Chicago: University of Chicago Press, 1945. 244 pp.
Born, 1895; wrote, c. 1944. Osage mother. Mathews was educated at the University of Oklahoma and Oxford. In 1932 he published Wah'Kon-Tah: The Osage and the White Man's Road (University of Oklahoma Press); not long thereafter he left the "roaring river of civilization" (p. 3) for a retreat in the Oklahoma hills. There he had a stone cabin built for himself, and there he lived "in rhythm" with the life about him, and there he "reached maturity and the stage of ornamentation, expressed by worry over the peace of the world, the future of [his] nation, the passing of the landmarks along the jungle river of time" (p. 241). Filled as it is, then, with closely observed accounts of, and ruminations upon, animals, people, plants, self, and seasons, this book is at once a narrative of Mathews's years of retreat and the fruit of his "maturity."
The book makes frequent use of Osage myth, nature lore, and history; but Thoreau's Walden seems to have been much

before Mathews's mind as well, as is perhaps especially evident in the care Mathews takes with his descriptions of the technological aspects of his self-consciously chosen primitive existence. This is an elegant and a sensitive book.

319   Maxidiwiac (F). GILBERT L. WILSON. Agriculture of the Hidatsa Culture: An Indian Interpretation (IP), University of Minnesota Studies in the Social Sciences, No. 9 (1917), viii + 129 pp.

Born, 1839; interviewed, 1912. Hidatsa. Wilson worked with Maxidiwiac's son, Goodbird (see no. 192), as interpreter, and Wilson "claims no credit beyond arranging the material and putting the interpreter's Indian-English into proper idiom" (p. 5). Wilson wanted to get a single informant's account of Hidatsa agriculture, rather than a composite picture from many informants, and this gently moving book is the result. Maxidiwiac tells of the mythic origins of her people, tells moral fables, and tells of her life in her fields. She provides ethnographic detail by the bushel--but she also allows us a wonderful sense of her self and of her feelings for her plants and their proper nurture. She talks about how methods have changed in her lifetime as a result of white contact, and something of her feelings toward those changes.

320   _____. _____. Wa-Hee-Nee: An Indian Girl's Story, Told by Herself.* St. Paul, Minn.: Webb, 1921. 189 pp.

Interviewed, 1908-18. Wilson fabricated this autobiography by putting many of the stories which Maxidiwiac had told him over the years of their collaboration into one continuous narrative. Occasionally Wilson fleshed out Maxidiwiac's accounts of certain events with information from Maxidiwiac's brother, Wolf-chief (nos. 541, 542), and other Hidatsa informants. One assumes that Wilson supplied transitions and the like as well. Wilson does repeat some material here which had already been published in no. 319, but there is much that is fresh and revealing. Maxidiwiac talks of what it was like to live in earth lodges, and of how much better the people liked these lodges than they did their summer skin lodges. "We thought the earth was alive and had a spirit like a human body." We read of her childhood, her coming to womanhood, her learning a woman's work; she tells about her marriage in detail, and her assumptions and feelings about child-rearing as well.

This book deserves to be reprinted, for this woman is one whom it behooves anyone interested in American Indians to come to know.

321   _____. _____. Hidatsa Horse and Dog Culture (IP), Anthropological Papers of the American Museum of Natural

History, XV, No. 2 (1924), 125-311.

See no. 319 for details of collaboration. Wilson's method is again to introduce us to certain aspects of Hidatsa culture by allowing individuals to talk about their remembrances and knowledge of traditional ways in regard to, in this case, horses and dogs. And here again, we get a nice sense of the narrators--Maxidiwiac and her brother Wolf-chief (nos. 541, 542). Maxidiwiac's contributions here are confined to pp. 199-224, 231-98.

322 McCarty, Darlene. JOHN R. MILTON. "A Day with Yaya," as found in the book cited in no. 184, pp. 119-25.

Born, c. 1950; wrote c. 1968. Yakima. McCarty reminisces here about her childhood and her grandmother.

323 McCortney, Lila. Blix Ruskay. Reminiscences* in the book cited in no. 28, pp. 106-09, 129.

Born, c. 1899; interviewed, 1975. Half Nisqually-Quinault. For the details of the collaboration, see no. 28. These are unconnected reminiscences of child-bearing, shop-keeping, ranching, etc.

324 McDaniel, Mary. EARLE SHORRIS. A narrative is to be found in Shorris, Death of the Great Spirit (P),* N.Y.: Simon and Schuster, 1971, pp. 191-97.

Born, c. 1915; interviewed, c. 1970. Hunkpapa father, Oglala Sioux mother. We are given no information about how this narrative was taken down, but internal evidence suggests that it came in response to particular questions, and that Shorris did some subsequent cutting and rearranging. The phrasing retains its colloquial flavor. McDaniel tells about growing up on the reservation and her bad experiences at boarding school. She also talks about marital relations ("A Sioux woman don't care nothing for her husband anyway. But my children are my flesh and blood," p. 195), her eventual removal to the cities of the West, and her poverty there. She claims to be the great-granddaughter of Big Foot and Chief Gall.

325 McDonald, Catherine. WINONA ADAMS. "An Indian Girl's Account of a Trading Expedition to the Southwest About 1841,"* The Frontier, X (May, 1930), 338-51, 67.

Born, c. 1827; narrated, c. 1875. Nez Perce (father, Mohawk and white). A few years after the trip she recounts here, Catherine married Angus McDonald. During the years of their marriage she told many stories to her children, and Angus wrote a number of these down in a huge ledger, which is still preserved. Whether the tales were originally in English or not, we do not know, but it is at least evident that Angus transformed his wife's tale into late nineteenth-century literary English. Adams has edited, then, one of these narratives, omitting some "incidental stories which have no relation to this journey" (p. 339), and occasionally altering puncuation.

This is a remarkable narrative. Catherine went with her mixed-blood father and the rest of a large party (Indians and whites) on a trapping expedition, a trip which began just west of what is now Yellowstone Park and continued all the way down to the Gulf of California. Along the way the group encountered hostile Indians, kidnaping Spaniards, Piutes, and others. One of the most interesting aspects of this narrative is the perspective Catherine has upon all that happened. At times she seems to identify quite comfortably with Indians. She speaks, for example, with appreciation of skirts made out of the scalps of enemies. At other times Indians may be "savages"--as when, for example, the men of their party, disregarding the recriminations of her father, murder many of the inhabitants of a defenseless desert Indian village because they suspect these hospitable people of having stolen five traps.

326 McLaughlin, Marie L. A narrative is to be found in McLaughlin, Myths and Legends of the Sioux, Bismark, N.D.: Bismark Tribune Co., 1916, p. 3.

Born, 1842; wrote, 1916. One-quarter Sioux. This auto-biography is less than a page long, simply an attempt to establish credentials for tales that follow.

327 Means, Russell. See nos. 60, 274.

328 Medicine Eagle, Brooke. JOAN HALIFAX. "Brooke Medicine Eagle,"* as found in the second book cited in no. 202, pp. 86-91.

Born, c. 1946; interviewed, 1976. Nez Perce and Sioux. The uncritically enthusiastic book cited here is a collection of narratives by shamans, some reprinted from sources cited elsewhere in this bibliography. Some, however, are the result of Halifax's interviews with contemporary shamans. No account is provided of the kind of editing Halifax performed upon these shamans' accounts, though internal evidence suggests that she did at least cut and edit for standard English. Medicine Eagle tells here of the vision quest which was preparatory to her becoming a shaman--all very much a self-conscious attempt to return to the old ways (see no. 234).

329 Merip okegei (F). A.L. KROEBER. Narrative in Kroeber, Handbook of the Indians of California (P), Berkley, Calif.: California Book Co., Ltd., 1953 [1925], pp. 65-66.

Born, probably c. 1835; interviewed, 1902. Yurok. Merip okegei tells about her two years of training to become a shaman, and a bit about the methods of her practice. This is the second wife of Sregon Jim (no. 467).

330 Merqusaq (M). KNUD JOHAN VICTOR RASMUSSEN. "A Tribal Migration,"* as found in the book cited in no. 50, pp. 23-26.

Born, c. 1840; narrated, c. 1902. Eskimo, Baffin Island and Cape York. For the details of the collaboration, see no. 50. This narrative is the result of Rasmussen's request for information from the survivors of a tribal migration from Baffin Island to Cape York in the far north of Greenland. As Rasmussen wrote, "This is probably the only example we come in contact with among the Eskimos" of an "actual tribal migration . . . lasting several years, from one polar region to another." And this happened without "any external influence," the people having "only their own primitive means to assist them" (p. 23).

One of the fascinating aspects of this remarkable narrative is Merqusaq's account of the cultural and technological differences between his own people and the Cape York people they came to live with. He tells, for example, about the items of technology which his people took over from Cape Yorkers, and vice versa.

331 Meyers, Chief. LAWRENCE S. RITTER. "Chief Meyers," as found in Ritter, The Glory of Their Times (IP),* N.Y.: Macmillan Co., 1966, pp. 162-76.

Born, 1880; interviewed, c. 1964. Cahuilla. This is an edited version of a taped interview, the editing limited to cutting and rearranging. Although Meyers does talk briefly about his people and about some of his youthful experiences, these reminiscences have almost entirely to do with Meyers's career in baseball. He played in the major leagues, 1909-17.

332 Miguel. JOHN ADAIR. "Life History of Miguel," as found in the book cited in no. 75, pp. 2-107.

Born, 1921; collaborated, 1947. Zuni. For the details of the collaboration, see no. 75. Miguel tells of his schooling, his courting, his time in the army (WW II), and his return to the reservation. The narrative is detailed, and Miguel says a good deal, at Adair's prompting, as to his feelings about his experiences. One of the most interesting aspects of this narrative is the bi-culturalism which is clearly evident, for example, in Miguel's belief in witchcraft and his simultaneous knowledge of the relationship of germs to disease. The witches use germs to do their evil.

333    Miguel, Albert (pseudonym). EVON Z. VOGT. "Albert Miguel:
       Life History," as found in the book cited in no. 42, pp. 199-
       217.
            Born, c. 1918; interviewed, 1948. Navajo. Vogt worked
       with an interpreter here. Vogt provides a nice account of
       Miguel's resistance to telling his life story, and of his own not
       entirely straightforward means of overcoming that resistance.
       For further details of the collaboration, see no. 42. Miguel's
       account of his life is dominated by his bad experiences at the
       boarding school--whippings, etc.--and of his army experiences
       (WW II).

334    Miguel, Pedro (pseudonym). ROBERT N. RAPOPORT. "Pedro
       Miguel--a Doubtful Galilean," in the book cited in no. 163, pp.
       121-25.
            Born, 1911; interviewed, 1949. Navajo. For the details of
       the collaboration, see no. 311. Marcos is a type of the Indian
       caught between two cultures. He did not achieve enough of
       white education to allow him to succeed in white society, but
       the years devoted to white schooling did deprive him of a
       knowledge of Navajo religion and mythology. His early life
       was very hard. We also read of his two marriages, his
       conversion to the Galileans, etc.

335    Miguelito, Frank (pseudonym). EVON Z. VOGT. "Frank
       Miguelito: Life History," as found in the book cited in no. 42,
       pp. 239-52.
            Born, c. 1922; interviewed, 1947. Navajo. Miguelito spoke
       English, and so there was no interpreter necessary here. See
       no. 42 for the further details of the collaboration. Miguelito
       tells about his childhood, his learning to herd sheep, his work
       on the railroad, and his feelings about being drafted into the
       army (WW II). He ends by hoping for better things for his
       children through education. He had no schooling.

336    Miranda, Mike. CHARLES F. VOEGELIN. "Autobiography,"
       as found in Voegelin, Tubatulabal Texts, California University
       Publications in American Archeology and Ethnology, XXXIV
       (1935), 223-41.
            Born, c. 1888; interviewed, c. 1934. Tubatulabal. Voegelin
       interfered very little with this narrative. The original
       Tubatulabal is printed on facing pages with a literal transla-
       tion. Miranda tells about childhood games, hunting, a gun-
       fight, marital difficulties, and other matters. Miranda is the
       nephew of Frances Philips (no. 392).

337    Mitchell, Charlie. EDWARD SAPIR. "A Navajo's Historical
       Reminiscences," in Sapir and Harry Hoijer, Navajo Texts (IP),
       Iowa City: Linguistic Society of America, 1942, pp. 336-97.

Born, c. 1850; interviewed, 1929. Navajo. Sapir exercised next to no control over this narration. Mitchell even translated his own narrative, with the help of a younger Navajo man, John Watchman. The native-language text appears on facing pages with the translation. The result is much more readable than are most such texts intended primarily for linguistic analysis. Of the time when he become old enough to bear arms Mitchell translates: "My arrows came into being" (p. 341). He remembers having spent his youth in a time of peace and laments that the Navajos were drawn into war.

338 MITCHELL, EMERSON BLACKHORSE. T.D. Allen. Miracle Hill: The Story of a Navajo Boy (IP),* Norman: University of Oklahoma Press, 1967. xvii + 230 pp.

Born, c. 1945; wrote, probably 1963-66. Navajo. Allen was Mitchell's writing teacher at the Institute of American Indian Arts in Santa Fe, and this book is the protracted result of an early assignment in writing autobiography. Allen did virtually no editing toward standard English, although she actively influenced the writing of narrative in other ways one would expect of a writing teacher. The book is fictionalized autobiography, written in the third person, telling about "Broneco," his childhood, his education (which he hopes will help him help his people), his sense of his past, his hopes--and his desire to write.

339 MITCHELL, FRANK. Charlotte J. Frisbie and David P. McAllester. Navajo Blessingway Singer: The Autobiography of Frank Mitchell, 1881-1967 (P), Tucson, Ariz.: University of Arizona Press, 1978. x + 446 pp.

1881-1967; interviewed, 1963-67. Navajo. Frisbie tape-recorded a nondirected life history and then, off and on during the remaining four years of Mitchell's life, she and McAllester recorded many hours of supplemental interviews with Mitchell. All of these data were carefully checked for accuracy against a wide range of evidence from documents and Navajo informants. The final editing involved cutting repetitious material and regularizing the English of three different trans-lators. "In some cases, this meant rephrasing a particular interpreter's various idiosyncratic usages, such as the some-times elaborate social science terminology developed by [one translator] during his work with Edward Sapir and his years as a Tribal interpreter." Frisbie and McAllester also incorporated some "verbatim materials given by Frank to other scholars," and arranged their material into chronological order. But throughout, the editors have tried to capture the "flavor, style and implication" of Mitchell's Navajo (p. 8). The editors also mention the present location of the tape recordings, for those interested to compare the book with the original.

This is one of the very few most fully and carefully annotated Indian autobiographies--and Mitchell's personality is quite sufficient to bear the weight of all these glosses. One of the most engaging aspects of the book is the evident interest Mitchell takes in it all. He wants to tell all he is allowed to tell, for example, about the Blessingway rites he practices. He considers them to be important and quintessentially Navajo. Anyone interested in Navajo ceremonialism will be delighted by this book. For the rest, Mitchell was one of the first Navajo children to attend the Fort Defiance boarding school. Later he worked as a handyman and interpreter at reservation missions and trading posts. He also was a wagon freighter in the days before motorized transport on the reservation.

340 Mitchell, Wayne. PETER ANASTAS. Reminiscences in Glooskap's Children: Encounters with the Penobscot Indians of Maine, Boston: Beacon Press, 1973, pp. 115-22.

Born, probably c. 1948; interviewed, c. 1971. Penobscot. The Mitchell narrative was cut, but evidently there has been little other editing. Mitchell tells of his family, his work in a mental institution, and his feelings about being an Indian.

341 MODESTO, RUBY. Guy Mount. Not for Innocent Ears: Spiritual Traditions of a Cahuilla Medicine Woman (P).* Angelus Oaks, Calif.: Sweetlight Books, 1980. 124 pp.

1913-80; collaborated, beginning 1976. Cahuilla. This book is a miscellaneous collection of Cahuilla history (written by Mount); Cahuilla folktales (narrated by Modesto); animadversions on modern medicine and adumbrations on the virtues of Cahuilla medicine, midwifery, and hallucinogenic spiritualism (all by Mount); and Modesto's brief autobiography (pp. 23-57). Mount even includes a twenty-eight-page high school curriculum, "Our Indian Heritage"--but before social studies teachers rush in, they should be warned that Mount is arguing for "a spiritual curriculum," one that would guide "the use of psychoactive plant experience [sic]" (p. 76). Mount mentions that the book is a result of two or three years of interviews with Modesto, and so we must suppose that the autobiography has been pieced together from several interviews. Beyond this the nature of the collaboration is not specified (although it is clear from internal evidence that Mount edited for standard, written English), but how far can we trust an editor who can proclaim:

> It is my hypothesis that large desert petroglyphs visible only from the air in their gigantic entirety were directional markers for medicine men and women who were

using their spirit flight as a visionary tactic for making long journeys. (p. 74)

We are not surprised, then, to read that Mount feels himself to be very much in Carlos Castaneda's debt--and clearly Modesto is to be Mount's Don Juan. Her autobiography is consequently largely concerned with her training for and practice of shamanism, her dreaming, her "spirit flights," her use of hallucinogens, her healings, powers, and trials.

342 MOISÉS, ROSALIO. Jane Holden Kelley and William Curry Holden. A Yaqui Life: The Personal Chronicle of a Yaqui Indian (P).* Lincoln: University of Nebraska Press, 1977. lviii + 251 pp. First published as The Tall Candle: The Personal Chronicle of a Yaqui Indian (1971).

1896-1969; collaborated, 1954-58, 1967-69. Yaqui. The history of this text is complex. Holden asked Moisés to write an autobiography in 1954. Although his best languages were Yaqui and Spanish, Moisés wrote in English, because that was the language in which he had received what little formal education he had had. During the next four years he produced over five hundred hand-written pages. The resulting manuscript (see no. 343), which Kelley describes as "solicited but undirected" (p. li), was then liberally edited by Holden. The English was regularized, some of the episodes were rearranged, and some material was added which Holden had elicted from Moisés over the years he had employed him as an informant. This manuscript was never published. In 1967 Holden turned the project over to his daughter, Kelley, who eventually worked out a compromise, staying close to Moisés's original manuscript, but filling out detail, filling in names, etc., as these were provided during her own interviews with Moisés, 1967-69. Moisés read and corrected each chapter as it was written, and Moisés and Kelley went over the final manuscript together as well. These interviews, by the way, were conducted in Spanish, in which Moisés was fluent.

The result of all of this is one of the very good Indian autobiographies. It is packed with detail of the kind which is valuable to the ethnographer, but which, in this case, seems also always to be necessary to the narrative. When we read that a well had to be dug in the river bed in order to supply water for Moisés's newly planted watermelon, chili, and pumpkin seeds, when we read that he had to carry two five-gallon cans of water to each of the eighty watermelon seeds he had planted, we feel the heat, the dust, the ache of muscles, and the hunger.

Moisés was born as the traditional Yaqui ways were disintegrating. We see in the life of Moisés the effects of Porfirio Díaz's dictatorship upon the Yaquis.

343 _____. _____. "Original Notebooks of Rosalio Moisés," folders A472a and A472b. Arizona State Museum Archives, Tucson, Arizona.

These are the unedited notebooks of Moisés, in manuscript (see no. 342).

344 Momaday, N. Scott (M). The Way to Rainy Mountain (P).* N.Y.: Ballantine Books, 1973 [1969]. 119 pp.

Born, 1934; wrote, 1966-69. Kiowa father, mother with an Indian great-grandmother. The frame for this book is Momaday's account of his journey to Rainy Mountain, his journey back to his own birthplace in the heartland of the Kiowas. Momaday asks us to see that his journey was analogous to the journey of the Kiowas--their great tribal migration--from the forests of the Rocky Mountains to the Oklahoma plains in the vicinity of that same Rainy Mountain. For the rest, the book is a collection of brief autobiographical narratives, juxtaposed with brief accounts of events in the historic and mythic past of his Kiowa forebears. Momaday shows us, then, the way his conception of himself as an Indian evolved, by showing us the constituents of his idea of himself. For other Indian autobiographers who combine personal, tribal, and mythic history to convey their sense of themselves, see nos. 186, 204, 265, 318, 385.

345 _____. The Names (P).* N.Y.: Harper and Row, Publishers, 1976. 170 pp.

Wrote, c. 1976. Momaday here abandons the Faulknerian narrative complexity of his Pulitzer Prize-winning House Made of Dawn and the stark juxtapositions of The Way to Rainy Mountain (no. 344) in favor of a straightforward narrative style (with occasional lapses into stream-of-consciousness); Momaday is here trying to "write in the same way, in the same spirit" as a traditional Kiowa storyteller (The Names; for an account of the evolution of Momaday's style, see Brumble, 1980).

The Names takes us up to Momaday's fourteenth year, when he left Jemez pueblo, where his parents were school teachers, to attend military school. This is a rich and gentle book--and, along with The Way to Rainy Mountain and Talking to the Moon (no. 318), it is by far the most literate of these autobiographies--almost certainly the most beautiful of the self-written Indian autobiographies.

346 Monongye, Preston. See no. 38.

347 Mountain Chief (Omaq-Kat-Tsa [M]). JOSEPH KOSSUTH DIXON. "Mountain Chief,"* as found in the book cited in no. 11, pp. 104-18.

C. 1848-1942; interviewed, 1909. Blackfeet. For the details of the collaboration, see no. 11. Reminiscences of boyhood, hunting, and war.

348 MOUNTAIN HORSE, MIKE. Thyrza Young Burkitt. My People, the Bloods (IP),* ed. Hugh A. Dempsey. Calgary, Alberta: Glenbow-Alberta Institute and the Blood Tribal Council, 1979. xiii + 146 pp.

1888-1964; wrote, 1936. Blood. Mountain Horse wrote this with the editorial help of Burkitt, but they were unable to find a publisher, so the manuscript was laid aside and then thought to be lost until a few years ago when Dempsey came upon a copy of it. Dempsey made numerous changes. First he added two historical pieces, which Mountain Horse had written for the Lethbridge Herald (1931, 1937). He then made "a few grammatical corrections," although many of Mountain Horse's idiosyncracies--and all of his high-flown diction--were allowed to remain. Dempsey also placed the "chapters in a more logical order than existed in the original document." Finally, he deleted such phrases as "this barbarous ritual" and "this revolting custom" and "a most horrible and sordid custom," arguing that Mountain Horse was writing for a white audience, an audience which he knew would disapprove of the old pagan ways of the Bloods. Such negative comments in the manuscript, then, were not so much an "indication of his feelings as they were a reflection of the attitudes of the 1930's which he believed he had to satisfy if he expected to get his manuscript published" (p. x). Dempsey knew Mountain Horse quite well during the latter years of his life.

All of this leaves us with a book that is close to Standing Bear's (no. 469) and Alford's (no. 6) in intent and point of view. Mountain Horse wants to improve his people's standing in the eyes of the white man, but he feels ambivalent about the old ways. Mountain Horse is thoroughly Christian, and he is thankful for all that the missionaries and the Mounted Police have done for his people. He is quite willing to criticize some aspects of the old ways (the treatment of women as drudges, for example) and to laugh at some of the traditional customs-- but he also feels a considerable pride in the past of his warrior people.

The book is devoted mainly to tribal history, although there are autobiographical details scattered throughout. For the most part these are confined to childhood, schooling, and WW I service.

349 Mountain Wolf Woman. NANCY OESTREICH LURIE. Mountain Wolf Woman, Sister of Crashing Thunder: The Autobiography of a Winnebago Indian (P). Ann Arbor: University of Michigan Press, 1961. xx + 142 pp.

1884-1960; interviewed, 1958. Winnebago. Lurie asked Mountain Wolf Woman to tape record her life history. The resulting autobiography, a transcription of which is printed as an appendix, was so brief, and Lurie's disappointment was so evident, that Mountain Wolf Woman offered to do another, longer life history, this time prompted along the way by Lurie's questions. She also did a third version in halting English. The autobiography as it is printed is a translation of the native-language text, supplemented by excerpts from Mountain Wolf Woman's English version and by bits of information obtained in other interviews.

This book is a fascinating account for many reasons: because of Mountain Wolf Woman's remarkably easy passage from the old ways to the new; because of her dual perspective --she can, for example, understand that her father would have been wise to take his land allotment, although she can also understand her father's reasons (land was a Bear clan concern; he was of the Thunder clan)--and because of the fact that she is the sister of Crashing Thunder (no. 129) and Sam Blowsnake (nos. 73, 74). The book is further remarkable for its utter lack of bitterness or sense of loss.

350 Moustache (Bidagh or Son of Many Beads or Jose Pino [see Kluckhohn and Vogt, 1955, for these names]). CLYDE KLUCKHOHN. "A Navajo Personal Document with a Brief Paretian Analysis," Southwestern Journal of Anthropology, I (1945), pp. 260-83.

1866-1954; interviewed, 1936. Navajo. Kluckhohn worked through an interpreter, but he did not direct the interview beyond asking for a life story. Kluckhohn even includes the dialogue between himself and Moustache which led up to the narration of the life story, the dialogue wherein Kluckhohn gave his reasons for wanting the life story and the terms of payment; and he gives Moustache's replies, his reasons for reluctance, and so forth. He also takes the trouble to specify certain of his interpreter's limitations. The text itself-- unfortunately only six pages long--is simply a transcription of the interpreter's words. Kluckhohn also includes a helpful analysis of some aspects of the life story. Kluckhohn was very much concerned with the problems and the possibilities of the personal document, and this is clearly an attempt to direct further work with autobiographies (see Kluckhohn, 1945). Moustache himself was a widely respected man, one of the few in his community still to wear his hair long, a traditionalist. Moustache was the half-brother of Marcos (no. 311).

351 Moves Camp, Ellen. See no. 60.

352 Mustache, Curly. See no. 24.

353. Nanabah (F). ROBERT N. RAPOPORT. A narrative is to be found in the book cited in no. 163, pp. 115-18.

Born, c. 1890; interviewed, 1949. Navajo. Rapoport worked here as he did with Marcos (no. 311). Nanabah is the mother of Sally Yazi, (no. 550) the half-sister of Mr. Moustache (no. 350), and the sister of Marcos (no. 311). Nanabah tells of an impoverished childhood, tending sheep, family relations, marriages, and her conversion to the fundamentalist Galilean faith. This last was partly the result of a miraculous cure and a miraculous rainfall.

354 Navajo, Buck. See no. 33.

355 Navaysa, Phil. See no. 38.

356 Nelly (pseudonym). ERIKA BOURGUIGNON. A Life History of an Ojibwa Young Woman, Microcard Publications of Primary Records in Culture and Personality, ed. Bert Kaplan, I, No. 10, Madison, Wis.: The Microcard Foundation, 1956, 42 pp.

Born, 1923; interviewed, 1946. Ojibwa. This is a typed transcript of Bourguignon's interviews with Nelly. It is quite rough, Bourguignon's paraphrases of Nelly all jumbled together with direct quotations. Descriptions of Nelly's actions during the course of the interview--"beams at child"--and Bourguignon's questions are set off by parentheses. It is all in English. Nelly talks about hard times, babies, her childhood fears, the mistreatment which she suffered at the hands of her husbands, etc.

357 Nelson, Alfred. See no. 39.

358 Nelson, Ernest. BRODERICK H. JOHNSON. "Ernest Nelson,"* as found in the book cited in no. 17, pp. 230-42.

Born, c. 1916; interviewed, 1976. Navajo. For the details of the collaboration, see no. 17. Nelson's narrative is mainly devoted to his years of schooling. For other narratives by Nelson, see nos. 24 and 33.

359 Neptune, Martin. PETER ANASTAS. Reminiscences* in the book cited in no. 340, pp. 69-81.

Born, 1950; interviewed, 1971. Penobscot. Neptune's narrative is cut, but otherwise evidently little editing was done. Neptune tells about dropping out of high school, his troubles with the police, and his dawning awareness of his rights and identity as an Indian.

360 Newland, Sam. JULIAN H. STEWARD. "Autobiography of Sam Newland," as found in "Two Piute Autobiographies,"

California University Publications in American Archeology and Ethnology, XXXIII (1934), 423-38.

Born, c. 1840; interviewed, 1927-28. Piute. Steward worked through an interpreter with both of these informants. Both were asked the bare minimum of questions necessary to keep the narrative going, because "those facts were chiefly desired which they themselves regarded as important and significant" (p. 425). The narratives are edited for standard English but are otherwise unembellished. These two old men provide quite different narratives. Newland never had much luck in hunting or gambling, while Steward's second Piute, Jack Stewart (no. 476), had much in both endeavors, and was constantly guided by dreams and visions as well. Newland, on the other hand, laments that he never received a power dream. Both he and Stewart would have achieved manhood before the time of extensive white contact.

361   Nez, Andres (pseudonym). EVON Z. VOGT. "Andres Nez: Life History," as found in the book cited in no. 42, pp. 92-111.

Born, probably c. 1925; interviewed, 1948. Navajo. Vogt worked through an interpreter here. See no. 42 for further details of the collaboration. Vogt mentions that this life history was related in Nez's mother's hogan, and that friends and relatives were present. Evidently the narrative was very much enjoyed by this audience--not surprisingly, since this is an engaging narrative. Nez tells of his childhood, his childish fears of the shadows cast by clouds, and of his childhood responsibilities as a shepherd. He goes on to tell of his life on the reservation up until 1948, all in a light mood.

362   Nez, Buster Hastiin. See no. 33.

363   Nez, John (pseudonym). EVON Z. VOGT. "John Nez: Life History," as found in the book cited in no. 42, pp. 368-84.

Born, c. 1922; interviewed, 1947. Navajo. Nez spoke English, so no interpreter was necessary here. For the rest of the details of the collaboration, see no. 42. Nez talks about his childhood and the sometimes unhappy times at boarding school. For the rest, the narrative is largely devoted to Nez's army experiences (WW II). Nez ends with a desultory account of his return home to the reservation.

364   Nikoline (Majuvartariaq [F]). KNUD JOHAN VICTOR RASMUSSEN. "A Temptation,"* as found in the book cited in no. 50, pp. 353-58.

Born, c. 1864; narrated, c. 1904. Eskimo, East Greenland. For the details of the collaboration, see no. 50. Nikoline tells of a fearful encounter with a shaman just prior to her conversion to Christianity.

365 Nolasquez, Carolina. JANE H. HILL. Recollections nos. I, IV, V, IX, XI, XII, XIII, XV as found in Hill and Rosinda Nolasquez, ed., Mulu'wetam, the First People: Cupeno Oral History and Language (P), Banning, Calif.: Malki Museum Press, 1973, pp. 46-52.

Born, before 1880; interviewed, 1919-21. Cupeno. Paul Louis Faye collected these recollections in the native language, but his work was filed away and forgotten until 1967 when Hill and Nolasquez began the work of translation and editing. Their literal translations are printed on facing pages with the Cupeno text. These recollections are but autobiographical jottings. Some passages, however, are well worth the reading: "And then we would go to play, we used to jump, we used to play the . . . bird game. And we played hopscotch, and we played jacks on the rocks, and we played dolls. And then they built the school, and we never played any more" (p. 46).

366 NOLASQUEZ, ROSINDA. Jane H. Hill. "Childhood in Cupa," in the book cited in no. 365, pp. 52-54.

Born, before 1900; interviewed, 1962. Cupeno. The native language text is on facing pages with Hill's and Nolasquez's literal translation. There is little here beyond what the title promises.

367 Norcross, Walker J. BRODERICK H. JOHNSON. "Walker J. Norcross," as found in the book cited in no. 34, pp. 97-115.

Born, 1895; interviewed, c. 1973. Navajo. For the details of the collaboration, see no. 34. Norcross tells about his childhood and his WW I experiences--including his transfer to play baseball for the army. For another narrative by Norcross, see no. 24.

368 Nowell, Charles James. CLELLAN S. FORD. Smoke from Their Fires: The Life of a Kwakiutl Chief (IP).* Hamden, Conn.: Archon Books, 1968 [1941]. xiv + 248 pp. The first few pages of chapter 5 are reprinted (without attribution) in Thomas E. Sanders and Walter W. Peeks, eds., Literature of the American Indian, Beverly Hills: Glencoe Press, 1973, pp. 432-34.

Born, 1870; interviewed, 1940. Kwakiutl. Nowell knew English, so it was "possible to take down the story of his life exactly as he told it," although rearranging was done to place the events "as nearly as possible in chronological sequence." Ford also performed some syntactic alterations, although many nonstandard features remain. "English aliases have been substituted for the real names of the girls with whom Charley had affairs. In all other respects the story has been repeated exactly as he told it" (p. 41). Internal evidence suggests that this narrative was largely guided by the anthropologist's questions.

As a child Nowell had very little contact with whites; so this is, in part, an account of the effects on the Kwakiutls of the coming of the whites. Despite his white education and extensive contact with white culture, Nowell himself retains his Kwakiutl values and beliefs. He still believes in witchcraft, for example, and he still believes in the values of the Potlach. This is a highly regarded book.

369  NULIGAK (M). Maurice Metayer. I, Nuligak (P).* Toronto: Peter Martin Associates Ltd., 1966. 208 pp.

Born, 1895; wrote, probably c. 1960. Eskimo, Mackenzie Delta. Meyers asked Nuligak to write his memoirs, but otherwise did not guide the narrative. Nuligak wrote in Eskimo, and Meyer translated, doing no editing other than cutting "useless repetitions" and redundant accounts of, for example, hunting experiences. On rare occasions the order of sentences was altered "in order to clarify what was said, but this was never done when this might in any way have altered the sense" (pp. 7-8).

This is a wonderful book. Substantial white contact in the North came so late that Nuligak can recall his youth with very few references to the white man and his ways. Although he was to become a trapper as an adult, for example, he recalls a time when the Eskimo "hardly ever set traps for foxes . . . the people had eyes for only one thing--what could be eaten" (p. 42). The book is full of detail and full of Nuligak's feelings about those details. One of the most appealing aspects of the book, however, is Nuligak's determination to do more than simply relate the incidents of his life. He has a rather definite idea of himself, an idea built up from the stuff of myth as well as personal history. As Meyer put it:

> Nuligak was orphaned when very young. The Eskimo legends of the . . . little orphan are continually recalled, as well as the misery and neglect suffered by him up to the day he became a great hunter. . . . No doubt these stories are but the projection of the ordinary life of a poor Eskimo orphan in the domain of legends and dreams. Nuligak was one of these and his life is quite close to the legend. (p. 9)

370  NUÑEZ, BONITA WA WA CALACHAW. Stan Steiner. Spirit Woman: The Diaries and Paintings of Bonita Wa Wa Calachaw Nuñez. New York: Harper and Row, 1980. xix + 243 pp.

1888-1972; written over the course of much of her adult life. Luiseno (?). Nuñez was taken from her mother at birth by a white woman who had been active in working for Indian rights in the southwest, taken to live with the woman and her husband in New York. There she was not allowed to forget that she was an Indian--she was dressed in beads and buckskins as a child; indeed, she seems to have been kept as a kind of curious exhibit. It was soon discovered that she was something of a child prodigy, and Nuñez gave her first women's rights speech at the age of ten. A self-taught painter, she spent much of her adult life working for Indian and women's rights, and she devoted a good deal of time as well to trying to discover who her parents were and gaining a real Indian identity for herself.

Internal evidence suggests that Steiner did very little sentence-level editing of the miscellaneous but compelling writings he fell heir to. Nuñez recalls a remarkably varied life--bohemian life in Greenwish Village, unsuccessful marriage, painting, life with her white family, and the search for her Indian identity. The book includes reproductions of her striking paintings and drawings, many in color.

371 Ojuvainath (M). KNUD JOHAN VICTOR RASMUSSEN. A hunting narrative* is to be found in the book cited in no. 50, pp. 260-65.

Born, c. 1862; narrated, c. 1902. West Greenland Eskimo and Danish. For the details of the collaboration, see no. 50.

372 OKA, MIKE. Harry Mills. "A Blood Indian's Story," Alberta Historical Review, III, No. 4 (1955), 13-16.

C. 1860-c. 1940; narrated, 1936. Blood. Oka delivered himself through his son, Mills, in English. Internal evidence suggests that there was little editing other than that required to put the narrative into standard English. These are disconnected reminiscences, historical and personal--although not much of the latter.

373 Old Man. ADOLF HUNGRY WOLF. A narrative* is to be found in the book cited in no. 20, pp. 352-53.

Born, c. 1877; interviewed, c. 1972. Blood. For the details of the collaboration see no. 20. This is Old Man's account of how he came by his power and his long life as a result of the ministrations of a holy woman.

374 Old Mexican (M). WALTER DYK. A Navaho Autobiography (P). Viking Fund Publications in Anthropology, No. 8 (1947), 218 pp.

Born, 1865; interviewed, 1933. Navajo. Dyk worked through an interpreter. For the most part, Old Mexican resisted Dyk's attempts to guide his narrative, and Dyk's editing preserves Old Mexican's chronological ordering with few alterations. Some minor cuts were made, but this autobiography can be taken as being much closer to the narrator's intent than is the case in many of these longer narratives. As Dyk put it: "I asked him to tell all that he remembered. But it is clear that he 'remembered' only what pleased him." Old Mexican related only that which "cast him, so he believed, in his proper role--that of a magnanimous and virtuous man, abused, imposed upon, and frustrated by an unappreciative world" (p. 6).

Old Mexican recalls little of his childhood, and even that little has to do with his preparation for adulthood. We read of his attempts to achieve greatness by gaining wealth, first by herding, then by farming. He is quite receptive to whatever white innovations will aid him in this farming, by the way. He also describes the woes of his marriage and his strong ties with his mother, at the time of whose death, in 1919, he ends his narrative. This is one of the very good autobiographies.

375 OLIVER, SIMEON (Nutchuk). Alden Hatch. Son of the Smokey Sea.* N.Y.: Julian Messner, Inc., 1941. viii + 245 pp.

Born, 1903; collaborated, c. 1940. Eskimo mother, white father, but raised in an orphanage with Aleuts on Attu Island. The nature of the collaboration here is unspecified, but it seems likely that Oliver wrote out his account of his life with Hatch making suggestions, editing, and rearranging. This volume covers the years 1903-25. Oliver tells us about being raised in an orphanage which provided warmth and good will in such large measure that he is able to remember his childhood as a time of real happiness and security. But his youth was also a time of yearning for "the outside." This yearning was in no small measure inspired by "Sears-Roebuck, whose catalogue was," as Oliver put it, "our most exciting reading" (p. 68).

Eventually Oliver realized his dream, and so we are treated to his remembrances of his first sight of a tree, of a city, of football, and of his life at Northwestern University, where Oliver studied first medicine and then music. Within a year, however, lack of money forced Oliver to go back north, this time to live with his mother's people, the Alaskan Eskimos. He remembers this return north as a journey of discovery; in his learning of the Eskimo ways he discovers himself, discovers that he must return south to the woman he loved and to his music.

376 _____. _____. Back to the Smokey Sea.* N.Y. Julian Messner, Inc., 1946. 225 pp. Illustrated by the author.

This second volume of Oliver's autobiography covers the years 1925-45, chronicling his musical training, his marriage, and his work as a concert and radio pianist (one enterprising radio entrepreneur brought Oliver to Louisiana, at a handsome wage, to play the piano--all sponsored by Igloo Ice Cream).

Eventually, after the untimely death of his wife, Oliver learned more and more about his people, and spent more and more time lecturing about Alaska and the Eskimos. Finally, the book describes Oliver's shocked response to the Japanese capture of Attu Island and of his hurried enlistment and subsequent service in the army in the Aleutians.

Both of Oliver's books are quite unassuming and self-effacing, but they are thoughtful as well. We are left with a clear sense of a man remarkably well able to balance his peculiar collection of cultures.

377  One-blue-bead (M). See no. 200.

378  One Bull, Oscar. H. INEZ HILGER. "The Narrative of Oscar One Bull," Mid-America, XXVIII (New Series: XVII), No. 3 (1946), 147-72.

Born, c. 1855; narrated, c. 1940. Teton Sioux. Hilger worked through an interpreter; probably she did very little cutting and rearranging. She even includes some of the questions asked of One Bull during the course of his narration. One Bull packs a good deal of detail into these twenty-five pages, beginning with an account of his relative Sitting Bull and continuing with striking tales of raids upon the Crows, of his ten wives, and of his visions and dreams and consequent powers. One Bull talks about the responsibility that fell to him to enact his horse vision in a public dance. (See nos. 66 and 537 for similarly motivated enactments of visions.) Hilger claims that One Bull spoke of such sacred matters only because his adopted son was present during his narration. He also talks briefly about matters of Teton diet, hunting, and technology, expresses his negative opinion of Custer, of the Peyotists and Ghost Dancers, and more.

379  Orr, Veronica. See no. 38.

380  Orulo (F). KNUD JOHAN VICTOR RASMUSSEN. A brief autobiography is to be found in Rasmussen, Across Artic America: Narrative of the Fifth Thule Expedition (IP),* tr. W.E. Calvert, N.Y.: Greenwood Press, 1969 [1927], pp. 140-53.

Born, probably before 1870; interviewed, c. 1922. Eskimo, Baffin Island. Rasmussen was fluent in the native language. This is an account, at least impressionistically, of the whole interview (although there has been cutting), with Rasmussen including his own questions. Orulo tells of being passed from one family to another, until she was finally taken by her husband, who had since made her very happy. She tells of famine and of song contests, and she speaks with confidence of having seen evil spirits. Another autobiographical narrative by Orulo is to be found in the book cited in no. 23, pp. 48-53.

Some of this material is repeated from the above, but Rasmussen does add some material here, especially about Orulo's experiences with shamans.

381 Otaq (M). KNUD JOHAN VICTOR RASMUSSEN. A narrative* is to be found in the book cited in no. 50, pp. 147-48.
Born, c. 1877; interviewed, c. 1902. Eskimo, Cape York. This narrative of a shaman's acquisition of power over his helping spirits is Rasmussen's literal translation retranslated into English. For further details of the collaboration, see no. 50.

382 Otterby, Thomas (Red Eagle). BIREN BONNERJEA. "Reminiscences of a Cheyenne Indian," Journal de la Société des Américanistes de Paris, XXVII (1935), 129-43.
Born, 1871; interviewed, shortly before 1935. Cheyenne. Otterby spoke English. His responses to Bonnerjea's questions were edited into a connected narrative. Bonnerjea did considerable editing, but Otterby's phrasing is preserved. Much ethnographic detail and little on attitudes and feelings.

383 Pahmit (M). FRANK FOREST LATTA. "Pahmit's Story," as found in Latta, Handbook of Yokuts Indians, Oildale, Calif.: Bear State Books, 1949 (Human Relations Area Files, NS 29), pp. 217-23.
Born, c. 1829; interviewed, 1928. Yokuts. Latta says that he prints this story just as it was related to him by Pahmit, allowing such sentences as "Now white man at Washington pay me seven dollar half, live one month" (p. 218). Remembrances of very early contact with white men and of the wiles of one Major Savage who pretended to catch bullets as a way of convincing the Yokuts that they ought to obey him. Pahmit talks too of being a chief of the Yokuts: "I big chief now, but got no Indian tribe. Just me; just my sister left" (p. 222) and a very few others.

384 Pat (M). MARCEL RIOUX. "Notes autobiographiques d'un Iroquois Cayuga," Anthropologica, I (1955), 18-36.
Born, c. 1900; interviewed, c. 1954. Cayuga Iroquois. Evidently this interview was accomplished in English, a second language for Pat. Rioux intersperses his own paraphrases of and comments upon sections of Pat's narrative with long quotations of Pat's English, translated into French. Pat is a conservative, and it is from this perspective that he comments upon social change in the course of telling of his life. Pat was an important member of his tribe's governing body.

385 PATENCIO, CHIEF FRANCISCO. Margaret Boynton. Stories

and Legends of the Palm Springs Indians.* Palm Springs, Cal.: Palm Springs Desert Museum, 1969 [1943]. xvi + 132 pp.

Born, c. 1860; narrated, 1939. Cahuilla. Patencio wrote at the end of his preface to this volume, "All of the words in this book are my words" (p. xiv). Certainly Boynton's editing did allow many of the idiosyncracies of Patencio's English to remain. It is not clear how much cutting was done, but that there was some cutting was made manifest by the recent publication of some of the gleanings (no. 386). Autobiographical elements are scattered throughout this volume, but there is a section entitled "Francisco's Life," which begins Part Two of the book. This is an appealing book, moving quite unpretentiously back and forth among history, myth, folklore, and personal reminiscences. In this way, Patencio's work here is much like Momaday's The Way to Rainy Mountain (no. 344).

386 _____. Kate Collins. Desert Hours with Chief Patencio, as Told to Kate Collins by Chief Francisco Patencio,* ed. Roy F. Hudson. Palm Springs, Calif.: Palm Springs Desert Museum, 1971. 38 pp.

In the late 1930's Kate Collins wrote down much material as it was narrated by Patencio--tales, tribal history, personal reminiscences, etc. Most of this material appeared in 1943 as Stories and Legends of the Palm Springs Indians (no. 385). Some of the material was not used and was stored away. Hudson gathered this material together and added a fictionalized narrator's voice as a frame for Patencio's largely autobiographical reminiscences. "I drew up my legs and listened to the words" of Chief Patencio (p. 7)--that sort of thing. This booklet does, however, preserve the idiosyncrasies of Patencio's English very nearly intact.

387 Paytiamo, James. Flaming Arrow's People: By an Acoma Indian.* N.Y.: Duffield and Green, 1932. 158 pp.

Born, probably before 1890; wrote, c. 1931. Acoma Pueblo. Paytiamo proceeds by alternating personal, tribal, and family history with the legends and beliefs of his people. In this he is like Momaday (no. 344), Kennedy (no. 265), and others. His account of himself, however, seems designed to allow the reader a better sense of what the Acomas were and are, while Momaday, on the other hand, provides his account of his Indian background in order to allow the reader to see how Momaday became the man he is. In this, not surprisingly, Paytiamo is closer to Yava, another Pueblo Indian (no. 547).

This is an ingenuous and artful book, providing a good deal of ethnographic detail in a very readable way, accounts of food preparation, sheepherding, shamans, witches, Paytiamo's ritual preparation for a life as a warrior--in a time when it was certain that he would not be called upon to go to war with his people's traditional enemies, the Apaches and the Navajos.

Paytiamo writes very much from the perspective of a man with a white education (Haskell Institute); he is convinced that his people's beliefs were "superstitions," and yet he is full of reverence for the old ways. His stance is like that of Standing Bear (no. 469) and Alford (no. 6); he is convinced that the old ways were "wrong"--and yet he feels that the old people were morally and physically better than the present generation of Indians. Paytiamo's striking illustrations accompany the text.

388    Pelletier, Wilfred. "Childhood in an Indian Village," This Magazine Is about Schools, III, No. 2 (1969), 6-22.

Born, probably c. 1920; wrote, c. 1969. Ottawa. Pelletier gives some account of his own childhood, but these recollections have almost entirely to do with the freedom granted children in his village to learn what and how they would--and the virtues of this kind of education are then compared to the confinements imposed by the white system of education, very much to the discredit of the latter. This is really a tract for "open" education, typical in its assumptions of much that was written about education in the late 1960's.

389    _____. Ted Poole. No Foreign Land: The Biography of a North American Indian.* N.Y.: Pantheon Books, 1973. xii + 211 pp.

Interviewed, c. 1972. Pelletier and Poole tape-recorded long conversations, and Poole worked from these: "selections were made from the tapes, sequences arranged, stories invented, passages written" (p. 4). The colloquial flavor of Pelletier's language is retained, and the whole narrative is in the first person. Pelletier tells of his youth, his experience of discrimination, his assimilation, his work as a hunters' guide, and of his eventual decision to reject, in a large measure, modern values and return to more nearly aboriginal Indian ways.

390    Peopeo Tholekt (M). See no. 509.

391    Peterson, Annie Miner. MELVILLE JACOBS. Narratives are to be found in Jacobs, Coos Narrative and Ethnologic Texts (IP), University of Washington Publications in Anthropology, VIII, No. 1 (1939), 22-23, 63-64, 96-97, 99-100, 104-14.

Born, c. 1860; interviewed, 1933-34. Coos. Jacobs collected texts for linguistic and ethnographic purposes. The native language texts are printed below Peterson's own English translation (edited to conform to standard English, except for certain lexical items). A proper autobiography is on pp. 104-14, the rest of the narratives being disconnected reminiscences. We read of Peterson's childhood fears, her marriages (the last to a white logger), her dreams, and her experiences with the spirits of the dead.

One of Peterson's narratives is a brief autobiographical account which she remembers having been told by a woman named Batter (pp. 103-4). Through Peterson, then, Batter tells of having been sold into marriage as a very young girl, and of finally surpassing an older wife in her husband's regard by playing well at shinny. She was, in fact, so good a batter that she was named Batter.

392 Philips, Frances. ERMINIE W. VOEGELIN. An autobiography is to be found in Voegelin, Tubatulabal Ethnography, University of California Publications in Anthropological Records, II, No. 1 (1938), 72-78.

C. 1863-1933; interviewed, 1933. Tubatulabal. Evidently Voegelin first elicited a life history and then asked specific questions. All of this material was rearranged into a continuous narrative in chronological order, little other editing being done. Philips's daughter served as interpreter. Considering the brevity of this autobiography, the quantity and freshness of detail is surprising. Philips tells, for example, about many of her experiences with shamans and their medicines, one of which medicines was live ants (had to be red ants), to be ingested packed in eagle down. She supposes that the subsequent pains she felt in her belly resulted from the bites of these insectivorous Jonahs. She also tells of the unhappy experience of her tattooing, her husband's murder, and a good deal else. This is the aunt of Mike Miranda (no. 336).

393 PITSEOLAK (F). Dorothy Eber. Pitseolak: Pictures Out of My Life.* Montreal: Design Collaborative Books, in association with Oxford University Press, Toronto, n.d. [c. 1971]. 93 unnumbered pp.

Born, c. 1900; interviewed, 1970. Eskimo, Baffin Island. Eber sought out Pitseolak because of her reputation as one of the best of the Cape Dorset artists. Eber knew no Eskimo, and the interviews were conducted through an interpreter. A transcript of Pitseolak's Eskimo narrative was submitted to Ann Hanson to be retranslated. The translation is printed along with the native text in syllabics, a phonetic system of writing in use among the Eskimos since the late nineteenth century. The book is lavishly illustrated with Pitseolak's art.

This autobiography is a gentle celebration of life, a book without bitterness. As Pitseolak put it: "It used to be okay without clocks, but it is okay with clocks too. Now I am used to watching the time." She tells about the old ways, her transition to the new ways, and of coming to earn her bread by drawing.

394   PITSEOLAK, PETER. Dorothy Eber. People from Our Side:
      A Life Story with Photographs (IP).*   Edmonton, Alberta:
      Hurtig Publishers, 1975. 159 pp.
            1902-73; wrote, 1972.  Cape Dorset Eskimo.  Pitseolak
      wrote up a history of his people in Eskimo syllabics and sent
      this, unsolicited, to Eber. Eber had the manuscript translated
      and then decided to supplement Pitseolak's writings with
      material from tape-recorded interviews with Pitseolak (1971-
      73, Eber working through an interpreter) and letters from
      Pitseolak's relatives responding to Eber's questions. Since the
      book evinces relatively little regard for sequence--Pitseolak
      says that in this his book is like the Bible (p. 66)--it would
      seem that Eber hung all of her supplementary material on the
      frame provided by Pitseolak's original manuscript. The book is
      illustrated with photographs taken by Pitseolak, some dating
      back to the 1940's, back to the last years, then, of camp life
      among the Baffin Island Eskimos.
            This book combines mythic, tribal, and personal history in
      such a way as to provide the reader with a keen sense of this
      gentle, intelligent man. We read of his hunting, his children,
      his work as a pilot for ships coming into Cape Dorset, his
      religion, and his attitudes and feelings--and all the while we
      realize that this man has experienced his people's transition
      from furs to cloth, from hunting to bartering, from wandering
      to town-dwelling.
            Pitseolak does, by the way, briefly tell the story of his
      grandfather Etidluie, upon whose life was based John Houston's
      novel The White Dawn.

395   _____ .  _____ . Peter Pitseolak's Escape from Death
      (P).*  Toronto:   McCelland and Stewart Ltd., 1977.    43
      unnumbered pp.
            Pitseolak wrote two versions of this narrative in Eskimo
      syllabics. Eber's edition draws upon both of these as they were
      translated for her.  This is an affectingly simple tale of a
      walrus hunt that ends in near tragedy on an ice floe. The book
      is illustrated with the author's felt-tip pen drawings.

396   Pitsualak, Markosie (M). See no. 5.

397   Plenty-coups (M). FRANK B. LINDERMAN. American: The
      Life Story of a Great Indian.*  N.Y.: John Day Co., 1930. xi +
      309 pp.  Reprinted as Plenty-Coups, Chief of the Crows (P),
      Lincoln: University of Nebraska Press, 1962.
            1847-1932; interviewed, c. 1928.  Crow.  Linderman gives
      us a sense of the whole process of the interview.  The text
      includes not only Linderman's questions and Plenty-coups'
      responses, but also some account of Linderman's motivations
      in asking particular questions, and of Plenty-coups' hesitations

in answering certain kinds of questions. Linderman also includes the comments of some of the old men who sat in on these sessions, and he records as well the changes in Plenty-coups' moods as he related the events of his life. The work does proceed chronologically, although Linderman is willing to sacrifice chronology occasionally in favor of preserving the sequence of Plenty-coups' remembrances. While the result is certainly not a verbatim account of the whole interview, all of this contributes to a pervasive air of authenticity. And nothing that I have read would contradict this impression. Linderman was one of the first to demonstrate a real sensitivity to the problem of the interviewer's interference in such life histories, and one of the first to resort to including the interviewer in the life history as a way of coping with the problem (see no. 380). Linderman knew sign language, but these interviews were conducted with the aid of an interpreter.

Some of the most interesting sections of this book have to do with Plenty-coups' struggling with his society's taboos in the face of Linderman's questions and the demands of the autobiographical mode as Plenty-coups came to understand it. Should he relate his power vision? Should he use the (sacred) names of the dead? He decides to abandon his taboos, and some nice points of comparison can thus be made with Black Elk's (no. 66) and Fine-day's (no. 175) quite different reasons for breaking such taboos.

This is a richly detailed and a deeply felt autobiography. We read of Plenty-coups' youth, his quests for vision and power, of Sun Dances, and Plenty Coups' feats of war. We also find that it was Plenty-coups who led the Crows to ally themselves with the whites against their ancient enemies, the Sioux.

398 Plummer, Rosie. WILLARD ZERBE PARK. Narratives in the first book cited in no. 202, pp. 17, 26-27, 30-31, 39, 41. Much of this is reprinted in the second book cited in no. 202, pp. 105-7.

Born, c. 1879; interviewed, 1934-36. Paviosto. Park worked through an interpreter. Plummer tells about the acquisition and use of her shamanic powers.

399 Pokagon, Chief Simon. O-Gi-Maw-Kwe Mit-I-Gwa-Ki (Queen of the Woods), Also Brief Sketch of the Algaic Language. Hartford, Mich.: C.H. Engle, Publisher, 1899. viii + 255 pp. Reprinted as Queen of the Woods, Pleasantville, N.Y.: Hardscrabble Press, Inc., 1972.

1830-99; wrote, c. 1898-99. Potawatomi. Pokagon wrote first in Potawatomi, then translated into English. His written English required the services of an editor (mainly for grammer and spelling; see Dickason, 1961). This book is fiction with autobiographical elements. Buechner (1933) is a help in sorting fact from fiction here, but Pokagon paints even the autobiographical with a coat of ripe romanticism.

Pokagon was something of an institution in his own day, a man who worked hard in his own people's behalf, a man regarded by whites as "the Indian Longfellow," a man devoted to the cause of temperance. He was the son of that Chief Pokagon who sold the land whereon Chicago now stands for three cents an acre, and he himself devoted most of his adult life to the pursuit of the payment to his people of those three cents an acre.

400    Pope, Bob. RONALD L. OLSON. "The Autobiography of Bob Pope," as found in the book cited in no. 317, pp. 182-83.

Born, c. 1835; interviewed, 1925-26.  Quinault.  Olson worked with an interpreter here. The translation is close to literal, and Olson did little or no other editing. Pope tells of hunting, the Potlatch, and shamanic doings.

401    Porcupine (M). GEORGE BIRD GRINNELL. A narrative is to be found in Grinnell, The Fighting Cheyennes (P), Norman: University of Oklahoma Press, 1956 [1915], pp. 265-67.

Fl., 1867; narrated, c. 1874.  Cheyenne.  Porcupine's narrative is printed here as it was taken down by Grinnell from his interpreter with little change. Porcupine tells of his first encounter with a railroad and of his band's subsequent attempt to derail a train.

402    Potts, Ronald. KENT GOODERHAM. "Ronnie,"* as found in the book cited in no. 188, pp. 77-79.  This is a transcribed excerpt from the film "Ronnie," by Ronald Potts, Image Productions, 1968.

Born, c. 1946; filmed, 1968.  Assiniboine.  This is an affecting narrative, devoted mainly to Potts's remembrances of his mother's death and the subsequent suicide of his father.

403    Preston, Scott. See no. 24.

404    Pretty-shield (F).  FRANK B. LINDERMAN.  Red Mother.* N.Y.: The John Day Co., 1932. 256 pp. Reprinted as Pretty-Shield: Medicine Woman of the Crows (P), Lincoln: University of Nebraska Press, 1974.

Born, c. 1857; interviewed, shortly before 1932.  Crow. Linderman worked with an interpreter, although Pretty-shield spoke to Linderman in sign language while she spoke to the interpreter in Crow. This allowed Linderman a constant check on the interpreter. As in his edition of Plenty-coups' autobiography (no. 397), Linderman includes himself in the narrative, includes his questions, his motivations for asking certain questions, and he includes an account of Pretty-shield's changing moods, of the interruptions of grandchildren, etc. The narrative is thus not always strictly chronological. While we can be certain that Linderman does not present all of this with perfect accuracy, we have no reason to doubt that the interviews went generally as they are described.

The result is one of the very interesting Indian autobiographies. Pretty-shield was a medicine woman, and a woman of keen mind. She tells of her life before the reservation days, and, like Two Leggings (no. 506), she refuses to tell of later times because "there is nothing to tell, because we did nothing" (p. 10). Included here are myths and grandmother tales.

405 Pretty Voice Eagle, Chief. JOSEPH KOSSUTH DIXON. "Chief Pretty Voice Eagle,"* as found in the book cited in no. 11, pp. 72-91.

Born, c. 1845; interviewed, 1909. Sioux. For the details of the collaboration, see no. 11. Reminiscences of war, the coming of the railroad, broken treaties, and conversion to Christianity. Dixon includes folktales as told by Pretty Voice Eagle.

406 Price, Anna (Her Eyes Grey). GRENVILLE GOODWIN. Narratives are to be found in the book cited in no. 85, pp. 19-20, 54, 76-79, 84, 89-91, 233-34, 244-45, 252, 330-32, 355, 380, 385-86, 389, 406-9, 470, 472, 482-85, 530, 560-61, 564, 670-90.

C. 1837-1937; interviewed, 1931. White Mountain Apache. For the details of the collaboration, see no. 85. There is a great deal of material here, although it gives us a much better idea of the way of life of the nineteenth-century Apache than it does of Price. She recalls trading, inter-band rivalry for land, relations with the Zunis and the Yavapais, her childhood, courtship, and married life, and thievery and rape. She also has a good deal to say about her father's activities as chief (see no. 407).

407 _____. _____. "Anna Price," as found in the book cited in no. 226, pp. 29-39.

"Price was the eldest daughter of Diablo, probably the most influential chief ever to appear among the White Mountain Apache" (p. 29). Most of Price's recollections here have to do with her father's exploits. For the rest, see no. 226.

408 Qappik, Paulosie (M). See no. 5.

409 QOYAWAYMA, POLINGAYSI (ELIZABETH Q. WHITE). Vada

Carlson. <u>No Turning Back: A True Account of a Hopi Girl's Struggle to Bridge the Gap between the World of Her People and the World of the White Man.</u> Albuquerque: University of New Mexico Press, 1964. 180 pp.

Born, c. 1892; collaborated, c. 1964. Hopi. Although this book is sometimes cited as autobiography, it is a biography. Qoyawayma did, however, provide the reminiscences upon which the book is largely based.

410 Ranco, Mike. PETER ANASTAS. Reminiscences in the book cited in no. 340, pp. 122-33.

Born, c. 1950; interviewed, 1971. Passamaquoddy. Anastas abridged Ranco's narrative, but evidently did little other editing. A University of Maine student, Ranco tells of his early concern for the welfare of his people and of his work with Indian education and politics.

411 Ration, Tom. BRODERICK H. JOHNSON. "Tom Ration,"* as found in the book cited in no. 17, pp. 299-335.

Born, 1901; interviewed, c. 1976. Navajo. For the details of the collaboration, see no. 17. Ration tells about his education, speaking appreciatively of both his formal and his traditional education. He also talks about the history of silversmithing, of his own silver work, and how he became a silversmith. Along the way, he tells a few traditional tales.

412 Rave, John. PAUL RADIN. "John Rave's Account of the Peyote Cult and of His Conversion," as found in Radin, <u>The Winnebago Tribe</u> (P), Lincoln: University of Nebraska Press, 1970 1923 , pp. 341-46.

Born, c. 1855; interviewed, c. 1910. Winnebago. Radin worked with an interpreter, although he had sufficient knowledge of the native language to allow him to check the translation. Radin edited the translation into standard English. Rave was the man who introduced the Peyote Cult to the Winnebagos, and he was for some time the leader of the Winnebago Peyote Cult. Consequently, this is an important narrative, and it can help us to understand the religious experience of Crashing Thunder (no. 129), Mountain Wolf Woman (no. 349), and Sam Blowsnake (nos. 73, 74).

This volume contains many other, briefer narratives of personal religious experiences--both traditional and peyote inspired. I will not try the reader's patience by listing each by name, since many are pseudonyms. See pp. 243-61 for traditional religious experiences and pp. 341-71 for peyote narratives.

413 Ray, Bill. PLINY EARLE GODDARD. "A Supernatural Experience," as found in Goddard, <u>Kato Texts</u>, <u>University of</u>

California Publications in American Archaeology and Ethnology, V, No. 3 (1907), 182, 237-38.
    Born, c. 1842; interviewed, 1906. Kato. The native language text appears first, with interlinear translation, then a free translation. Nothing beyond what the title promises.

414    Red Bear (M). See no. 423.

415    Red Cloud, Chief. JOSEPH KOSSUTH DIXON. "Chief Red Cloud,"* as found in the book cited in no. 11, pp. 118-21.
    Born, c. 1859; interviewed, 1909. Oglala Sioux. For the details of the collaboration, see no 11. This son of the warrior chief Red Cloud reminisces here about his first war party, but he says, "The greatest event in my life was when I stopped the old Indian custom of fighting and adopted what the white man told me to do--live in peace" (p. 121).

416    Red Crow (M). ROBERT N. WILSON. "The Life History and Adventures of Red Crow, Late Head Chief of the Bloods (Blackfoot Confederacy)," as found in Samuel H. Middleton, Kainai Chieftainship: History, Evolution and Culture of the Blood Indians, Lethbridge, Alberta: The Lethbridge Herald, 1953, pp. 113-64. Excerpts* are to be found in the book cited in no. 20, pp. 239-54.
    C. 1830-1900; narrated, 1881. Blood. Wilson, one of the original members of the Northwest Mounted Police, knew the native language and so evidently worked with Red Crow without an interpreter. Internal evidence--a relative disregard for chronological ordering, for example--suggests that Wilson's editorial hand was not heavy. Red Crow limits himself, like Two Leggings (no. 506), to the "principal adventures" of his life (p. 164). This richly detailed narrative, then, is devoted almost exclusively to intertribal warfare and raiding. Some deeds are recounted the likes of which one does not find elsewhere, the massacre and scalping, for example, of close to one hundred Cree women--after which, as Red Crow assures us, "There was great jubilation" (p. 131).
    Adolf Hungry Wolf, the editor of the second source cited above, abridged Wilson's text and simplified much of its phrasing as well.

417    Red Eagle. JAMES WILLARD SCHULTZ. "The First Fire Boats"* and "Laugher, the Story of a Tame Wolf,"* in the book cited in no. 228, pp. 113-26, 175-90.
    Born, c. 1810; told these tales, 1877-87. Blackfeet. Schultz was living with the Blackfeet at this time, and he heard these and many other tales around the fire, heard them, that is, as they were told by a gifted storyteller in the Blackfeet oral tradition. Schultz, throughout this volume and

elsewhere, provides a nice sense of what happened on those evenings when the stories flowed. The gist of these two episodes in the life of the narrator may be inferred from the titles. For more about Schultz's work and methods, see no. 31.

418　Red Elk. See no. 509.

419　Red Feather. JAMES LARPENTUR LONG. Autobiographical fragments* are to be found in the book cited in no. 27, pp. 30-31, 180-82.

　　　Born, c. 1850; interviewed, 1939. Assiniboine. For the details of the collaboration, see no. 27. Red Feather tells of the circumstances of and his fears concerning his (traditional) marriage. He also tells about what he remembers as the first meeting of the Assiniboines and the Santee Sioux.

420　RED FOX, CHIEF. Cash Asher. The Memoirs of Chief Red Fox.* N.Y.: McGraw Hill Book Co., 1971. xii + 209 pp.

　　　Born, 1870 (according to Red Fox); Asher claims that Red Fox did his writing in 1968. Sioux. Asher claims that Red Fox wrote up, on his own, some notes about his own life and his people's history. These notes were sufficient to fill sixty-eight typewritten pages, double spaced. The fact that Asher's reworking of these notes covers over two hundred printed pages is some indication of the degree to which this book is Asher's rather than Red Fox's. And then there are other problems: the book was a "nearly successful act of plagiarism. A significant portion of the contents was taken from J. H. McGregor's The Wounded Knee Massacre: From the Viewpoint of the Sioux" (Hodge, 1976, p. 159). For those who are determined to be interested it should be noted that Asher does include sixteen pages of transcription from Red Fox's "notebooks" in an appendix. Asher's Red Fox claims to have seen Crazy Horse killed in battle with General Custer. He claims also to have been a member of Buffalo Bill's Wild West show.

421　Red Horse (M). See no. 132.

422　REDSKY, JAMES (ESQUEKESIK). James R. Stevens. Great Leader of the Ojibway: Mis-quona-queb (P),* ed. Stevens. Toronto: McClelland and Stewart Ltd., 1972, pp. 13-17.

　　　Born, c. 1899; collaborated, 1969-72. Ojibwa. Stevens began working with Redsky in 1969, in the hope of collecting Ojibwa myths. Some months later Redsky brought to Stevens some fifty pages of a biography of Mis-quona-queb. Stevens immediately began the work of editing. Redsky continued to write, and Stevens tape-recorded interviews with Redsky. The introduction to this book, then, includes autobiographical passages by Redsky, wherein he tells about his childhood, schooling, employment, and WW I experiences.

423  Red Star (M). O. G. LIBBY. Narratives by Red Star and others are in Libby, ed., The Arikara Narrative of the Campaign against the Hostile Dakotas, June, 1876 (IP), N.Y.: Sol Lewis, 1973, ix + 219 pp. This is a reprint (with new introductory matter by Dee Brown and D'Arcy McNickle) of the work first published in the North Dakota Historical Collections, VI (1920).

   That Crow Indians fought on the side of Terry and Custer is well known; that Arikaras also served is less well known. In 1912 "the nine survivors of some forty of these scouts met at the home of Bear's Belly on the Fort Berthold Reservation," and there they related to Libby, through an interpreter, each his role in, and remembrances of, the campaign of 1876. "Each of the scouts gave that special portion of the whole with which he was most familiar. The narrators were very scrupulous to confine themselves to just that portion of the common experience to which they were eyewitnesses .... After the whole story was put in form it was submitted to the Indians to be read and corrected through their interpreters" (pp. 9-10). The result has been highly praised by Brown and McNickle (in their preface and introduction, respectively, to the 1973 edition) and by W. A. Graham (see no. 132), but those interested in autobiography will be disappointed to find that most of the narratives were edited into the third person; Libby was after historical accuracy, not individual perspectives. Only the narratives of Red Star (born, 1858; excerpted in no. 132) and Red Bear (born, 1853) may be said to have remained autobiographical.

424  Red Whip, Chief. JOSEPH KOSSUTH DIXON. "Chief Red Whip,"* as found in the book cited in no. 11, pp. 40-44.

   Born, c. 1854; interviewed, 1909. Gros Ventre. For the details of the collaboration, see no. 11. Red Whip reminisces about two of his war experiences.

425  Richardson, Molly. BRODERICK H. JOHNSON. "Molly Richardson,"* as found in the book cited in no. 17, pp. 266-72.

   Born, c. 1885; interviewed, c. 1976. Navajo. For the details of collaboration, see no. 17. Richardson tells of being a witness to a murder and of her part in the subsequent trial.

426  RICKARD, CLINTON. Barbara Graymont. Fighting Tuscarora: The Autobiography of Chief Clinton Rickard (IP). Syracuse: Syracuse University Press, 1973. xxviii + 182 pp.

   1882-1971; collaborated, 1965-71. Tuscarora. Graymont's interviews with Rickard were very much guided interviews; she argued to overcome his reticence to speak on certain topics, etc. The interviews were conducted for the most part in English, in which Rickard was fluent. Graymont checked the manuscript with Rickard continuously, and he was able to approve the final draft of the complete book shortly before his death. The arrangement of the book, then, is Graymont's in collaboration with Rickard. The phrasing is Rickard's with minor editing.

Rickard tells of his life and education, and of the importance of Tuscarora cultural traditions to him even as he came to be a leader and educator not only of Indians but of whites. Rickard was the founder of the Indian Defense League of America.

427 Riegert, Wilbur A. I Am a Sioux Indian. Rapid City, S.D.: Fenwyn Press, 1967. 24 pp.

Born, probably c. 1900; wrote, c. 1967. Ojibwa! This is not autobiography. It is a brief, very elementary, illustrated account of Sioux religion and symbols.

428 Rogers, John (Chief Snow Cloud). Red World: Memories of a Chippewa Boyhood (IP), with a foreword by Joseph W. Whitecotton. Norman: University of Oklahoma Press, 1974. xvii + 153 pp. Published in 1957 as A Chippewa Speaks.

Born, 1890; wrote, shortly before 1957. Ojibwa. Rogers writes for the most part about his boyhood, including an account of his experiences at the Indian schools. This is another autobiography of a man caught between two cultures.

429 Romero, Luke (pseudonym). EVON Z. VOGT. "Luke Romero: The Life Story," as found in the book cited in no. 42, pp. 127-74.

Born, 1909; interviewed, 1947. Navajo mother, Laguna father. Romero spoke English; no interpreter was involved here. For further details of the collaboration, see no. 42. Romero devotes but one page to his preschool childhood, most of the rest of the narrative being devoted to his boarding school experiences and to his life in the navy (WW II). Romero is rather unlike the rest of the men Vogt studied--and he feels himself to be so.

Vogt supplies more commentary with this narrative than he does for most of the other narratives in this collection, and this commentary makes it clear that much of the interest here is in what is left out. Vogt goes so far as to say that, given all of the trouble Romero actually experienced after his return from the navy, his blithe account of his readjustment to the reservation verges on fantasy.

430 Rope, John. GRENVILLE GOODWIN. Narratives are to be found in the book cited in no. 85, pp. 52, 79-80, 82-83, 95, 124,

396-97, 462, 464, 465, 468, 475-76, 485-86.
Born, c. 1850; interviewed, 1932. White Mountain Apache. For the details of the collaboration, see no. 85. Rope tells about inter-band warfare, trading with the Zunis, relations with other Pueblo Indians, and fur traders. He recalls as well his childhood games, his hunting, raids into Mexico, and Apache justice.

431 _____. _____. "John Rope," as found in the book cited in no. 226, pp. 92-185. An abridged version of this narrative was published in the Arizona Historical Review, VII, 1 and 2 (1936).
For the details of the collaboration, see no. 226. Rope was a scout for the U.S. forces during the Apache wars. This narrative is largely, but not entirely, devoted to warfare.

432 Rosetta, Johnny. See no. 38.

433 Rosetta, Marlene. See no. 38.

434 Rowland, Willis. GEORGE BIRD GRINNELL. A narrative* is to be found in the book cited in no. 401, pp. 429-33.
Fl., 1876; narrated, c. 1880. Cheyenne. No interpreter was necessary here, since Rowland knew English. Grinnell edits toward standard English, while leaving something of the colloquial flavor of Rowland's speech. This is Rowland's account of his scouting for General Miles.

435 Running Fisher, Chief. JOSEPH KOSSUTH DIXON. "Chief Running Fisher,"* as found in the book cited in no. 11, pp. 98-101.
Born, c. 1853; interviewed, 1909. Gros Ventre. For the details of the collaboration, see no. 11. Reminiscences of the Sun Dance and war.

436 Runs-the-Enemy (M). JOSEPH KOSSUTH DIXON. "Chief Runs-the-Enemy,"* as found in the book cited in no. 11, pp. 62-72.
Born, c. 1849; interviewed, 1909. Teton Sioux. For the details of the collaboration, see no. 11. Reminiscences of training for the hunt and war, and of war. Dixon includes a folktale by Runs-the-Enemy.

437 Sanapia (pseudonym [F]). DAVID E. JONES. Sanapia, Comanche Medicine Woman (P). N.Y.: Holt, Rinehart and Winston, 1972. xvii + 107 pp.
Born, 1895; interviewed, 1968. Comanche. Jones proceeds here by interspersing long quotations from Sanapia (virtually unedited, save for some standardization of the English) with

his own narrative and comments. The book details the events of Sanapia's life and the herbs and methods of her healings. We are also provided an account of her seven happy years at a mission school and of the acquisition of her powers. This is one of the Indian autobiographies wherein the purpose of the autobiographer is clear; Sanapia wants this book to serve as a means for training future healers. The book is also interesting in that Sanapia managed, in her work, to combine elements of her father's Christianity, her uncle's Peyotism, and the traditional vision quests of the plains.

438   Sanimuinak.   G. HOLM.   "Sanimuinak's Account of How He Became an Angakok," as found in William Thalbitzer, ed., The Ammassalik Eskimo:   Contributions to the Ethnology of the East Greenland Natives, pt. 1, Copenhagen:   Bianco Luno, 1914, pp. 298-300.   An abridgment is in the second book cited in no. 202, pp. 110-13.
    Born, probably before 1840; narrated, 1885.  Angmagsalik Eskimo.   Holm took down this narrative verbatim from his interpreter, and his interpreter interrupted the narrative whenever necessary to assure the accuracy of the translation. Holm admits that this must have affected the narrator (p. 229).   Holm also bowdlerized the narrative and abridged it considerably.  What remains is a fantastic account of the trials and visions Sanimuinak endured on his way to becoming a shaman.  He tells of self torture and sea monsters, and of having been killed and eaten by a bear.

439   Sappier, Jim.   PETER ANASTAS.   Brief autobiography in the book cited in no. 340, pp. 159-68.
    Born, c. 1939; interviewed, 1971.   Penobscot.   Sappier's narrative is cut, but evidently little other editing was done. Sappier describes his childhood, his brief army experience, his work in Connecticut factories, his marriage, and his work as an Indian political activist.

439a  Sat Okh (Stanislaw Suplatowicz).   Les Fils de Grand-Aigle, trans. from Polish, Michel Clement.  Paris:   Farandole, 1967. 201 pp.  Originally, Ziemia Slonych Skal.
    Born, 1920; wrote, c. 1960.  Although this book has at least once been cited as an autobiography, it is romantic, warriors-and-lances fiction.   The author claims to be the son of a Canadian Indian chief and a Polish mother.   But since the claim is that his father was Shawnee, and that his Indian family "hélas, a péri dans un des derniers combats des Shawanèses pour leur indépendence"--at some time after 1936, in Canada, I think that we may be allowed some doubts.

440   Satterlee, John V.   LEONARD BLOOMFIELD.   Narratives to

be found in the book cited in no. 154, pp. 20-23, 28-29.

Born, probably before 1860; narrated, 1920-21. Menomini. For the details of the collaboration, see no. 154. Buying a canoe and a hunting experience.

441 SAVALA, REFUGIO. Kathleen M. Sands. The Autobiography of a Yaqui Poet (P). Tucson: University of Arizona Press, 1980. xxiii + 228 pp.

Born, 1904; wrote, 1964-c. 1969. Yaqui. Although he had but a few years of formal education, Savala was fluent in Yaqui, Spanish, and English. Indeed, he was hailed as a poet and a man of letters as early as 1941, but it was not until 1964--ill and in a nursing home--that he began to write down his remembrances in a systematic way. Muriel Painter, for whom Savala had done some translation, urged him to write more personally: "She told him to write about what he knew best, Yaqui culture, but to explain it in terms of his family's participation" (p. viii). Savala then wrote, in nonstandard English, a chronological series of disjointed episodes. In 1974 this manuscript was turned over to Sands, who standardized the language, combined episodes into chapters, added some of Savala's poems at the beginning of chapters, but evidently did virtually no reordering of Savala's material. She did do "considerable cutting of the last ten 'episodes' . . . since they dwell on his surgery, bodily functions, etc., none of which were very readable and which undercut the intent of the earlier part of the narrative" (Sands, personal communication). Sands also adds a long and helpful section of her own which provides historical background and interpretation--and this section includes long quotations from Savala's poetry, prose, and recorded conversations.

Savala was born just south of the U.S. border at a time when the Mexican government was systematically deporting or executing Sonoran Yaquis, and the first part of this narrative is devoted to an account of his family's flight from the "heartless killers" of Mexico. The family settled in southern Arizona, along with many other fugitive Yaquis. Through Savala's eyes, then, we see the rebirth and growth of Yaqui culture in a strange land.

The book is full of the kind of detail we might expect from a poet. As he thinks back fifty years, for example, to a trip into town for supplies, he recalls his burros coming to him after a night's foraging: "I knew they had drunk yuku ba'ampo [in a rainwater pool] because of their muddy feet" (p. 35). Savala's senses seem never to have been at rest; the man himself seems always to have been at peace.

442 Scratches-face (M). See no. 201.

443 SEKAQUAPTEWA, HELEN. Louise Udall. Me and Mine: The
Life Story of Helen Sekaquaptewa (P).* Tucson: The
University of Arizona Press, 1969. 262 pp.
    Born, 1898; collaborated, shortly before 1968. Hopi.
Sekaquaptewa spoke English. Few details are provided, but it
would seem that Udall--Sekaquaptewa's friend and religious
co-worker--did the usual editing and rearranging to conform to
chronology. This autobiography deals with Sekaquaptewa's
early years as the daughter of "hostile" parents, parents who
actively resisted the attempts of white and Indian authorities
to take their children away to school. She also discusses, quite
straightforwardly, rituals, kachinas, traditional beliefs. All of
this is interesting to compare with Don Talayesva's accounts
(no. 483), since both he and Sekaquaptewa are from Oraibi.
    Sekaquaptwea also provides an account of her conversion
as an adult to the Mormon church. The book does not become
a religious tract as do the autobiographies of some other
converted Indians, but in one chapter she does talk about the
ways in which Mormon doctrines have allowed her more fully
to understand traditional Hopi teachings, and about the ways
in which her knowledge of Hopi ways allows her more fully to
comprehend Mormon doctrine. In this she seems very much
like Alford (no. 6) and Eastman (no. 161), but it should be
remembered that Mormon doctrine has a good deal to say
about the American Indian.
    Sekaquaptewa raised a family of achievers: two of her
children are businessmen, one has a master's degree, one is
executive secretary of the Hopi Tribal Council, and one was a
director of the local Office of Economic Opportunity.

444 Senungetuk, Joseph E. Give or Take a Century: An Eskimo
Chronicle (P).* San Francisco: Indian Historian Press, 1971.
x + 206 pp.
    Born, c. 1940; wrote, c. 1970. Eskimo. This book combines
autobiography with family history, the history of the Eskimo
people, and pro-Eskimo polemics. Senungetuk writes about the
consequences of the coming of the white man for his family
and his people, about the differences, then, between his
father's generation and his own. The impact of the oil
companies is discussed in some detail.

445 SEWID, JAMES. James P. Spradley. Guests Never Leave
Hungry: The Autobiography of James Sewid, a Kwakiutl Indian
(IP). New Haven: Yale University Press, 1969. xi + 310 pp.
    Born, 1913; collaborated, 1967-68. Kwakiutl. Sewid spoke
English well enough for the purposes of these interviews.
Spradley looked at family records and scrapbooks, asked
questions, and took straight narration on tape. Sewid some-
times insisted on bringing in family and acquaintances in order

to verify his remembrances. All of this resulted in over five hundred pages of typed transcript, which Spradley then edited, rearranging, cutting, and altering syntax a bit. The final manuscript was read and approved by Sewid. Sewid was chosen for this work because of his success in straddling two cultures. A successful entrepreneur, he owned his own fishing vessel and hired his own crew to work it, yet he retained his tribal identity as well. He was an Anglican and a Kwakiutl too.

446  Shadlow, Ann. See no. 215.

447  Shattock, Tobias. JAMES DOW McCALLUM. Letters are to be found in the book cited in no. 18, pp. 201-9.
       1742-68; wrote, 1765-67. Narraganset. For the details of the writing and the editing of these letters, see no. 18. Shattock writes about his efforts to unite the Narragansets and about his trip to England to get support for the preservation of the lands of the Narragansets. He also writes about his labors among the Indians as a teacher.

448  Shaw, Anna Moore. A Pima Past (P).* Tucson: University of Arizona Press, 1974. xv + 263 pp.
       Born, 1898; wrote, shortly before 1974. Pima. Shaw was active in religious matters as a teacher and tribal functionary. This autobiography begins with a brief history of her people. Throughout, Shaw is concerned to compare the old and the new ways, mindful of the benefits of education and running water, yet aware that new living patterns tend, for example, to leave the elderly without the support and company the old, close-knit social patterns allowed them. She is convinced that "minority people can climb the ladder of success by hard work" (p. 166).

449  Sheen, Pete. See no. 24.

450  Shoots Them (Nick Alverz). JAMES LARPENTUR LONG. An autobiographical fragment* is to be found in the book cited in no. 27, pp. 162-64.
       Born, c. 1853; interviewed, 1939. Assiniboine. For the details of the collaboration see no. 27. A supernatural experience.

451  Shot in Head. See no. 509.

452  Shot-on-Both-Sides, Jim. ADOLF HUNGRY WOLF. "Our Head Chief, Jim Shot-on-Both-Sides,"* as found in the book cited in no. 20, pp. 332-33.
       Born, c. 1900; interviewed, c. 1972. Blood. See no. 20 for

the details of the collaboration. What little is here is of some interest because this chief of the Bloods is a participant in the attempt to revive and maintain traditional ceremonies. "If we start to live a holy life again, maybe there won't be so many deaths" (p. 333).

453  Simms, Maxey. GUNTER WAGNER. "Maxey Simms' Life Story," in Wagner, Yuchi Tales (IP), Publications of the American Ethnological Society, XIII (1931), 20-29, 244-57.
Born, c. 1876; narrated, 1928-29. Yuchi and Creek. This is a nondirected life history. Wagner prints the Yuchi text, a literal translation, and a free translation. He also includes a brief but interesting account of how Simms's knowledge of especially biblical English has resulted in a "broad and lengthy style" (p. x). Simms tells of his childhood fears, a smallpox epidemic, his first visit to town, of preachers, and other matters which must have been familiar enough to many Indian boys growing up in late-nineteenth-century Indian Territory. He also talks about his separation from his family, his conversion, his marriage, and even his brother's trial for murder.

454  Simpson, Louis. EDWARD SAPIR. "A Personal Narrative of the Paiute War," as found in Sapir, Wishram Texts (IP), Publications of the American Ethnological Society, II (1909), 204-27.
Born, c. 1830; interviewed, 1905. Wishram. Sapir was aided by an interpreter. The Wishram text is printed on facing pages with a free English translation, without rephrasing, cutting, or rearranging. This is a vivid, detailed, and quite self-conscious account of visions and prophecies which preceded the warfare.

455  Sinyella (M). LESLIE SPIER. "Historical Tales," as found in Spier, Havasupai Ethnography (IP), Anthropological Papers of the American Museum of Natural History, XXIX, pt. 3 (1928), 111-12, 222-23, 226-27, 238-41, 246-48, 251-53, 279-81, 322-23, 333-34, 356-80.
Born, c. 1845; interviewed, c. 1920. Havasupai. Spier worked through an interpreter. Pages 356-80 contain a connected historical narrative about Sinyella's people from about the time of his birth (1845) to the end of the warfare among Havasupais, Apaches, and Yavapais (1870). This is, however, history nicely mixed with autobiography. Other, briefer autobiographical narratives are scattered throughout the book (Sinyella was Spier's principal Havasupai informant), and, taken together, we have quite enough to allow us a wonderful sense of this man. We read about his relations with the shamans, his hunts for bear and mountain lion, his father's attempt to keep a wandering Navajo woman to wife--we even

read an account of Sinyella's wet dreams.

456  Sitting Bull (M). See no 132.

457  SMALLBOY, ROBERT.  Eugene Steinhauer.  "Decision to Leave Hobbema," Western Canadian Journal of Anthropology, I, No. 1 (1969), 111-18.  Also appeared as "A Narrative Told by Robert Smallboy," The Northian, VII, No. 3 (1970), 25-27.

Born, 1887; narrated, 1968.  Cree.  Steinhauer here translates the second in a series of Cree-language radio programs "taken on the spot in Kootenay Plains . . . by the Alberta Native Communications Society" (p. 111).  Smallboy explains the events which resulted in his decision to lead 150 of his people away from the Hobbema Reserve--and away from the reserve system--to camp on government land in the Kootenay Plains.

458  Smith, Charlie. EVE BALL. A narrative is to be found in the book cited in no. 138, pp. 102-4.

Born, c. 1878; interviewed, c. 1955.  Chiricahua Apache. No interpreter was necessary. For the rest see no. 138.  Smith recalls his childhood in Geronimo's band in the days before surrender.

459  Smith, John.  Being the Life History of Chief John Smith, As Narrated by Himself and Interpreted by His Adopted Son, Thomas E. Smith. Walker, Minn.: The Cass County Pioneer, n.d. [c. 1920].  12 unnumbered pp.

1802-1932; narrated, c. 1920.  Ojibwa.  The birthdate is that given by the narrator, and the unnamed editors claim to have confidence in the date.  Internal evidence and common sense, however, argue a later date.  Smith tries to make his autobiography worthy of the 1802 birthdate, claiming to remember early prophecies of the coming of the white men and of their double dealing, and early prophecies as well of his own longevity. He also recounts his war experiences, his seven marriages, his hunts, his late conversion to Christianity, and his "pet car."

460  Smith, John (Navajo). See no. 24.

461  Smith, Louisa.  LEO J. FRACHTENBERG.  "The Story of Louisa Smith's Childhood," as found in Frachtenberg, Lower Umpqua Texts (IP), New York:  Columbia University Press, 1914 (Columbia University Contributions to Anthropology, IV), pp. 100-102.

Born, c. 1825; interviewed, 1911.  Umpqua.  What little is here is given us in Umpqua and in literal translation on facing pages.  The narrator was well along the way to senility when she was asked for her life story.

462   Smoking-star. CLARK WISSLER. "Smoking-star, a Blackfoot Shaman," as found in Elsie Clews Parsons, American Indian Life by Several of Its Students (IP), N.Y.: Viking Press, 1925 [1922], pp. 45-62. Reprinted as American Indian Life, Lincoln: University of Nebraska Press, 1967.
     Born, probably before 1820; narrated, c. 1905. Blackfeet. A word must first be said about the volume in which this narrative appears. Parsons persuaded a distinguished group of anthropologists to invent narratives about Indian life, and so we have fictional but true-to-life narratives here by A.L. Kroeber, Edward Sapir, Robert Lowie, Paul Radin, and others. According to Kroeber (1952, p. 234), "Wissler, and apparently Sapir, used actual autobiographies, at least as a base." Sapir turned his material into a third person narrative, but Wissler's remains a first-person autobiography. Wissler's introduction to the narrative--"I sat before the tepee fire of my host, Smoking-star," etc.--is almost certainly a fictional framework. Probably the narrative is one of those collected and translated for Wissler by David C. Duvall, a mixed-blood Piegan who served as Wissler's interpreter and co-worker for about eight years. The beginning of the narrative shows evidence of Wissler's packing in ethnological detail--"Also I suppose that my mother laid aside all ornaments and affected carelessness of person" (p. 45)--but the rest is probably close to a straight translation of Smoking-star's narrative. This turns out to be one of the best of the brief autobiographies, full of detail, humor, and life. Smoking-star tells about his training for the hunt, about his days as a warrior, his raids upon the Crows, his courtship and marriage, his vision quest, his training as a shaman, and more.

463   Snow, John. These Mountains Are Our Sacred Places: The Story of the Stoney Indians (IP).* Toronto: Samuel Stevens, 1977. xiv + 186 pp.
     Born, 1933; wrote, 1969-77. Assiniboine. Quite a bit of autobiographical detail is woven into the later chapters of this history of the Stoney, or Assiniboine, Indians. Snow writes a good deal, for example, about his work in tribal government and affairs, and about his work in the pan-Indian movement.

464   Sorqaq (M). KNUD JOHAN VICTOR RASMUSSEN. A bear-hunting story* is found in the book cited in no. 50, pp. 40-41.
     Born, sometime before 1860; narrated c. 1902. Eskimo, Cape York. For the details of the collaboration, see no. 50.

465   Sowloapik, Josepee (M). See no. 5.

466 Spotted Horn Bull, Mrs. (Pte-San-Waste-Win). JAMES McLAUGHLIN. "Mrs. Spotted Horn Bull's View of the Custer Tragedy," in My Friend the Indian, Boston: Houghton Mifflin Co., 1926 [1909], pp. 162-78.

Born, c. 1833; interviewed, c. 1908. Hunkpapa Sioux. Mrs. Spotted Horn Bull, a cousin of Sitting Bull and an important member of her tribe, was asked to relate the events of the Custer battle. This she did, although her narrative was frequently interrupted by questions, some of which she ignored. McLaughlin does represent some of these questions and interruptions in the text, but for the most part he edited toward consecutive narrative. McLaughlin's wife (see no. 326) was almost certainly the interpreter here.

Mrs. Spotted Horn Bull recounted these events on an earlier occasion, likewise arranged by McLaughlin (McLaughlin's wife interpreting). Her account on this occasion was reported (in the third person) in the St. Paul Pioneer Press (May 19, 1883), and this is reprinted in the book cited in no. 132, pp. 81-87.

467 Sregon Jim (Sra'mau). A.L. KROEBER. "A Yurok War Reminiscence: The Use of Autobiographical Evidence," Southwest Journal of Anthropology, I (1945), 318-32.

Born, c. 1825; interviewed, 1902. Yurok. Kroeber would have worked through an interpreter, though he did have a knowledge of the native language. Biographical information on Sregon Jim and his shaman wives may be found in Robert Spott and Kroeber (1942), pp. 142-256. For an autobiographical narrative by Sregon Jim's second wife, Merip okegei, see no. 329.

468 Standing, William (Fire Bear). "The Illustrator," as found in the book cited in no. 27, pp. lxvii-lxx.

Born, c. 1905; wrote, 1942. Assiniboine. Standing's brief autobiography is a part of the prefatory material for a book on the Assiniboines which he illustrated. Standing briefly tells about his life, education, art training, and his successes as an artist.

469 STANDING BEAR, LUTHER. E.A. Brininstool. My People the Sioux (P),* with an introduction by Richard N. Ellis. Lincoln: University of Nebraska Press, 1975 [1928]. xx + 288 pp.

1863 (1868?)-1939; wrote, c. 1928. Oglala Sioux. Standing Bear hoped, as he put it, to present his people to his white audience "in a true and authentic manner" (p. v), and indeed, according to Ellis, the book did help to create sympathy for the Indians at a crucial time. The pattern of the book is to compare, more or less continually, Indian customs, foods, etc., with white counterparts, almost always in favor of the former.

The result is an explicitly Edenic (p. 190) conception of the pre-reservation Sioux, not so extreme, but along the same lines as Eastman's account (no. 161) and Alford's (no. 6).

Standing Bear was precisely of an age to allow him all of the traditional Indian education but virtually none of the application of that education. He describes all of the training that went into preparing him to become a hunter of buffalo-- but he killed only one before he was whisked off to be a student in the first class at Carlisle. There is a good deal of ambivalence here, however. Standing Bear's hard-won education allows him to laugh with his readers at what he remembers as instances of Sioux credulity and superstition, yet there remains a lingering sense that something is viable in Sioux mysticism.

Standing Bear tells of witnessing the Ghost Dance uprising at Pine Ridge and of his travels with Buffalo Bill's Wild West show. He was entrusted with various responsible positions in tribal affairs, and he worked in the pan-Indian movement.

470    . Land of the Spotted Eagle.* N.Y.: Houghton Mifflin Co., 1933. xix + 259 pp. Reprinted (P): Lincoln: University of Nebraska Press, 1978.

For the most part this book is Standing Bear's description of his culture and people, with frequent autobiographical references. The intent throughout is, as it is in no. 469, to better the Indian in the eyes of white readers. This book is somewhat more outspoken in its criticism of the government's treatment of Indians, however, than My People the Sioux.

471    . My Indian Boyhood.* N.Y.: Houghton Mifflin Co., 1931. 190 pp.

Standing Bear wrote this account of his youth for children "with the hope that the hearts of the white boys and girls . . . will be made kinder toward the little Indian boys and girls" (front matter). The book follows Standing Bear up to his eighth year, when he killed his first, and only, buffalo. The book includes a good deal of Indian lore along the way, romanticized in the same way, but hardly to the same degree, as Eastman romanticizes his youth (no. 161).

472 STANDS IN TIMBER, JOHN. Margot Liberty. Cheyenne Memories (P). Lincoln: University of Nebraska Press, 1972 [1967]. xv + 330 pp.

1884-1967; collaborated, 1956-67. Cheyenne, self-appointed and widely respected tribal historian for the Cheyennes. This book is the result of tape-recording sessions wherein Stands in Timber's memory was aided by the mountains of documents and newspaper clippings which he had accumulated over the years. No translation was necessary.

Liberty retains Stands in Timber's diction and enough of his grammatical "errors" to preserve a unique voice. Sections written in the first person are scattered throughout, but the first 285 pages are devoted to tribal history. A brief autobiography, however, does appear on pp. 286-301. It would seem that Stands in Timber's oral sequencing was preserved here, for there is no real attempt to proceed from first to last. Throughout we are presented with a man who never "took part in" the Indian religion, but who has a firm commitment to the past and a firm belief in the importance of its preservation. There is also the sense here, as in so many others of these autobiographies, that things were better in the old days-- except that, for Stands in Timber, the old days, when there was more of morality, were in the 1920's, long after the move to the reservation.

473    Stanley, Mrs. Andrew. GRENVILLE GOODWIN. "Mrs. Andrew Stanley," as found in the book cited in no. 226, pp. 204-19.
    Born, c. 1866; interviewed, 1931. White Mountain Apache. For the details of the collaboration, see no. 226. Stanley's narrative begins around 1880, with a journey that ended with her capture by a band of renegade Chiricahuas. She tells of "her escape from the Chiricahuas and how, after a series of thoroughly extraordinary adventures, she finally made her way back to her own people" (p. 205).

474    STANLEY, GEORGE. A.E. Peterson. "An Account of the Frog Lake Massacre," Alberta Historical Review, IV, No. 1 (1956), 23-29.
    Born, c. 1868; interviewed, 1931. Cree. Peterson interviewed Stanley, and the resulting Cree-language narrative was translated by George Fidler. Stanley recalls one of the bloody events of the Riel Rebellion, the massacre of nine residents of Frog Lake, Alberta, and the destruction of that settlement. Stanley and other Woods Crees were witnesses of but not participants in these events.

475    STEWART, IRENE. Doris Ostrander Dawdy and Mary Shepardson. A Voice in Her Tribe: A Navajo Woman's Own Story (P). Socorro, N.M.: Ballena Press Anthropological Papers No. 17, 1980. 93 pp.
    Born, 1907; wrote, beginning 1965. Navajo. Stewart was one of the first people Shepardson met when she began her anthropological field work among the Navajos in 1955. After ten years of association and friendship, it occurred to Shepardson to ask Stewart to write her life story. Stewart complied in a series of letters, beginning 1965, directed along the way, to some degree, by Shepardson's questions. These letters were edited by Dawdy, who revised their order and

standardized grammer and spelling. Stewart was one of the first women to enter into Navajo tribal politics (1955), but this book is perhaps most attractive for its extended treatment of the years of Stewart's schooling and her struggle with the two cultures. She was at first so terrified by the thought of going away to school that she had to be fetched by a policeman; by the fifth grade she was so happy at school that she was reluctant to return home. After her years at Haskell (beginning 1922) she decided that she would leave the hogan for the white man's way. Only years later was she able to find peace and satisfaction in a return to the hogan. In Stewart we see a Christian, a Navajo, and an educated, ambitious, woman.

476 Stewart, Jack. JULIAN H. STEWARD. "Autobiography of Jack Stewart," as found in the work cited in no. 360, pp. 425-32.
  Born, c. 1837; interviewed, 1927-28. Piute. For the details of the collaboration, see no. 360. Stewart was good at hunting and gambling, and he was very often lucky, a very sucessful man by the standards of his people. He also was guided by frequent dreams and visions, some of which are recountered here. Stewart tells of his early years, the years before real white contact.

477 Sun Bear (attribution in doubt [M]). THOMAS B. MARQUIS. "A Cheyenne Old Man," as found in the book cited in no. 194, pp. 27-37.
  Born, c. 1843; interviewed, 1927. Cheyenne. Marquis worked sometimes with interpreters, sometimes, relying on sign language, without. For further details of the collaboration, see no. 194. Tales and miscellaneous reminiscences.

478 Susanne. KNUD JOHAN VICTOR RASMUSSEN. "The Invulnerable Uase,"* as found in the book cited in no. 50, pp. 339-46.
  Born, c. 1840; narrated, 1904. Eskimo, East Greenland. For the details of the collaboration, see no. 50. Susanne's personal recollections of the doings of a murderer.

479 Sweezy, Carl. ALTHEA BASS. The Arapaho Way: A Memoir of an Indian Boyhood.* N.Y.: Clarkson N. Potter, Inc., 1966. xvi + 80.
  c. 1881-1953; narrated, probably shortly before 1953. Arapaho. Bass writes: this book is "an account of what Carl Sweezy told me in our frequent visits together. Except to rearrange it by subject matter and to add a few dates, I have not altered it" (p. x). One assumes that this means that the book is a rendering of Sweezy's conversations from notes, for the book certainly does not read like a transcription of oral

conversation. This will say that one cannot, probably, assume that any given phrase is Sweezy's own.

Sweezy is quite conscious of having grown up on the boundary of the old ways and the new ways. Throughout, the book breathes Sweezy's pride in the old ways and his acceptance of the new. He provides a good deal of tribal history, as well as an account of his schooling, his attitudes toward religion, his marriage, and his work. Sweezy also reminisces quite fondly about the anthropologist James Mooney, who worked off and on among the Arapahos between 1891 and 1918. It was in the summer of Sweezy's fourteenth year that Mooney gave him his start as an artist. Sweezy was to go on to achieve some fame as an artist, and he credits Mooney with having provided him with his aesthetic: " . . . don't paint rocks and trees and things that aren't there. Just paint Indian. So I am still painting, and painting Indian . . . . I call it the Mooney way" (p. 63).

480     Sword (M). J. R. WALKER. A brief autobiography is to be found in The Sun Dance and Other Ceremonies of the Oglala Division of the Teton Dakota, Anthropological Papers of the American Museum of Natural History, XVI (1917), 159.

Born, probably before 1865; wrote, probably c. 1910. Oglala Sioux. Walker tells us only that Sword was at work on an autobiography when he died, and that Sword wrote in Lakota. What Walker prints, then, is a translation of a very brief autobiography, which nevertheless takes us from Sword's days as a shaman to his days as a deacon for "the church."

481     Tahan (M). See no. 208.

482     Takornaq (F). KNUD JOHAN VICTOR RASMUSSEN. A narrative is to be found in the book cited in no. 23, pp. 23-32.

Born, probably before 1870; interviewed, c. 1922. Iglulik Eskimo. For the details of the collaboration, see no. 50. Takornaq provides us with a fascinating account of her childhood and supernatural experiences. She tells us that, since she was born with the aid of an ice loon, which is half bird and half human, she has always had trouble distinguishing between the living and the spirits of the dead. Another autobiographical narrative by Takornaq is to be found in the book cited in no. 380, pp. 16-17, where she recalls a woman who ate her own children in order to save herself from starvation.

483     Talayesva, Don (Sun Chief). LEO W. SIMMONS. Sun Chief: The Autobiography of a Hopi Indian (P). New Haven: Yale University Press, 1974 [1942]. xx + 460 pp.

Born, 1890; collaborated, 1938-41. Hopi. Simmons was quite assertive. He insisted, for example, that Talayesva provide much fuller accounts of the Hopi rituals than he wished to. Talayesva's eventual compliance with these requests was, at least initially, a source of some pain, although he was quite eager, on the other hand, to provide an endless stream of detail about the daily fetching in of horses, daily menus, and other such homely matters. After a time Simmons asked that these repetitious accounts be curtailed. Talayesva wrote in English and voluminously--Simmons worked from a manuscript of more than 8,000 handwritten pages, supplemented with material obtained from three years of interviews with Talayesva. "Possibly not more than one fifth of the data are presented here, but the remainder is, for the most part, monotonous repetitions of the daily details of life, legends, and additional dreams"; however, the book is in the first person, and it is "almost always in Don's own words or in words which he readily recognized in checking the manuscript" (p. 7). The result has been much praised for its authenticity and detail, but it should be remembered that it is not such a narrative as Talayesva would have written had he been without direction. Quite the contrary.

The narrative itself is fascinating. Talayesva was white-educated, but his outlook remained essentially that of the traditional Hopi. He tells of witches, journeys, and participation in rituals. He also tells of being frightened by a certain kachina when he was a child, and of how his remembrance of those fears shaped his own performance, as an adult, in the role of that same kachina. Another unusual, if not quite unique, aspect of this book is the fact that it includes an account of the effect of the anthropologist upon the life of the autobiographer.

484  Tangled Yellow Hair, James. THOMAS B. MARQUIS. "James Tangled Yellow Hair, a Cheyenne Scout,"* as found in the book cited in no. 194, pp. 38-45.
Born, c. 1866; interviewed, 1927. Cheyenne. Marquis worked sometimes with an interpreter, sometimes in sign language. See no. 194 for further details of the collaboration. Tangled Yellow Hair does tell about childhood experiences, but for the most part this is devoted to scouting in the Dakotas.

485  Tate, Albert. "A Winter Buffalo Hunt," Alberta Historical Review, VI, No. 4 (1958), 25-29.
Born, c. 1858; wrote, ?. Cree and white. Tate vividly recounts the procedures and events of a buffalo hunt by impoundment (winter of 1867-68).

486  Taylor, James, Jr. EDWARD M. BRUNER. Life History of a Fort Berthold Indian Psychotic, Microcard Publications of Primary Records in Culture and Personality, ed. Bert Kaplan,

II, No. 9, Madison, Wis.: Microcard Foundation, 1957, 28 pp.

Born, 1912; interviewed, 1952. Mandan-Hidatsa and white. This is an unedited transcript of a taped, English-language life history. Beyond his initial request for a life history, Bruner did very little to direct Taylor. This is a remarkable narrative. Although he asserts that he has always been in "complete control" of himself (p. 15), Taylor was diagnosed as a schizophrenic in 1935, after several scrapes with the law. He was committed to a mental asylum. He managed to escape, however, much as he managed to leave the army after a nine-month stay--"one day" he just "decided to walk off" (p. 13). For the rest, Taylor tells of his childhood under the strict eye of his father, and he tells of his hobo life.

487   Teio, Mrs. LESLIE SPIER. A narrative is to be found in the book cited in no. 88, pp. 243-44.

Born, c. 1860; interviewed, c. 1925. Wishram. I presume that Spier worked through an interpreter here. Teio recounts an experience with a shaman.

488   Tens, Isaac. MARIUS BARBEAU. "The Career of a Medicine Man, According to Isaac Tens, a Gitksan," as found in Barbeau, Medicine Men of the Pacific Coast, National Museums of Canada, Bul. 152, Anthropological Series No. 42 (1958), 39-55. Excerpts reprinted in the second book cited in no. 202, pp. 183-91.

Born, probably, c. 1880; interviewed, probably 1954. Gitksan. Barbeau worked through an interpreter. Tens, who practiced in and around Hazelton, British Columbia, in the 1920's, talks about the acquisition of his shamanic powers and his exercise of those powers. He sings some of the songs he used in healing the sick, and he tells of his rise in prestige (and of the simultaneous rise in his fees). He also talks about the loss of his original power after he began to use church prayers for his healings. This is one of the most interesting of the accounts of shamanic powers.

489   Tetlaneetsa (M). MARIUS BARBEAU and GRACE MELVIN. Some narratives are to be found in Barbeau and Melvin, The Indian Speaks,* Caldwell, Idaho: Caxton Printers, 1943, pp. 58-74.

Born, probably c. 1850; interviewed, 1912. Thompson River. Barbeau worked through an interpreter when he collected this material for the National Museum of Canada. While the details of this reworking of that material for a popular audience are not specified, we can assume that Barbeau did some rephrasing, some cutting, and some rearranging--although this was probably not very extensive. Tetlaneetsa tells here of his vision quests from the age of fifteen on.

490    Tetso, John. Trapping Is My Life (P).* Toronto: Peter Martin
       Associates, Ltd., 1970. xi + 116 pp. This edition contains
       letters from Tetso to Claire V. Molson which were not printed
       in the 1964 edition (Fort Simpson, North West Territory:
       Sacred Heart Mission).
           C. 1921-64; wrote, during the early 1960's. Slave. This is a
       lovely, unpretentious collection of autobiographical sketches,
       each filled with woodland lore, each full of Tetso's passion for
       the hunt and the outdoors.

491    Thompson, Jean (Sipsis). PETER ANASTAS. Reminiscences in
       the book cited in no. 340, pp. 52-69.
           Born, 1941; interviewed, 1971. Penobscot. This is an
       abridged but otherwise little-edited interview with Thompson
       and her white husband. Thompson talks about the frustrations
       of her schooling and her early work as a social worker.
       Eventually she began working to develop Indian leadership
       programs and school curricula appropriate for Indian school
       children.

492    THRASHER, ANTHONY APAKARK. Gerard Deagle and Alan
       Mettrick.    Thrasher . . . Skid Row Eskimo (IP).* Toronto:
       Griffin House, 1976. xii + 164 pp.
           Born, 1937; wrote, c. 1970-75. Eskimo. Thrasher began to
       write down disjointed personal anecdotes while he was in jail
       awaiting trial for the murder of a man whom he claims never
       to have seen. Encouraged by his lawyer, Thrasher continued to
       write after he had been convicted and sentenced. Eventually
       these writings were given to Deagle and Mettrick, two journal-
       ists, for editing. One suspects that their editorial hand was
       quite heavy on Thrasher's earlier efforts, lighter on the later
       material, which he wrote while he was educating himself in
       the prison school. There is no indication as to which parts of
       this autobiography were written when, other than internal
       evidence which seems to suggest that Thrasher wrote his
       account of his prison years late. Deagle and Mettrick supple-
       mented the written record with their own tape recordings of
       his recollections.
           The result is an extraordinary book. Thrasher was born in
       the same year that the Catholic and Anglican missions were
       founded in Tuktoyaktuk, Thrasher's corner of the Arctic. As
       he grew up he learned to hunt and trap, and by the time his
       father suffered a stroke, Thrasher was able to take his father's
       place as provider for his family--at the age of twelve. By the
       time he was nineteen, however, he was prevailed upon by the
       government to go south for job training. He saw his first flush
       toilet on the airplane to Edmonton. The government's best

expectations, and Thrasher's life, soon crumbled. He promptly became an alcoholic, began his stumbling progress from bar to bar, soup kitchen to soup kitchen, job to job, woman to woman, and jail to jail, until he was finally convicted of murder.

Thrasher's account of his life as a prisoner--his life among madmen, as he puts it--is as vivid as it is predictable: racial tensions, riots, homosexuality, beatings, killings, drugs. And all of this is made to seem the more stark and cruel by occasional lapses into remembrances of the freedom and the cold and the ways of the North. This is one of the very good autobiographies.

493     Three Suns (Big Nose [M]). JAMES WILLARD SCHULTZ. "Battle on Sun River," and "Three Suns' War Record,"* as found in the book cited in no. 31, pp. 252-70.

C. 1823-96; narrated, probably in the 1880's. Piegan. Schultz wrote this tale down at least forty years after he head it --although he did hear it several times, evidently. For further detail about the collaboration, see no. 31. Three Suns, the last war chief of the Piegans, tells about a battle wherein he and his men killed a large number of Crows. "Three Suns' War Record" is a verbal account of twenty pictographs by Three Suns (1845-81). The verbal account is Three Suns'--but at third hand. The pictographs themselves are not included.

494     Thunderchild, Chief. EDWARD AHENAKEW. "The Stories of Chief Thunderchild," as found in Ahenakew's Voices of the Plains Cree (P),* ed. Ruth M. Buck. Toronto: McClelland and Stewart Ltd., 1973, pp. 27-76.

1849-1927; narrated, 1923. Cree. Ahenakew, himself a Cree, spent a year collecting tales from old Cree storytellers, and Chief Thunderchild was his prime source. As Ahenakew noted in his journal, he paid Thunderchild "$1.00 a night . . . for story-telling" (p. 11). Ahenakew took notes in English while Thunderchild spoke. These notes then lay fallow until after Ahenakew's death in 1961, when they were sent to Buck. Buck, who had known Ahenakew well, then worked the notes into readable prose.

The result is as vivid a set of autobiographical tales as I have read, tales of winter starvation, horsemanship, warfare, stealing horses, racing, and the Sun Dance. These tales are the more effective, perhaps, for being in a form much closer to the autobiographer's traditional narrative form than is the case for so many of the other works listed in this bibliography.

495     Tilden, Sam (Suhm-Keen). ROWENA L. and GORDON D. ALCORN. "Old Nez Perce Recalls Tragic Retreat of 1877," Montana, XIII, No. 1 (1963), 66-74.

Born, 1867; interviewed, 1962. Nez Perce. No interpreter

was necessary here, although the Alcorns have edited Tilden's narrative into standard English. This is an account of Tilden's part in the Nez Perce wars and the retreat to Canada in 1877. This includes Tilden's remembrances of Chief Joseph. The Alcorns proceed here by telling the tale in their own words, with long quotations from Tilden along the way. Only about half of this, then, is in the words of Tilden himself.

496 Tin-Tin-Meet-Sa (M). JOSEPH KOSSUTH DIXON. "Chief Tin-Tin-Meet-Sa,"* as found in the book cited in no. 11, pp. 59-62.
Born, c. 1831; interviewed, 1909. Umatilla. For the details of the collaboration, see no. 11. Flickering remembrances of raids against the Sioux and clashes with the Piutes during the Bannock war.

497 Tisnado, Alasco (M). See no. 114.

498 Tom (Sayachapis). EDWARD SAPIR and MORRIS SWADESH. The "Tom" narratives in Sapir and Swadesh, Nootka Texts (IP), Philadelphia: Linguistic Society of America, 1939, pp. 128-209.
Born, probably before 1830; interviewed, 1910-14. Nootka. Tom knew no English. Sapir had some knowledge of Nootka but collected this material with the aid of interpreters. The native text is presented on facing pages with a literal translation. Swadesh assisted in the work of translation. This material is of considerable interest, since Tom incorporated songs, visions, and much else into his account of his life. The accounts of his Potlatches are particularly intriguing.

499 Tom, John. See no. 24.

500 Tracy, Bernard, BRODERICK H. JOHNSON. "Bernard Tracy," as found in the book cited in no. 34, pp. 86-96.
Born, 1925; interviewed, c. 1973. Navajo. For the details of the collaboration, see no. 34. Tracy tells of his experiences as a Marine in the Pacific during WW II.

501 Tracy, Deescheeny Nez (M). BRODERICK H. JOHNSON. "Deescheeney Nez Tracy,"* as found in the book cited in no. 17, pp. 149-72.
Born, 1900; interviewed, c. 1976. Navajo. For the details of collaboration, see no. 17. Although he could neither read nor write, Tracy managed to become a stone mason and a member of the stone mason's union. Still a believer in the Navajo religion, he experienced the stock reduction, and is convinced that that program caused the decline in rainfall and verdure in his area.

502    Tso, Curly. See no. 24.

503    Tubbe, Laah (F). See no. 504.

504    Tubbee, Okah (William Chubbee). L. LEONIDAS ALLEN. A
Thrilling Sketch of the Life of the Distinguished Chief Okah
Tubbee, Alias Wm. Chubbee, Son of the Head Chief, Mosholeh
Tubbee, of the Choctaw Nation of Indians.    N.Y.: n.p.
[probably Cameron's Steam Power Presses], 1848. 43 pp.
            .    LAAH CEIL MANATOI ELAAH TUBBEE.    A
Sketch of the Life of Okah Tubbee.  Springfield, Mass.: H. S.
Taylor, 1848. 85 pp.
       Born, c. 1805; written, c. 1847.  Choctaw, but see below.
Tubbee was raised as a slave in Natchez, but as he recalls his
life, he fought not only against this servitude, but against the
very idea that he was black.  He remembered, he says, two
moments of his life as an Indian before his capture and
enslavement.  He was eventually convinced that he was, in
fact, the son of a chief of the Choctaws, and eventually he
won his freedom upon this claim (c. 1840), at a point shortly
after which the first book cited above ends.  Whether Indian or
black in fact, Tubbee does allow us a vivid impression of the
latitude allowed the "town" slaves, the slaves apprenticed to
trades--and a vivid impression of their special problems.
       The second book includes all this, and then goes on to tell
of Tubbee's work as a wandering musician (c.  1840-48) of a
rather unusual stamp.  He was a self-taught flutist, and he
played as well upon the sauce-pananna, an instrument he made
from a sauce pan, all according to the dictates of a dream.
His dreams also directed Tubbee to try to "harmonize" the
races, white and Indian.  And he conceived of his mission
largely: he was to be an emissary to the whites to earn
compassion for the Indians, to convince whites that the Indians
ought to be allowed to maintain their then boundaries; he was
an emissary to the Indians to civilize them, to "harmonize"
their souls--and all by music.
       Tucked away in the second book (pp. 77-81) is a brief
autobiography by Laah Tubbee (born, 1817; Mohawk father,
Delaware mother).  She tells of her childhood--and she too was
a dreamer of dreams.  She dreamed that she must be Christianized and schooled; she dreamed that she was to marry
Tubbee, even as he had dreamed that he was to marry her.
She tells as well of their travels and successes together as
musicians.   These are two extraordinary people, full of
purpose, full of a sense of the nobility of their Indian forebears, and withall convinced that Indians ought to be civilized
and Christianized.
       But however clear all of the above may be, the texts
themselves are beset with problems.  The account I provide

below is quite tentative. Probably, then, Tubbee met Allen in some military connection. Tubbee held several musical posts in the military (fife major, etc.), Allen was a military chaplain, and both served in New Orleans. Since Tubbee was urgent throughout much of his life to convince both friends and enemies that he was an Indian, a good and useful human being, and no "nigger," he might himself have initiated the autobiography. Allen had, however, written other books, and it is certainly quite possible that he urged the labor upon Tubbee; or, indeed, Laah Tubbee, who was quite literate, might have initiated the book. But however the plan originated, almost certainly it was Laah who took down her husband's story in writing--with polite embellishments at the sentence level, but probably little other alteration--and posted it to Allen for "corrections" (see p. 30 of first book).

As to Allen's work, one knows not whether to praise him for his fidelity to the text as he received it, or to damn him for his sloppy editing. Remembrances of events quite outside the normal chronological order frequently interrupt the narrative, quite in the manner one would expect of an oral history, but of course with none of the cues with which an oral version would alert its audience to changes of setting and time. These kinds of problems do strongly suggest that this autobiography is remarkably close to Tubbee's original oral version; the misprints, of course, fall entirely to Allen's credit.

The second book probably had Laah Tubbee acting as sole editor, although almost all of Allen's prefatory material is retained--reordered and reparagraphed. Some of the misprints of the first are corrected in the second; whole new passages are inserted (sometimes making nonsense of what had been coherent passages; see, for example, pp. 16-18 of the second book); and then there are added some thirty pages treating of the years 1840-48. One cannot but suspect, however, that Laah's influence in the second goes beyond editorial emendations. One suspects that her interest in visions is more pronounced than Okah's. Certainly there is much more of visions and the dictates of dreams in her edition than in Allen's.

505 Tupuhse (F). RUTH LANDES. Narrative to be found in the book cited in no. 254, pp. 233-39.

Born, probably some time before 1880; narrated, shortly before 1936. Cree, but lived with and shared the customs of the Ojibwas. For the details of the collaboration, see no. 254. This narrative is concerned exclusively with matters of courtship, separation, enmity between husband and wife, etc.

506 Two Leggings (M). PETER NABOKOV. Two Leggings: The Making of a Crow Warrior (P).* N.Y.: Thomas Y. Crowell

Co., 1967. xxv + 226 pp.

C. 1847-1923; interviewed, beginning 1919. Crow. The history of the composition of this autobiography is complex. William Wildschut interviewed Two Leggings via an interpreter. He then imposed chronological order upon the resultant reminiscences, embellished the prose, added mood, and checked the manuscript with Two Leggings. Wildschut's manuscript then lay idle until Peter Nabakov was apprised of its existence nearly forty years after its completion. Nabokov then undertook to edit the manuscript, paring down the prose in such a way as to leave almost every sentence leaner, while not otherwise abridging the manuscript. Nabokov provides an appendix which includes before-and-after passages which demonstrate his method. Wildschut's prose was so ornate, and Nabokov works so sensibly, that one cannot but applaud Nabokov's bold license.

Although we are thus at four removes from Two Leggings, this is one of the most interesting of the Indian autobiographies. Three reasons: first, because of the very complexity of the process of its composition. Second, because Two Leggings manages to shape the autobiography in such a way that it serves purposes of his own definition. He wanted desperately to be remembered. If in the old times the exploits of the great warriors were told around the campfire, Wildschut provided Two Leggings the opportunity for immortality in a new mode. When, for example, Two Leggings reaches the time when the wars and the raiding end, he quits abruptly, although he had lived for thirty-five years after the point at which he chooses to end his narration. "Nothing happened after that. We just lived .... There is nothing more to tell" (p. 197). Third, because the book transmits an unusual personality. Two Leggings so keenly yearned to succeed that he was willing to transgress his society's rules in order to succeed in his society's terms.

507 Two Moon (or Two Moons [M]). HAMLIN GARLAND. "Custer's Last Fight as Seen by Two Moon,"* McClure's, XI (May, 1898), 443-48. Reprinted in Hamlin Garland's Observations on the American Indian, 1895-1905 (IP), ed. Lonnie E. Underhill and Daniel F. Littlefield, Jr., Tucson: University of Arizona Press, 1976, pp. 159-64. Also reprinted in the book cited in no. 132, pp. 101-3. An abridgment is in Let Me Be a Free Man (IP),* ed. Jane B. Katz, Minneapolis: Lerner Publications, 1975, pp. 99-106.

C. 1847-1917; interviewed, 1898. Northern Cheyenne. Garland worked through an interpreter, and this text includes interpolations by Garland as to, for example, Two Moon's gestures, his mood, etc. Two Moon here tells of the events leading up to the Custer battle, and of his own part in that battle. The abridgment cited above does not include Two Moon's final paragraph:

> I am now old, and my mind has changed. All that [fighting] is past. I think of these things now: first that our reservation shall be fenced and the white settlers kept out and our young men kept in. Then there will be no trouble. Second I want to see my people raising cattle and making butter. Last, I want to see my people going to school to learn the white man's ways. (P. 448)

508       . JOSEPH KOSSUTH DIXON. "Chief Two Moons,"* as found in the book cited in no. 11, pp. 121-28.

Interviewed, 1909. For the details of the collaboration, see no 11. Remembrances of marriage customs and war.

509 Two Moons (M). LUCULLUS VIRGIL McWHORTER. Autobiographical narratives in McWhorter, Hear Me My Chiefs: Nez Perce History and Legend, ed. Ruth Bordin, Caldwell, Idaho: Caxton Printers, Ltd., 1952, pp. 31-49, 199-203, 245-48, 282-83, 340, 352-53, 459, 553-54.

Born, c. 1830; interviewed, 1909. Nez Perce. The book cited here is a history primarily of the Nez Perces in the age of Chief Joseph, and at the center is the Nez Perce war of 1877 and the events which precipitated that war. The method is to write with constant reference to, and frequent--and often quite extended--quotations from, Indian and white informants. Many brief but moving autobiographical narratives by Nez Perces are thus included here, narratives by Two Moons, Black Eagle, Chelooyeen, Chuslum MoxMox, Shot in Head, Many Wounds, Peopeo, Tholekt, Red Elk, and others (all named here are male). Judging from the method of his work with Yellow Wolf (see no. 554), we can assume that McWhorter did very little tampering with these narratives beyond abridging them. In the case of Two Moons, McWhorter even includes some of the questions he asked.

For the most part all of these narratives have to do with the 1877 war, its antecedents and its aftermath. Two Moons is singled out for separate citation here because he tells us something about other periods of his life as well, about his youth, his warfare with the Crows, his powers, etc.--and then there is much more material here by Two Moons than there is by the others.

510 Umapine, Chief. JOSEPH KOSSUTH DIXON. "Chief Umapine,"* as found in the book cited in no. 11, pp. 51-59.

Born, c. 1853; interviewed, 1909. Umatilla. For the details of the collaboration, see no. 11. After some prefatory remarks about his love for President Taft and what a wonderful work Dixon is accomplishing, Umapine recounts various war experiences.

511 Valenzuela, Salvadora. PAUL-LOUIS FAYE. Recollections II and X in the book cited in no. 365, pp. 46-50.
Born, before 1880; interviewed, 1921. Cupeno. For the rest see no. 365.

512 Valor, Palmer. GRENVILLE GOODWIN. "Palmer Valor," as found in the book cited in no. 226, pp. 40-71.
C. 1837-1933; interviewed, 1932. White Mountain Apache. Valor tells of a time when "there was no sickness among us and it seemed as though the people didn't die" (p. 43). Valor mentions some details from his childhood, but for the most part this narrative is devoted to warfare and raiding. Valor ranged widely on these forays, once as far as the Gulf of California. For the rest, see no. 226.

513 Wadsworth, Annie. ADOLF HUNGRY WOLF. "Mrs. Annie Wadsworth,"* as found in the book cited in no. 20, pp. 339-41.
Born, c. 1892; interviewed, c. 1972. Blood. For the details of the collaboration, see no. 20. Wadsworth tells of her early marriage and her feelings about leaving home.

514 Wapiti, Marisa (pseudonym for Marie Belanger?). Ashes of Fire: Manuscript of Just a Little Halfbreed and Ropes of Sand: Manuscript of Just a Little Halfbreed. Smithers, B.C.: Tanglewood Press, 1972. 237 pp.
Born, c. 1925; wrote, mid 1960's. Métis. Printed by mimeograph with little editing, the two parts of Wapiti's narrative have more the appearance of a first draft than a published work. Wapiti says that she writes in the hope that she will awaken in her daughter a sense of pride in her Métis heritage. Wapiti tells about her childhood, her work--mining camps, etc.--and her life in the cities and villages of British Columbia as a Métis. Probably there is a fair mixture of fiction here.

515 Watches-All (F). A. L. KROEBER. "Watches-All's Narrative," as found in the book cited in no. 69, pp. 216-21.
Born, c. 1837; interviewed, 1901. Gros Ventre. Brief but interesting account of a woman's war experiences--being captured, sold, etc. For details of collaboration, see no. 69.

516 Waterman (M). See no. 132.

517 Waybenais, Myrtle. BRODERICK H. JOHNSON. "Myrtle Waybenais," as found in the book cited in no. 34, pp. 129-33.
Born, 1908; interviewed, c. 1973. Navajo. For the details

of the collaboration, see no. 34. Waybenais talks about her work with Navajo education, the government's stock-reduction program, and her service in the Women's Army Corps (WW II).

518  Weasel Tail (M). JAMES WILLARD SCHULTZ and JESSIE LOUISE DONALDSON. A narrative* is to be found in the book cited in no. 157, pp. 166-92.
 Born, c. 1857; narrated, c. 1927. Blood. For the details of the collaboration, see no. 157. Weasel Tail recounts deeds of war.

519  Webb, George. A Pima Remembers (P).* Tucson: University of Arizona Press, 1959. 126 pp.
 Born, 1893; wrote, during the late 1950's. Pima. A cattleman, farmer, grocery store owner, and associate justice of the tribal court, Webb wrote this book, as he says, largely to acquaint younger Pimas with "the customs and habits of their forefathers" (p. 7). The book is a connected collection of mythic and historical tales and personal reminiscences.

520  Welmas, Carolina. PAUL-LOUIS FAYE. Recollections III, VI, VII, VIII in the book cited in no. 365, pp. 47-48.
 Born, before 1880; interviewed, 1921. Cupeno. For the rest, see no. 365.

521  White-arm (M). See no. 200.

522  WHITE BULL, CHIEF JOSEPH. James H. Howard. The Warrior Who Killed Custer (IP),* trans. and ed., James H. Howard. Lincoln: University of Nebraska Press, 1968. xix + 84 pp.
 Born, 1850; wrote, 1931. Teton Sioux. White Bull was persuaded to write an account of his life in 1931. He wrote more than was requested of him and added thirty-nine illustrations in pencil, ink, and crayon. All of this lay in manuscript until 1960, when Howard took up the work of translating and editing. This volume includes the original Dakota text and the illustrations, many in color, as well as the translation and notes.
 White Bull was a renowned warrior, and this autobiography is fairly exclusively devoted to his deeds in war and on the hunt. This is one of the most important of the American Indian autobiographies, because it is almost entirely the product of White Bull's own sense of his past. He writes in response to a request for a life history, but past that it is entirely his own creation. It is interesting to compare White Bull's concerns, for example, with those of Indian autobiographers more influenced by their white collaborators and/or Western education. Much could be done, too, by comparing

the winter count which White Bull includes with the structure of his own life history.

523 _____ . STANLEY VESTAL. "The Man Who Killed Custer,"* American Heritage, VIII, No. 2 (1957), 4-9, 90-91.

Interviewed, 1932. Vestal here writes an account of the Custer battle which centers on the experiences of White Bull-- an account which includes events leading up to and including the death of Custer at the hands of White Bull. Vestal alternates his own historical narrative with passages from White Bull's first person narrative. I assume that Vestal worked through an interpreter. Vestal includes three of White Bull's own illustrations, White Bull's own copies of the illustrations mentioned in no. 522.

524 White Calf, Chief (Running Wolf, James Jacobs). RICHARD LANCASTER. Piegan: A Look from Within at the Life, Times, and Legacy of an American Indian.* Garden City, N.Y.: Doubleday and Co., 1966. 359 pp.

Born, 1857 (according to White Calf's own account); narrated, 1962. Piegan. Lancaster kept a very complete journal during an extended visit with White Calf, his adoptive father. Of this work Lancaster wrote:

> My original journal was very detailed . . . but not all portions of this volume appeared therein. Some of the Chief's stories were on tape and had to be transcribed in their entirety and inserted in a manner duplicating the time and the place of their original telling. . . . my subsequent visits with the Chief . . . have produced information which has been added in the form of foot-notes. Otherwise nothing has been changed--and absolutely nothing has been contrived: these are the words and the actions; these are the feelings and the thoughts; these are the people. (p. 6)

Lancaster's book, then, is a smoothly edited and augmented journal. We are given not only Lancaster's light-hearted accounts of daily life with White Calf and White Calf's tales (most of which are autobiographical), but also Lancaster's edited transcriptions of White Calf's son's interpretations of White Calf's tales. White Calf tells about his childhood, his first war parties, of political actions, trips to Washington to negotiate with the government, and a good deal else.

525 White Grass (M). JAMES WILLARD SCHULTZ. A narrative* is to be found in the book cited in no. 219, pp. 148-68.

Born, probably before 1835; narrated, 1922. Piegan. For the details of the collaboration, see no. 219. White Grass recounts deeds of war.

526 White Horse (M). JOSEPH KOSSUTH DIXON. "White Horse,"* as found in the book cited in no. 11, pp. 91-96, 209-11.

Born, c. 1850; interviewed, 1909. Yankton Sioux. For the details of the collaboration, see no. 11. White Horse tells of his reluctance to become a warrior. He also says that the most important event in his life came when his people were placed on the reservation and he was appointed "head farmer over the Indians" (p. 93). He also tells of his missionary work. White Horse's account puts before us the very epitome of the passively assimilated, though nostalgic, Indian which was the goal of Dixon and many other Indian enthusiasts of his day.

527 White Horse Eagle (M). EDGAR VON SCHMIDT-PAULI. We Indians: The Passing of a Great Race, trans. Christopher Tirner. N.Y.: E.P. Dutton and Co., 1931. 256 pp.

Born, 1822 (according to White Horse Eagle's claim); collaborated, 1929. Osage. Von Schmidt-Pauli took down White Horse Eagle's narrative in English, and then wrote up the autobiography in German, trying "to reproduce his ingenuous and racy style" (p. 33). The book cited, then, is an English translation of a German translation of White Horse Eagle's English.

It is difficult to evaluate this book. Von Schmidt-Pauli's introduction takes itself very seriously, but it is nonetheless engagingly idiotic, claiming, as it does, that White Horse Eagle is quite capable of sensing the presence of gold, silver, or water if there be any in the earth beneath his feet. Von Schmidt-Pauli's chief is also, of course, quite capable of reading Egyptian hieroglyphics, and this in turn is evidence that Africa and America were once joined. Since White Horse Eagle himself is convinced that the only reason the Indians allowed the whites to land in America in the first place was that the whites greeted the Indians with ancient Masonic-cabalistic signs, one begins to feel that White Horse Eagle deserved his collaborator.

But while the work can thus hardly be trusted for the purpose of ethnographic research, it is a kind of treasure trove for those interested in romantic attitudes toward race in general and the Indians in particular. The book is a supreme enunciation of the assumptions that guide Dixon's work (no. 11), and the early Eastman's too (no. 161).

528 White-Man-Runs-Him. JOSEPH KOSSUTH DIXON. "White-Man-Runs-Him,"* as found in the book cited in no. 11, pp. 130-38, 152-58.

Born, c. 1848; interviewed, 1909. Crow. For the details of

the collaboration, see no. 11. White-Man-Runs-Him tells of his boyhood training for the hunt and war, and he tells too of his war experiences and his work as a scout for Custer. For another narrative by White-Man-Runs-Him, see no. 132.

529   White Quiver (M). JAMES WILLARD SCHULTZ. "The White Quiver Saga,"* as found in the book cited in no. 31, pp. 210-24.
       C. 1850-1931; narrated, probably before 1900. Piegan. For the details of the collaboration, see no. 31. This is a coup tale, White Quiver's tale of his lone raid upon the Crows--a year after the Indian agents pronounced that there were to be absolutely no more such raids.

530   Whitewater, Hosteen (M). See no. 24.

531   White Wolf, Eddie. See 60.

532   Whitewolf, Jim (pseudonym). CHARLES S. BRANT. Jim Whitewolf: The Life of a Kiowa Apache Indian (IP). N.Y.: Dover Publications, Inc., 1969. xii +144 pp.
       C. 1878-c. 1955; narrated, 1948-49. Kiowa Apache. Brant sought Whitewolf out because he was "an ordinary member of his tribe" (p. vii). Whitewolf spoke fairly fluent English but was more comfortable conversing in his native language, so Brant made use of an interpreter. Though he did recognize that Whitewolf "tended strongly to think and speak in terms of dualities of actions and events much more than in temporal terms," and even though Brant believed that "this habit may well be due to the influence of his native language, which stresses aspects and qualities and does not pay the attention to time and chronology that English does," still Brant did do some rearranging in order to provide "some semblance of chronology" (p. viii). Brant does, however, do relatively little such editing, and the result is a text that conveys a fair sense of Whitewolf's disdain for chronology.
       Whitewolf works extended passages of tribal history and myth into his narrative, and so the book provides a nice point of comparision for Momaday's much more self-conscious juxta-posings of personal, tribal (Kiowa), and mythic history in The Way to rainy Mountain (no. 344).

533   Wikis (pseudonym [M]). GEORGE BIRD GRINNELL. When Buffalo Ran (P).* Norman: University of Oklahoma Press, 1966 (1920). 114 pp.
       Born, c. 1845; spoke with Grinnell, 1874. "The boy Wikis and his people are not identified, but internal evidence is that they were Northern Cheyennes" (p. 8). This is an artificial autobiography. Grinnell interviewed Cheyennes when he went

on the Custer expedition to the Black Hills in 1874. It is probable that the incidents Grinnell recounts are authentic, but one cannot know to what extent Wikis is a composite of several different informants. Grinnell says in his introduction that "the life of those days" has "passed away and will not return" (p. 10). It would seem that Grinnell has selected his material and arranged it in such a way as to maximize the nostalgic effect and minimize the bitterness toward the white that is usually found in these autobiographies.

534  Willetto, Carla. See no. 39.

535  Willis, Jane. Geniesh: An Indian Girlhood.* Toronto: New Press, 1973. 199 pp.
    Born, 1940; wrote, c. 1973. Cree mother, white father. Willis writes of growing up in the care of her Cree grand-parents, and of her twelve very unpleasant years at Indian boarding schools. She writes of the Canadian government's determination, and the schools' determination, to treat her and her people as children--and of her final determination to live independent of government paternalism. She writes too of the pride in her Indian heritage which that break allowed her. This book is bitter, lively, and ironic.

536  Willoya, William. "An Eskimo in Search of God," in Willoya and Vinson Brown, Warriors of the Rainbow: Strange and Prophetic Dreams of the Indians, Healdsburg, Calif.: Nature-graph Co., 1962, pp. 65-76.
    Born, 1939; wrote, c. 1962. Alaskan Eskimo, part white. This is an account of a spiritual odyssey which took Willoya from his adopted Eskimo grandmother's teachings through Christianity to a pan-Christian, pan-Indian, pan-Asian religion.

537  Wilson, Maggie. RUTH LANDES. Narratives are to be found in Ojibwa Religion and the Midewiwin, Madison: University of Wisconsin Press, 1968, pp. 208-22.
    Born, c. 1880; narrated, 1932. Cree and Ojibwa. Wilson was one of Landes's main informants for the book cited here. Wilson narrated in English, and Landes's editing was limited to minor sentence-level alterations. Wilson recounts her "common dreams" and her great vision. The latter is of considerable interest, since she goes on to recall her response to the vision, her indecision, and finally her determination to make the vision public for enactment in dance. Wilson also tells about how her vision affected other visionaries and shamans--and how their visions subsequently influenced her dreams and her vision's dance. All of this, I think, can be of help to us as we look at Black Elk's (no. 66) response to his great vision.

538    Wilson, Richard.  See no. 60.

539    Winnie, Lucille (Jerry).    Sah-Gan-De-Oh:    The Chief's Daughter.* N.Y.: Vantage Press, 1969. 190 pp.
Born, c. 1905; wrote, shortly before 1969. Seneca and white. Winnie writes about her years on the reservation and her schooling at Haskell, but this is really the autobiography of a thoroughly modern woman who happens to be an Indian. She writes at some length, for example, of her experiences in the air industry--she knew Amelia Earhart and worked for Howard Hughes. At the end of the book, however, she tells of her desire to return to the reservation to help her people.

540    Wolf-chief (M).  ROBERT H. LOWIE.  A narrative is to be found in Lowie, "Sun Dance of the Shoshoni, Ute, and Hidatsa," Anthropological Papers of the American Museum of Natural History, XVI, pt. 5 (1919), pp. 421-27.
Born, 1849; interviewed, c. 1910. Hidatsa. Lowie worked through an interpreter, but otherwise, according to his own account, he gives us Wolf-chief's narrative very much as he preserved it in his notes.  Wolf-chief here recalls the Sun Dance in general, and two Sun Dances in particular. In neither of these was he a dancer, but one occasioned a fast and vision quest. He also provides a spirited account of a battle with a band of Crow warriors who interrupted a Sun Dance on a horse-stealing raid.

541    _____.  GILBERT L. WILSON.  Hidatsa Horse and Dog Culture (IP), Anthropological Papers of the American Museum of Natural History, XV, No. 2 (1924), 125-311.
Interviewed, beginning 1908.  Wolf-chief knew some English, but Wilson worked through an interpreter, Wolf-chief's nephew, Goodbird (see no. 192). Wilson did little editing other than standardizing the interpreter's imperfect English and "arranging materials." Wolf-chief shares these pages with his sister, Maxidiwiac (see no. 321). Wolf-chief's contributions are to be found on pp. 125-230 and 290-311. Wilson's method was to have individual informants tell everything that they knew about some specific aspect of their culture. The result in this case is a fascinating blend of folk wisdom, folk technology, and personal history. The many illustrations were done under the eye and with the approval of Wolf-chief.

542    _____.  _____.  Hidatsa Eagle Trapping (IP), Anthropological Papers of the American Museum of Natural History, XXX, No. 4 (1928), 99-245.
See no. 321.  This is another of Wilson's attempts to describe Hidatsa culture from the perspective of individual participants in that culture. Wolf-chief provides a good deal

of autobiographical detail here.

543 Wolf Child, Guy. ADOLF HUNGRY WOLF. "Guy Wolf Child,"* as found in the book cited in no. 20, pp. 337-38.
   Born, c. 1882; interviewed, c. 1972. Blood. For the details of this collaboration, see no. 20. Wolf Child recalls his prowess as a dancer.

544 Wood, Ellen. ELIZABETH COLSON. "Life History of Ellen Wood," and "Autobiography of Ellen Wood," as found in the book cited in no. 2, pp. 109-94, 211-14.
   Born, c. 1882; interviewed, 1941. Pomo. For the details of the collaboration, see no. 2. Wood is the most voluble of Colson's informants: she talks of her childhood, puberty, and adult life, all of which took place while the traditional ways were slowly receding in the face of white contact. Wood is at pains to compare Pomo customs, especially marriage customs, with those of the whites.

545 Wooden Leg (M). THOMAS B. MARQUIS. Wooden Leg: A Warrior Who Fought Custer. Lincoln: University of Nebraska Press, 1962 [1931]. vii + 384 pp. Excerpts in the book cited in no. 132, pp. 103-7.
   1858-1940; interviewed, c. 1927. Cheyenne. Marquis says that he and Wooden Leg were fluent enough in sign language that an interpreter was usually unnecessary. Marquis did some editing and rearranging, and the account is occasionally corrected by other informants. When this occurs, however, Marquis notes it.
   This is one of the very good Indian autobiographies, filled with detail, told by a man who has come to appreciate, in his old age, the security of the reservation, but who still longs for the old days when a man had to be brave. Much space is devoted to the Custer battle. It is clear that Marquis was asking for as much about Custer as Wooden Leg could responsibly provide--and yet the fascination is there for Wooden Leg as well. Wooden Leg, for example, clearly relishes his memories of the thirtieth and fiftieth anniversaries of the Custer battle, upon which occasions the Indians convened to talk about it all.
   One of the interesting aspects of this book is that while Wooden Leg will attempt explanations for unusual phenomena in nature--in the case of the "claw marks" on the Devil's Tower, for example, the explanation is that "it must have been a monster of a bear" (pp. 50-55)--he makes no attempt to find larger significances lurking behind these explanations, none of the kind of allegory that Black Elk (no. 66) supplies in similar contexts. Another aspect of the book is worthy, perhaps, of attention. As distinct from such Indians as Luther Standing

Bear (no. 469, 470), Wooden Leg is not quite at ease with his newly fashioned pan-Indian sentiments. He says that he now feels sympathy for his old enemies, the Crows, but it is plain at times that his anti-Crow feelings are still simmering.

546 X, Doctor (pseudonym). GERTRUDE TOFFELMIER and KATHERINE LUOMOLA. "Dreams and Interpretations of the Diegueno Indians," Psychoanalytic Quarterly, V (1936), 195-225.
Born, before 1885; interviewed, 1934. Diegueno. The authors quote extensively from Doctor X's account of his dreams, his interpertations of his dreams, and other matters having to do with the acquisition, maintenance, and use of his shamanic powers.

547 YAVA, ALBERT. Harold Courlander. Big Falling Snow: A Tewa-Hopi Indian's Life and Times and the History and Traditions of His People (IP).* N.Y.: Crown Publishers, Inc., 1978. xiv + 178 pp.
Born, 1888; interviewed, 1969-71. Tewa-Hopi. Yava's tape-recorded narrative was transcribed and edited by Courlander, with Yava checking the manuscript at each stage. Yava added and deleted at will. Courlander did minor editing toward standard English. The first twenty-six pages are personal recollections. While the remainder is largely devoted to tribal history and folklore, personal observations and reminiscences are scattered throughout. Yava knew Don Talayesva (no. 483), for example, and comments upon his autobiography and on Son of Old Man Hat (no. 283). There are some fascinating differences between Yava's autobiography and Talayesva's, some of which have to do with the reticence that Yava maintains as opposed to the candor that Simmons urged upon Talayesva. Yava is quite aware of these differences.

548 Yazi, Charles (pseudonym). ROBERT N. RAPOPORT. "Charles Yazi--a Staunch Galilean," in the book cited in no. 163, pp. 109-15.
Born, 1890; interviewed, 1949. Navajo. For the details of the collaboration, see no. 163. Yazi tells of the stern discipline meted out during his youth. He also provides an account of the superstitions of the Navajos (this from his perspective as a convert to the Galilean faith). He tells of his marriages, his conversion, etc.

549 Yazi, Jo (pseudonym). EVON Z. VOGT. "Jo Yazi: Life History," as found in the book cited in no. 42, pp. 227-38.
Born, c. 1925; interviewed, 1947. Navajo. Yazi spoke English, and so there was no interpreter here. For further

details of the collaboration, see no. 42. This is mainly devoted to a grade-by-grade account of schooling and to army experiences (WW II). Yazi does speak briefly about his dissatisfactions with reservation life.

550 Yazi, Sally (pseudonym). ROBERT N. RAPOPORT. A narrative is to be found in the book cited in no. 163, pp. 118-21.

Born, c. 1920; interviewed, 1949. Navajo. Rapoport worked here as he did with Marcos (see no. 311). Yazi tells of her early hard life with her mother, Nanabah (no. 353); of her marriages and promiscuity; and of her eventual conversion to the fundamentalist Galilean faith. Yazi's latest husband was Jim Domingo (no. 149).

551 Yazzie, Dan. See no. 24.

552 Yellowhair, Chester. "I Was Born in the Dark Ages,"* Desert Magazine, XXIII, No. 11 (1960), pp. 17-18.

Born, c. 1912; wrote, c. 1960. Navajo. Beginning with the sentence "Until I was eight or nine years old I did not know there were people on earth other than my family," Yellowhair tells of his childhood--herding sheep at the age of four, horses at seven--schooling, and his eventually learning the art of silversmithing at high school in Santa Fe.

553 Yellowhair, Marvin. See no. 39.

554 Yellow Wolf. LUCULLUS VIRGIL McWHORTER. Yellow Wolf: His Own Story. Caldwell, Idaho: The Caxton Printers, 1940. 324 pp. Long excerpts are included in Harvey Chalmers, The Last Stand of the Nez Perce, N.Y.: Twayne, 1962.

C. 1855-1935; interviewed, 1908-35. Nez Perce. McWhorter employed no less than fifteen interpreters in the course of his work with Yellow Wolf, and he came to be quite discriminating in his choice of interpreters. He also made it a practice to conduct his interviews in front of witnesses who could correct or corroborate Yellow Wolf's account immediately.

McWhorter worked very carefully with the material which Yellow Wolf provided him during the course of their long collaboration, and he allowed Yellow Wolf to exert a good deal of control over the shaping of the narrative. Yellow Wolf himself was determined that the work should be a true account of the Nez Perce war of 1877, its causes, conduct, and consequences. In response to McWhorter's suggestion that they incorporate an account of Yellow Wolf's early life "as a prelude to his war career," Yellow Wolf responded: "It is not right for me to tell of my growing-up life. That does not belong to history. . . . I do not want to hurt, to spoil what I did in the war" (p. 24). By 1931 Yellow Wolf was intent upon setting the record straight: "White people are smothering my Indian rights. The young generation behind me, for them I tell the story. It is for them! I want the next generation of whites to know and treat the Indians as themselves" (p. 18). This is a deeply felt and a minutely detailed account. McWhorter did, by the way, manage to scrape together enough bits and pieces to provide a first chapter about the "Youth of the Warrior."

555 Yoimut (F). FRANK FORREST LATTA. "Yoimut's Story," as found in the book cited in no. 383, pp. 223-76.
  C. 1855-1933; interviewed, 1930-31. Yokuts. Yoimut spoke English, and Latta retains her phrasing without editing. The narrative has been cut, but it would seem that Latta did virtually no rearranging. This narrative is packed with ethnographic detail. Yoimut tells about her childhood, games, hardships--and all with a full awareness that she is the last Chenut Yokut left, that with her will die the Chenut language.

556 York, Laurine. T. D. ALLEN. "The Death of a Friend,"* in the book cited in no. 92, pp. 157-58.
  Born, c. 1956; wrote c. 1972. Choctaw. For the details of the collaboration, see no. 92. York recalls the events associated with the death of her father.

557 YOUNG, LUCY. Edith V. A. Murphey. "Out of the Past: A True Indian Story," California Historical Society Quarterly, XX (1941), 349-64.
  Born, c. 1848; interviewed, 1939. Wailaki. Young's English is printed here with little or no editing. There survive, thus, such sentences as: "Grown son carry him in great basket on his back, every place" (p. 349). Most of this has to do with injustices experienced by the Indians at the hands of the whites in the 1860's; indeed, although this narrative is the result of questions posed by Murphey, Young says that she is speaking in order to show "what white man do to Inyan. That's the reason I tell it" (p. 358).

558 Young Bear, Severt. See no. 60.

559 Young Jackrabbit. See no. 201.

560 Zah, Henry. See no. 24.

561 Zahne, Herbert. See no. 24.

562 Zitkala-Sa (Gertrude Bonnin). "Impressions of an Indian

Childhood,"* <u>Atlantic Monthly</u>, LXXXV (Jan., 1900), 37-47.

_____ . "The School Days of an Indian Girl,"* <u>Atlantic Monthly</u>, LXXV (Feb., 1900), 185-94.

_____ . "An Indian Teacher among Indians,"* <u>Atlantic Monthly</u>, LXXXV (Mar., 1900), 381-86.

_____ . "Why I Am a Pagan,"* <u>Atlantic Monthly</u>, XC (Dec., 1902), 801-803.

These are reprinted, complete, in Zitkala-Sa, <u>American Indian Stories</u> (IP),* Glorieta, N.M.: Rio Grande Press, Inc., 1976 [1921], pp. 7-107.

1875-1938; wrote, c. 1899-1902. Sioux. The first three of these pieces form a continuous narrative, while the fourth is Zitkala-Sa's response to one reader's Christian criticism. Zitkala-Sa writes first of her memories of her life with her mother, from age seven to the time of her being seduced by missionaries (she was promised luscious apples) to attend boarding school. Her mother, bitterly anti-white, opposed this. The next piece tells of her fearful trip to the school and of the fearful school itself, while the third piece tells of her beginning as a teacher and of her antipathy toward her colleagues, whom she saw as self-interested. In the final piece she talks about the limitations of the Christians she has had to deal with and of her determination to seek God in nature, rather than in churches.

563 Zuni, Lina. RUTH BUNZEL. "An Autobiography," as found in Bunzel, <u>Zuni Texts</u> (IP), <u>Publications of the American Ethnological Society</u>, XV (1933), 74-96. Excerpts are reprinted in the book cited in no. 28, pp. 62-64.

Born, c. 1856; interviewed, 1926. Zuni. Zuni knew no English. Her daughter, Flora Zuni, served as interpreter. Bunzel cut some material, but it would seem that she did no rearranging. Zuni tells about her growing up, her relations with her family, and of how she exhorts her children to cleave unto the old ways. She also tells about her troubles with the Navajos and her father's slaves.

564 Various. RAMON I. HARRIS. <u>Oyate Iyechinka Woglakapi: An Oral History Collection</u> (IP), Vols. I-IV, ed. Harris. Vermillion, S.D.: American Indian Research Project, University of South Dakota, 1970.

This is a descriptive catalog of the hundreds of tapes of Indian music, Indian storytelling, and interviews with Indians (Sioux, Ojibwa, Crow, Flathead, and Winnebago, for the most part) recorded by the American Indian Research Project, beginning c. 1967. Many of these tapes contain autobiographical narratives, and typed transcripts of some of the tapes are available. A few short excerpts of this material are to be found in the book cited in no. 28.

565    ? (M and F). Sister Inez Hilger. Narratives are to be found in
Arapaho Child Life and Its Cultural Backgrounds (IP), Smithsonian Institution Bureau of American Ethnology, Bul. 148
(1952).
    Some born as early as 1848; interviewed, 1935-41.
Arapaho. All of the names of these informants are provided
by Hilger, but none of the informants are linked to particular
narratives. Hilger worked through an interpreter. Hilger
proceeds here by alternating her own descriptions and analyses
with Arapaho recollections of childhood and adolescence, up to
and including marriage.

566    ? (M).   A. L. KROEBER.   "Autobiographies," as found in
Walapai Ethnography (IP), Memoirs of the American Anthropological Association, XLII (1935), 204-29.
    Born, before 1885; interviewed, 1929. Walapai. These are
brief autobiographies by four men, collected by Fred Kniffen,
Gordon Macgregor, Robert McKennan, Scudder Mekeel, and
Maurice Mook, all with the aid of interpreters. Kroeber edited
the material.

567    ? (F).   ALEXANDER H. and DOROTHEA C. LEIGHTON.
"Story II," as found in the second work cited in no. 205, pp.
109-19.
    Born, c. 1886; interviewed, c. 1940.   Navajo.   The
Leightons explained to this woman that they would like her to
tell them "everything she could remember from the first thing
right up to the present. . . . Scarcely any questions were asked
during the recounting, and the story is in her words, as
translated by another Navaho" (p. 109).

568    ? (M).   ALEXANDER H. and DOROTHEA C. LEIGHTON,
"Story III," as found in the second work cited in no. 205, pp.
119-31.
    Born, 1890; interviewed, c. 1940.  Navajo. For the details
of the collaboration, see no. 567.  This narrative includes a
good account of the unfortunate early years of the Indian
schools. This informant went on to become a curer.

569    ? (F). TRUMAN MICHELSON. "The Autobiography of a Fox
Indian Woman," 40th Annual Report of the Bureau of American
Ethnology to the Secretary of the Smithsonian Institution
1918-1919 (Washington, D.C., 1925), pp. 291-349.
    Born, probably before 1875; interviewed, 1918.  This Fox
woman, who asked to remain anonymous, offered this narrative in response to Michelson's interpreter's request for a life
story. No direction was imposed upon the narrator, and the
narrative is printed in the order in which it was spoken. One
wishes that the few sentences which Michelson deleted as

being "too naive and frank" for European tastes (p. 295) had been allowed to remain, but otherwise virtually no editing was done. The Fox text is printed on facing pages with the English translation. This autobiography is remarkable for the extent to which it disregards tribal concerns. No sense is provided here of the condition of the Fox Indians at any time during this woman's life. The narrative has to do with childhood games, with the taboos that affected her, with her marriage, separations, and child-bearing.

570  ? (F). TRUMAN MICHELSON. "The Narrative of a Southern Cheyenne Woman," Smithsonian Miscellaneous Collections, LXXXVII, No. 5 (1932), 13 pp.

Born, probably c. 1870; interviewed, 1931. Cheyenne. Michelson prints this narrative just as it came to him, written down by an interpreter-intermediary (except for slight editing toward standard English). This is a fascinating account, especially good as to the experiences of a Cheyenne girl. She tells about her games, of piercing her doll's ears, and of other play that served as training for Cheyenne domesticity. She tells as well about the honor of being bought as a bride and about her feelings upon going as a bride to a stranger.

571  ? (F). TRUMAN MICHELSON. "Narrative of an Araphao Woman," American Anthropologist, XXXV (1933), 595-610.

Born, 1855; interviewed, 1932. Arapaho. This was taken down by an intermediary-interpreter for Michelson, who was himself not present for the narration. Michelson printed this translation verbatim, except for slight corrections of its English. Especially considering the brevity of this piece, a lot of space is devoted to sexual habits and mores. It appears that Michelson wanted this narration to serve as a refutation of those anthropologists who had claimed that Arapaho women were morally lax. See Michelson's introduction. This woman sees the present world as fallen, but there is little bitterness here--and nothing at all about the whites.

572  ? (M). JOHN M. ROBERTS and MALCOLM J. ARTH. An autobiographical interview is to be found in Roberts and Arth, "Dyadic Elicitation in Zuni," El Placio, LXXIII, No. 2 (1966), 27-42.

Born, probably before 1900; interviewed, 1959. Zuni. The method explained and exemplified in this article is an attempt to overcome, to some degree, the problems of unnaturalness in the usual informant-ethnographer or informant-interpreter-ethnographer interviews. Roberts and Arth directed a younger Zuni man to ask questions of an older member of his family-- just as he would do if he were seeking information for himself. According to Roberts and Arth, the resultant elicitations "stand high in quality when they are compared with similar materials elicited through the familiar . . . techniques used so often by anthropologists" (p. 40). Two dyadic interviews are printed here, but only the second, pp. 31-39, is really autobiographical. Both are translated from the Zuni; both are cut but otherwise unedited. The older man, the man being questioned, was once a governor in Zuni. He tells of his feelings about his office, his modes of action, troubles with the missionaries, etc.

573  ? (M). GEORGE D. SPINDLER. Autobiographic Interviews of Eight Menomini Indian Males, Microcard Publications of Primary Records in Culture and Personality, ed. Bert Kaplan, II, No. 12, Madison, Wis.: Microcard Foundation, 1957, 105 pp.

Interviewed, 1948-56. Spindler prints unedited transcripts of eight autobiographic interviews (including his own questions). All of the informants but one (case 20) were interviewed in English, and each may be regarded, according to Spindler, as representative of one of four levels of acculturation: native oriented, Peyote Cultist, transitional, and acculturated. For the results of Rorschach testing of these men, see volume II, No. 11, in this same series.

Case 20, pp. 4-16. Born, c. 1884. Menomini. Interpreters were used here. Considerable detail here, especially about the way he was reared and his relationship with his son. Also talks of his feelings about the old ways, medicine, etc.

Case 9, pp. 17-31. Born, c. 1914. Menomini and Potawatomi. A good deal of sustained narrative here. Tells of his upbringing, his schooling, etc. He tells as well of running away from school and hoboing for a time in the 1920's. Medicine Lodge and dream experiences.

Case 11, pp. 32-44. Born, c. 1910. Menomini and Ojibwa. Childhood, school, Peyote Cult experiences, hunting, etc.

Case 2, pp. 45-59. Born, c. 1901. Menomini. A good deal of sustained narrative here. This man is widely read and is acculturated, but not as thoroughly as he would like to be. He is dissatisfied with the society of his Indian neighbors and regrets the lack of education which keeps him excluded from the society of professionals (except for the occasional visits of such anthropologists as Spindler).

Case 35, pp. 60-76. Born, c. 1922. Menomini and Potawatomi. Childhood, schooling, army experiences (WWII), feelings about his conversion to Catholicism as an adult, etc.

Case 41, pp. 77-91. Born, c. 1916. Menomini and Potawatomi. Quite a bit of detail here about life at various schools, particularly Haskell Institute. He tells too of being severely disciplined as a child, his experience in jail, logging, his election to tribal office, and a good deal else.

Case 13, pp. 92-96. Born, c. 1918. Menomini. Childhood, school, Peyote experience, army life (WW II), etc.

Case 74, pp. 97-105. Born, c. 1921. Menomini and French. School, travels as a musician in a swing band, logging, etc.

574 ? (M). GEORGE D. SPINDLER. Personal Documents in Menomini Peyotism, Microcard Publications of Primary Records in Culture and Personality, ed. Bert Kaplan, III, No. 13, Madison, Wis.: Microcard Foundation, 1957, 37 pp.

Ten males, probably all born after 1900; interviewed, c. 1950. Menomini. For the details of the collaboration, see no. 573. These narratives are quite rich in detail. Peyote visionary experiences, accounts of ceremonies, conversion experiences, etc.

575 ? (F). LOUISE SPINDLER. Sixty-one Rorschachs and Fifteen Expressive Autobiographic Interviews of Menomini Indian Women, Microcard Publications of Primary Records in Culture and Personality, ed. Bert Kaplan, II, No. 10, Madison, Wis.: Microcard Foundation, 1957, 302 pp.

Spindler prints unedited transcripts of fifteen "expressive autobiographical interviews"--which is to say that these women were asked to relate their life story and Spindler asked questions along the way. All of the informants spoke English. Spindler includes a great deal of other information about these women as well: Rorschachs, Murray Thematic Apperception Tests, letters, health data, etc. These women may be regarded, according to Spindler, as representative of "four levels of acculturation" (p. 4): native oriented, Peyote Cultist, transitional ("marginal identification with both native oriented and Western oriented religious groups" [p. 4]), and acculturated.

Case 1, pp. 11-26. Born, c. 1920. Menomini, one-fourth white. "Native oriented." Tells of happy days at school, how she was reared as a child, of the differences between genera- tions, of drinking, etc.

Case 2, pp. 27-32. Born, c. 1922. Menomini and Potawatomi. "Native oriented." Tells of school, parents, differences between the generations, a bit about shamanistic curing, etc.

Case 6, pp. 44-52. Born, c. 1923. Menomini and Potawatomi. "Native oriented." Tells of the Medicine Dance and shamanistic matters as well as her childhood, marriage, etc.

Case 11, pp. 56-64. Born, c. 1914. Menomini and Ojibwa. "Native oriented." This is a poignant narrative. In her hesitance and in her awareness of, but her lack of knowledge concerning, the old ways, she seems to personify, reluctantly, the passing of the old. School, the Peyote Cult, etc.

Case 12, pp. 65-74. Born, 1912. Menomini and Potawatomi. "Peyote Cult." Childhood, conversion to the Peyote Cult, life in Chicago, marriage, etc.

Case 15, pp. 81-87. Born, c. 1900. Menomini. "Peyote Cult." Childhood, school, Medicine Dance, Peyote.

Case 21, pp. 117-23. Born, c. 1920. Menomini and Ojibwa. "Transitional." Tells of the traditional fragments of her upbringing, her brush with the Peyote Cult, the Catholic baptism of her children. She also talks about witchcraft, etc.

Case 23, pp. 141-47. Born, c. 1907. Menomini. "Acculturated." Childhood, school, witchcraft, life in Chicago, marriage, etc. This is a troubled woman.

Case 28, pp. 155-61. Born, c. 1929. Menomini. "Acculturated." Witchcraft, school, life in Oshkosh, old ways vs. Catholicism, etc.

Case 32, pp. 162-72. Born, c. 1899. Menomini. "Acculturated." Childhood reminiscences, native cures, shamanism, witchcraft, first menstruation, etc.

Case 33, pp. 173-80. Born, c. 1889. Menomini and Irish. "Acculturated." Marriage at age thirteen, marriage problems, witchcraft, etc.

Case 35, pp. 181-87. Born, c. 1915. Menomini father, Menomini and French mother. "Acculturated." School, witchcraft, life in Milwaukee, etc.

Case 44, pp. 213-33. Born, c. 1916. White father, Menomini mother. "Acculturated." Most of the interviews in this book are too brief or too fragmented to be of much interest individually. This one is an exception. The narrator was raised by her Menomini mother and spoke only Menomini until her seventh year. She tells of tangled and troubled family relationships, her first menstruation, and her first awareness of sexuality; she talks about her attitudes toward witchcraft, schooling, Indian medicines, her feelings about being fired from her job, and more.

Case 53, pp. 259-67. Born, c. 1919. Menomini and white. "Acculturated." Family, school, work as a maid, etc.

Case 54, pp. 268-76. Born, c. 1897. Menomini and white. "Acculturated." Childhood, Catholic schooling, her work as a cook, her parents' reticence about sexual matters, etc.

576  ? (M). W. D. WALLIS. Narrative to be found in The Sun Dance of the Canadian Dakota, Anthropological Papers of the American Museum of Natural History, XVI (1919), pp. 331-33.

Born, probably before 1875; narrated, 1914. Santee Sioux. The monograph cited above includes many accounts of Sun Dance experiences. All except the one cited here specifically, however, are third-person accounts of Sun Dances. To some of these the narrators were witness, some the narrators know only by oral tradition. The exception is a vivid account of a

Sun Dance performed c. 1910, an account which includes a recitation of a power song which the dancer received in a dream just before his ordeal. Wallis would have worked through an interpreter, but evidently he did little or no cutting or rearranging.

577    ? (M). LESLIE WHITE. "Autobiography of an Acoma Indian," as found in White, New Material from Acoma, Smithsonian Institution, Bureau of American Ethnology, Bul. 136, Anthropological Papers, No. 32 (1943), 326-37.

Born, 1868; interviewed, 1941. Acoma Pueblo. This man narrated in English. Internal evidence suggests that this narrative was guided by questions posed by the interviewer. White did some cutting and some editing toward standard English. The result is a sometimes vivid account of growing up as a Pueblo Indian. The narrator, for example, tells about his fears of the whipping kachinas and about the whipping he endured upon entrance into one of the kiva societies--and he tells too of his family's crying with him when they saw his torn and bleeding back.

# References

1   Aberle, David Friend (1951). The Psychosocial Analysis of a Hopi Life-History, Comparative Psychology Monographs, XXI, No. 1.

2   Angell, Robert (1945). "A Critical Review of the Development of the Personal Document Method in Sociology," in Louis Gottschalk, et al., The Use of Personal Documents in History, Anthropology and Sociology, Social Science Research Bulletin, No. 53, pp. 175-232.

3   Allport, Gordon (1942). The Use of Personal Documents in Psychological Science. Social Science Research Bulletin, No. 49.

4   Bad Heart Bull, Amos (1967). A Pictographic History of the Oglala Sioux. Lincoln: University of Nebraska Press.

5   Bahr, Donald (1975). Pima and Papago Oratory: A Study of Three Texts. San Francisco: Indian Historian Press.

6   Bedford, Denton R. (1974). "Lone Walker, the Small Robe Chief," The Indian Historian, VII, No. 3, 41-54.

7   Brumble, H. David III (1980). "Anthropologists, Novelists and Indian Sacred Materials," Canadian Review of American Studies, XI, No. 1, 31-48.

8   Bruss, Elizabeth (1976). Autobiographical Acts. Baltimore: Johns Hopkins University Press.

9   Buechner, Cecilia Bain (1933). "The Pokagons," Indiana Historical Society Publications, X, No. 5, 279-340. Includes a bibliography of Pokagon's writings and public addresses.

10  Castro, Michael (1979). "Poetic License in Neihardt's Black

164

Elk Speaks," paper presented at a special session of the Modern Language Association devoted to American Indian autobiography.

11  DeMallie, Raymond J. (1978). "George Bushotter, Teton Sioux, 1864-1892," Margot Liberty, ed., American Indian Intellectuals, St. Paul: West Publishing Co., pp. 91-104.

12  Dempsey, Hugh A. (1978). "Sylvester Long, Buffalo Child Long Lance," as found in Margot Liberty, ed., American Indian Intellectuals, St. Paul: West Publishing Co., pp. 197-204.

13  Dickason, David H. (1961). "Chief Simon Pokagon: 'The Indian Longfellow'," Indiana Magazine of History, LII, 127-40.

14  Dollard, John (1935). Criteria for the Life History. New Haven: Yale University Press.

15  Garraty, John (1957). The Nature of Biography. New York: Knopf.

16  Goody, Jack, and I. Watt (1962-63). "The Consequences of Literacy," Comparative Studies in Society and History, V, 304-26, 332-45. An abridgment is in Pier Paolo Giglioli, Language and Social Context, Baltimore: Penguin Books Ltd., 1972, pp. 311-57.

17  Goody, Jack (1977). The Domestication of the Savage Mind. Cambridge: Cambridge University Press.

18  Gottschalk, Louis (1945). "The Historian and the Personal Document," in Gottschalk, et al., The Use of Personal Documents in History, Anthropology and Sociology, Social Science Research Bulletin, No. 53, pp. 1-75.

19  Hart, Francis R. (1970). "Notes for an Anatomy of Modern Autobiography," New Literary History, I, 485-511.

20  Heizer, Robert F. (1977). Bibliography of California Indians. N.Y.: Garland Publishing, Inc.

21  Hodge, William (1976). A Bibliography of Contemporary North American Indians. N.Y.: Interland, Inc.

22  Holly, Carol T. (1979). "Black Elk Speaks and the Making of Indian Autobiography," Genre, XII, 117-36.

23  Horton, Robin, and Ruth Finnegan (1973). Modes of Thought. London: Faber and Faber.

24   Kluckhohn, Clyde (1945). "The Personal Document in Anthro-
pological Science," in Louis Gottschalk, et al., The Use of
Personal Documents in History, Anthropology, and Sociology,
Social Science Research Bulletin, No. 53, pp. 77-173.

25   _____ and Evon Z. Vogt (1955). "The Son of Many Beads,
1866-1954," American Anthropologist, LVII, 1036-37.

26   Kroeber, A.L. (1952). The Nature of Culture. N.Y.: Columbia
University Press.

27   Kroeber, Theodora (1970). Alfred Kroeber: A Personal Config-
uration. Berkeley: University of California Press.

28   _____ (1971). Ishi in Two Worlds. Berkeley: University of
California Press. (Theodora Kroeber's Ishi: Last of His Tribe is
a fictionalized version of the above.)

29   Laird, Carobeth (1975). Encounter with an Angry God: Recollections of My Life with John Peabody Harrington. Banning,
Calif.: Malki Museum Press.

30   Langness, L. L. (1965). The Life History in Anthropological
Science. New York: Holt, Rinehart and Winston.

31   Leo, John Robert (1978). "Riding Geronimo's Cadillac: His
Own Story and the Circumstancing of Text," Journal of
American Culture, I, 818-37.

32   Lévi-Strauss, Claude (1962; English translation, 1966). The
Savage Mind. Chicago: University of Chicago Press.

33   _____ (1979). Myth and Meaning. N.Y.: Schocken.

34   Lowie, Robert H. (1959). Robert H. Lowie, Ethnologist: A
Personal Record. Berkeley: University of California Press.

35   Mandel, Barrett John (1968). "The Autobiographer's Art,"
Journal of Aesthetics and Art Cricitism, XXVII, No. 2, 215-26.

36   Mandelbaum, David G. (1973). "The Study of Life History:
Gandhi," Current Anthropology, XIV, No. 3, 177-96.

37   McClusky, Sally (1972). "Black Elk Speaks, and So Does John
Neihardt," Western American Literature, VI, 231-42.

38   Melody, Michael Edwards (1977). The Apaches: A Critical
Bibliography. Bloomington: Indiana University Press.

166

39    Miller, David Reed (1978). "Charles Alexander Eastman, the 'Winner': From Deep Woods to Civilization," as found in Margot Liberty, ed., American Indian Intellectuals, St. Paul: West Publishing Co., pp. 60-73.

40    Misch, Georg (1949-50). Geschicte der Autobiographie, vol. I (in two parts): Das Altertum. 3rd rev. ed., Bern: Francke.

41    Mooney, James (1898). Calendar History of the Kiowa Indians. Reprinted, Washington, D.C.: Smithsonian Institution Press, 1979.

42    O'Brien, Lynne Woods (1973). Plains Indian Autobiographies, Western Writers Series, No. 10, Boise, Idaho: Boise State College.

43    Pascal, Roy (1960). Design and Truth in Autobiography. London: Routledge and Kegan Paul.

44    Passin, Herbert (1942). "Tarahumara Prevarication: A Problem in Field Method," American Anthropologist, XLIV, 235-47.

45    Sayre, Robert F. (1964). The Examined Self: Benjamin Franklin, Henry Adams, Henry James. Princeton: Princeton University Press.

46    _____ (1969). "The Proper Study--Autobiographies in American Studies," American Quarterly, XXIX, 241-62.

47    _____ (1971). "Vision and Experience in Black Elk Speaks," College English, XXXII, No. 5, 509-35.

48    Schultz, James Willard (1907). My Life as an Indian. Reprinted, Greenwich, Conn.: Fawcett Publications, Inc., n.d.

49    Shea, Daniel B., Jr. (1968). Spiritual Autobiography in Early America. Princeton: Princeton University Press.

50    Smith, Sidonie (1974). Where I'm Bound: Patterns of Slavery and Freedom in Black American Autobiography. Westport, Conn.: Greenwood Press.

51    Spott, Robert, and A. L. Kroeber (1942). Yurok Narratives, California University Publications in American Archeology and Ethnology, XXV, 142-256.

52    Steward, Julian H. (1973). Alfred L. Kroeber. N.Y.: Columbia University Press.

53 Tedlock, Dennis (1977). "Toward an Oral Poetic," New Literary History, VIII, pp. 507-19.

54 Vogt, Evon Z., and Ethel M. Albert (1966). People of Rimrock: A Study of Values in Five Cultures. Reprinted, N.Y.: Atheneum, 1975.

55 Weintraub, Karl J. (1975). "Autobiography and Historical Consciousness," Cricital Inquiry, I, 821-48.

56 _____ (1978). The Value of the Individual: Self and Circumstance in Autobiography. Chicago: University of Chicago Press.

# Index of Editors, Anthropologists, Ghosts, and Amanuenses

# Index of Tribes

Acoma Pueblo: 387, 577.
Apache: 11, 35, 52, 56, 85, 111, 114, 115, 121, 138, 186, 226, 261, 262, 263, 266, 267, 289, 295, 312, 406, 407, 431, 455, 458, 473, 512, 532.
Arapaho: 132, 282, 479, 565, 571.
Arikara: 132, 423.
Assiniboine: 127, 153, 265, 276, 308, 402, 419, 450, 463.

Beaver: 9.
Blackfeet: 54, 59, 97, 157, 158, 185, 219, 220, 228, 279, 305, 417, 462.
Blood: 20, 140, 176, 188, 234, 307, 348, 372, 373, 416, 452, 513, 543.

Cahuilla: 150, 331, 341, 385, 386.
Cherokee: 38, 93, 151, 222.
Cheyenne: 47, 48, 132, 157, 215, 238, 382, 401, 472, 477, 484, 507, 508, 533, 545, 569.
Chippewa: see Ojibwa.
Choctaw: 232, 504, 556.
Chuructos: 174.
Comanche: 437.
Coos: 391.
Cree: 98, 148, 175, 280, 416, 457, 474, 485, 494, 505, 535, 537.
Creek: 453.

Crow: 90, 132, 137, 158, 189, 201, 212, 289, 378, 397, 404, 423, 509, 528, 529, 540, 545, 564.
Cupeno: 365, 511, 520.

Delaware: 99, 288, 504.
Diegueno: 134, 546.

Eskimo: 5, 22, 23, 50, 116, 122, 136, 139, 203, 237, 255, 259, 330, 364, 369, 371, 375, 376, 380, 381, 393, 394, 395, 438, 444, 464, 478, 482, 492, 536.

Flathead: 564.
Fox: 215, 569.

Gitksan: 488.
Gros Ventre: 54, 69, 424, 435, 515.

Halfbreed: see Métis.
Havasupai: 214, 455.
Hidatsa: 192, 319, 320, 321, 486, 540, 541, 542.
Hopi: 38, 104, 169, 245, 255, 443, 483, 547.
Hunkpapa Sioux: 132, 142, 324, 466.
Huron: 210.

Iroquois: 10, 98.

Jlli: 19.

# Subject Index

176

305, 312, 336, 347, 360, 369,
378, 389, 394, 395, 400, 430,
436, 440, 455, 459, 464, 469,
476, 485, 490, 492, 522.

Indian Defense League of America:
426.

Joseph, Chief: 509, 554.

Lincoln, President Abraham:
281.
Livestock-reduction program
(Navajo): 24, 46, 501, 517.

Marriage: 75, 99, 139, 205, 254,
286, 296, 320, 324, 336, 353,
356, 370, 374, 376, 378, 380,
391, 406, 419, 439, 453, 455,
459, 462, 504, 505, 508, 544,
548, 565, 569, 570, 571, 575.
Masons: 527.
Missionaries: 14, 18, 19, 99, 124,
163, 180, 241, 339, 348, 526,
562, 572.
Mormons: 163, 311, 443.
Murray Thematic Apperception
Test: 42, 75, 575.

Naming: 13, 155, 184.
Navajo Code-Talkers: 81, 96.
Northwestern University: 375.

Pan-Indianism: 165, 230, 469,
536, 545.
Peyote: 13, 73, 74, 129, 133,
138, 156, 267, 270, 341, 378,
412, 437, 573, 574.
Pictographs: 305, 493, 522.
Potlatch: 240, 368, 400, 498.
Preaching: 14, 128, 251.
Prison: 35, 44, 111, 115, 138,
186, 256, 261, 262, 266, 273,
492, 573.
Psychics: 281, 288.

Railroads: 401, 405.
Riel, Louis: 101, 474.
Rodeo: 71, 221.

Romanticism: 11, 12, 161, 222,
224, 241, 399, 439a, 469, 471,
527.
Roosevelt, President Theodore:
186, 214.
Rorschach Test: 42, 75, 575.

Sand Creek Massacre: 47.
Schooling: 2, 3, 6, 8, 13, 17, 28,
38, 39, 40, 46, 63, 70, 72, 75,
86, 92, 96, 104, 118, 120, 144,
145, 147, 148, 155, 163, 171,
173, 181, 187, 188, 195, 211,
213, 232, 243, 255, 256, 260,
271, 275, 284, 299, 304, 311,
313, 314, 332, 333, 335, 338,
339, 348, 358, 359, 365, 375,
387, 411, 422, 426, 428, 429,
437, 443, 447, 448, 468, 469,
475, 479, 483, 491, 492, 504,
507, 535, 549, 552, 563, 568,
573, 575.
Sentence Completion Test: 42,
75.
Sexual experience: 13, 181, 214,
283, 455, 492, 575.
Shamanism: 23, 24, 26, 33, 65,
66, 107, 108, 116, 131, 139,
163, 175, 179, 181, 202, 205,
237, 247, 273, 299, 303, 317,
328, 329, 339, 341, 364, 373,
380, 381, 387, 392, 398, 400,
404, 437, 438, 462, 467, 480,
487, 488, 546, 568, 575.
Sitting Bull: 177, 281, 378, 466.
Slavery (includes children taken
captive): 88, 238, 285, 391,
473, 504, 515, 564.
Social Darwinism: 161, 208.
Sun Dance: 97, 160, 220, 397,
435, 494, 540, 576.

Technology, folk: 25, 169, 203,
234, 243, 264, 314, 319, 320,
321, 330, 378, 387, 541, 542.
Tecumseh: 6.
Thoreau, Henry David: 318.
Trapping: 10, 219, 222, 325, 369,
490, 492.